FLYING AS IT WAS

TRUE STORIES FROM AVIATION'S PAST

GERRY A. CASEY

FIRST EDITION

FIRST PRINTING

Printed in the United States of America

Library of Congress Cataloging in Publication Data

Casey, Gerry A.
Flying as it was . . . .

Includes index.
1. Aeronautics—History. I. Title.
TL515.C327 1987 629.13'09 86-23091
ISBN 0-8306-2403-1 (pbk.)

Cover photograph by Brown Brothers.

Contents

FOREWORD

Every once in a while, a book appears that brings back the nostalgia of the past while giving brief insights of history in the making.

Flying As It Was is such a book, and when Gerry Casey asked me to write the Foreword, I agreed but told him, "First, I'd like to read the manuscript."

My wife Neva thought I was nuts to take on this added burden, having already created a monster in my crusade to save the lives of pilots with "Safe Action In Flight Emergency" (SAFE). I had to agree with her but when, thumbing through the pages, I caught glimpses of some pretty exciting bits of forgotten aviation history, I told Neva it was a wonderful opportunity to do this Foreword because it's kin to the excitement an archeologist experiences in uncovering some ancient bit of history.

Gerry Casey's *Flying As It Was* is an exciting account of aviation some 60 years ago—back to the 1920s when aviation was thought to be more of a fool's delight for thrill-seekers than anything really worthwhile.

Gerry recounts his own very early exposure to flight as a young boy in the mid-1920s, and the many fliers of that period who befriended and helped him along. The book reminds me of my own quest for a place in aviation; his heroes were also my heroes.

Flying As It Was is a delightful and accurate account of what made aviation tick in its 1920s infancy, on through the 1930s and right smack into the jaws of World War II.

It's great reading! Buy it, you'll like it.

Tony LeVier

Tony LeVier, a retired Lockheed test pilot, started flying in 1928. He authored *Pilot* in 1954.

INTRODUCTION

Since mankind first imitated creatures of flight, society has termed his quest a "disease." Most of us recognize this word as denoting a sort of illness, something injurious to life and limb. The dictionary's reference to disease is: "Any deranged or depraved condition such as mind, society, etc."

Alas. Though some who fly tend to be contemptuous of this interpretation, it conveys a degree of truth. I am a prime example.

As a toddler I watched as an old DH-4 mailplane steadily plowed its way across my field of vision. Knowing few words then—and to the consternation of my mother—I loudly proclaimed the contraption, "Daddy." That my parents were going through a divorce then hardly added to the peaceful coexistence of the three of us. As a child, I was unaware of such human frailties; the disease of flying had instantly invalidated all else in my consciousness.

Before I could manage the English language, I sensed I had to fly. In that way, I may be a kindred soul to all of you who read this book and chase an obsession called flying.

Society claims diseases must be cured. But who can argue that this supposed malady is bad for our health? We who fly know our psyche can remain viable only if we are flying. Would we not beg, borrow, or steal to spread our mechanical wings? As you read on, you'll discover that I've done all three—with a total lack of shame.

It's ironic that aviation-minded people expect nonflyers to understand our causes. But then how would the ant know what the eagle feels in flight?

So, turn the pages of history and come fly with me . . . .

Part 1

Barnstorming and Early Aviation Curiosities

1 GUS, THE AVID FLYER

In 1922, quite unobtrusively, Gus became the unofficial flight operations manager of Pacific Marine Airways. Devoting long hours, Gus would oversee each takeoff and landing of the awkward and underpowered old Curtiss HS-2-L flying boats as they departed and arrived with passengers to and from Catalina Island.

When one of the more crass pilots of the world's smallest airline suggested to management that Gus should be better paid, the brass sarcastically answered, "So, throw him a fish!"

Despite this apparent contempt, Gus was not one of those hated armchair pilots. Flying at every opportunity, Gus used his spare time to visit all the nearby airports, searching for more professional airplane savvy.

Always flying in an exemplary manner when entering airport's traffic patterns, Gus would space himself precisely behind the last airplane on the downwind leg, adjust his speed accordingly and, after an impeccable flare, glide to a perfect landing. His landings were an expression of flying artistry and no pilot was ever heard to fault his techniques.

His touchdowns caught everyone's attention for he would land precisely in the center of the runway, and use the least distance, no matter the wind.

Though some had agreed that in flight, Gus was as graceful as a ballet dancer, as all amphibians, he was ridiculously inept in taxiing. After each of his landings all eyes would be upon him as he wobbled uncertainly to the flight line. Upon his arrival, some would doff their hats to his prowess while others would laugh up-roariously as he taxied.

When Gus would leave, those same pilots would snicker and hoot as they watched his struggle to maintain dignity as he wobbled to the runway for a takeoff. But when Gus would face the wind and apply power for takeoff, his uncertain wobbling would metamorphose into beautiful flight precision.

"Looks like an overweight pelican!" roared one of the watching pilots.

And he was correct. Gus, the airman's friend, was indeed an overweight, overfed and very old pelican . . ..

Paul Haaron and Art Burns, Pacific Marine Airways owners, remembered that Gus had assumed his honorary job soon after the airline had commenced operations.

Stationing himself on a nearby dock, Gus would sit on the railings and carefully study the flights of the balky flying boats. Weeks later and after seemingly absorbing all that he could from a distance, Gus began to clamber over the seaplanes. Airline personnel watched with amusement as he studied all the details of the planes inside and out. After each inspection and as passengers came down the ramp to the boarding dock, Gus would scan each one and loudly squawk his approval or disapproval of each character.

Pilots noted that Gus never soiled any part of the airplane as he probed their innards. "Damned if he don't love that ugly plane!" Haaron noted. Others would nod their heads in agreement. It was inevitable that in time, the pilots would accept Gus as a flying compatriot.

As time passed, Gus astonished all by riding on the planes' bows during their takeoffs, watching for logs and obstructions to flight. As the flying boats gathered speed, Gus would ride rock-solid with his great beak pointed into the wind as if some probing specter of ancient times. When he would see any obstruction, he would emit great thunderous screeches and squawks. Moments before liftoff, Gus would stretch his mighty wings and soar away until the next plane was ready.

Appreciating all this and secretly feeling Gus was an actual pilot wearing some wonderful birdlike camouflage, the pilots took pains to constantly feed him. Of course, this

Curtiss HS-2L seaplane used by Pacific-Marine Airways, the world's shortest airline. Drawing courtesy of Bill Neale.

eventually made for an extra-heavy wing-loading on an already huge bird.

Pacific Marine personnel also noticed that whenever any airplane flew over, Gus would carefully study its actions. Once a small biplane practicing aerobatics flew overhead and captured Gus' attention completely. Later, the pilots observed Gus climb high above their heads, deliberately execute a copied half roll of the biplane and then split-ess into a screaming dive for the harbor waters. They were quick to note that when he reappeared, he had caught a fish much larger than usual.

"Damned if he hasn't figured out a way to dive deeper for bigger fish!" one pilot shouted.

Another watching pilot snorted, "Well, hell, you knew he wasn't stupid!"

A mechanic shook his head, observing, "Nope, Gus ain't no dumb bird!" A bystander would think they were discussing another human being rather than a graying pelican.

Though he lived happily with the small airline and its people for several years, one evening near dark when Gus was flying under a cloud spilling rain, all his innate skill failed to help him.

Soaring gracefully under the cloud as always, Gus saw a fish peddler's truck hit a bump, pitching a large fish onto the wet street. But to Gus, flying in the rapidly deepening gloom of the rainshower, the shining wet street appeared as a canal.

Several pilots watched in horror as Gus pointed his beak straight south, executed a perfect half-roll on a point, slowed inverted, then plunged at terrific speed straight down.

Those who witnessed his great and final dive to oblivion wept unashamedly.

Next day, Pacific Marine Airways closed their operation while Gus was buried with honors at the edge of a flying field nearby.

Years later, pilots still talked about Gus. Many claimed he had to be a reincarnated combat pilot from World War I. One affirmed, "Hell, he had to be an ace who got himself killed in the war. How else could a dumb pelican do such perfect split-esses and half-rolls?"

They would all nod their agreement. No one dared contest the points made about Gus. Those who are alive and remember know that the story of Gus is entirely true.

2 SANTA MONICA'S LADY SKYDIVER

The day was bright and cool with light Southern California breezes. It was November 13th, 1927. Next year I would enter my teens. This year I was still so unsophisticated that I was unaware the 13th was supposed to be an unlucky day. For a lovely young woman of 19, this day would be one of the luckiest in her life.

The event was promoted as the third annual *World Flight Commemoration Air Meet*. It was a hallmark day for Donald Douglas and his world cruiser biplanes. Officials of Santa Monica were justly proud of their genius airplane designer and manufacturer and wanted to promote his future success.

Scheduled to appear for the show was the Army Air Corps who would display a bevy of aerobatic Curtiss Hawk biplanes. Another event that had drawn pilots from all corners of the state was the loudly touted "Jenny" pylon race. Hard cash had been raised as prize money and hungry pilots had responded well to the incentive.

As a specialty act, the promoters had discovered a glamorous 19-year old female parachutist who recently had moved to the southland from St. Paul, Minnesota. The printed program boasted that she would electrify everyone by leaping from a barnstormer's airplane. When the 50,000 gaily printed red, white and blue programs sold out, the promoters knew it would be a very good day.

Reveling in her new southern California homeland, Miss Jean Devereaux West was laughing brightly at the clever sayings of the pilots gathered around her. As glamorous as any movie actress with blonde curls tucked into a white kid-leather flying helmet and a skin-tight flying suit, Jean was surrounded by men, men, men.

For her impending jump my father had offered her the services of his airplane and pilot. Bubbling, she thanked him profusely but when father introduced her to our pilot, Eddie Angel, she blushed deeply. So did Eddie who stammered while trying to make a favorable impression upon this astonishing beauty. Even at my young age, I thought something was brewing.

When a man from the crowd offered to prepare her 'chute, she smiled and nodded assent then continued her animated conversation with Eddie. At that moment she could not have expected the next day's newspapers to term her a flying flapper. Nor could she have imagined that her airshow act would hold 50,000 witnesses spellbound.

All this was no big deal for Jean, for she'd already accomplished more than 80 successful jumps in the East. She felt certain that this day would be hers.

Ordinarily, 24-year-old Eddie Angel as the pilot would be carefully overseeing all details of a jumper's equipment and the preparations. But this day his mind had gone slightly awry. *He silently wished she wouldn't look at him that way!* No one could foresee that Eddie's unusual inattention would result in serious consequences.

Aviation was still in diapers back in 1927 and parachutes were of the least sophisticated devices.

Jean's 'chute was the common exhibition parachute used by most of the barnstormers of that day. Packed in a large inverted canvas bag about two foot square, it was tied to a lower wing strut with rope. The jumper's harness was then wrapped with a rubber band and tied above the 'chute to a strut or other part of the airplane.

To jump, the chutist had to exit the cockpit and walk to where the chute was affixed, then untie the risers and harness package before snapping it onto his or her own 'chute straps. Sitting on the leading edge of the wing, the jumper would leap out at the proper time and her weight would break the weak twine that held the 'chute in its bag. All old hat for Jean.

Taking off, Eddie felt a special glow. The Jenny had been washed and waxed and displayed a large number "19" on each side of its fuselage in preparation for the coming Jenny race. Watching Jean wave to the spectators as they left the ground caused Eddie to feel that even for a few moments of flight, this lovely lady was technically his.

Nearing the jump point, the girl turned in her seat, blew Eddie a kiss and crawled out of the cockpit toward the wing leading edge and the parachute. Blushing, Eddie set the Jenny into a slow, flat glide and watched as Jean fastened her straps and prepared to jump. Confidently, she leaped clear of the propeller and dropped. But instead of the chute breaking loose from its pack, the cord—that the helper had installed—was too strong and fouled the release.

With a bump, Jean swung back and was pinned under the wing with her feet trailing. Seeing this, Eddie was shocked.

Usually slow-moving but always fast of thought, Angel circled the airport while he considered the best plan for landing without injuring Jean.

On the ground, there was a frantic rush. One airplane took off and climbed toward them with a cameraman in the rear cockpit. Two others soared away with wingwalkers who intended a plane-to-plane change for a rescue of the frustrated jumper. No way, Eddie decided, were others going to add more risk to an already dangerous situation. He alone would do the rescue.

Waving the other planes away, Angel began a wide gliding circle as slowly as he could possibly fly. Down they came toward the landing area. The announcer had told the audience of Jean's plight and all eyes were riveted upon the girl hanging helplessly below the Jenny's lower wing.

When the pair were barely a foot off the ground and the airplane neared a full stall, Eddie let it drop to a perfect three-point landing. But at the moment the wheels touched, he swung the plane into a groundloop toward Jean's side. Pilots watching this thought Eddie had lost control of the plane. But they were not aware of the unusual skill of this veteran pilot. At the moment when it appeared control would be lost, Eddie added power, straightened the plane and it rolled to a stop having used no more than 150 feet. Jean West was safe and bore not a scratch.

Two months later, Miss Jean Devereaux West flew with Eddie to the famed Mission Inn in Riverside, California, where she became Mrs. Eddie Angel.

3 GRAF ZEPPELIN

The dream of carrying passengers over land and sea began in 1852 near Paris, France, when Henri Giffard's steam-powered dirigible flew downwind for 16 miles at the fearful speed of three knots. That dream ended 84 years later.

When the Hindenburg exploded over Lakehurst, New Jersey, after crossing the Atlantic Ocean from Germany, the era of the airship literally died away. Since then, experts in lighter-than-air flight and aviation historians have speculated that had the cause of the Hindenburg's disaster been proven, the age of airships might still be with us. But to this day, no one knows, if the giant airship's final catastrophe was caused by a flash from static electricity or from an act of sabotage.

Whatever, public opinion stressed that such aerial behemoths were structurally unsound and obviously at nature's mercy. The three failures of America's best design efforts only underlined the public's disapproval.

Despite all the emotional outcry, straightforward facts belied the dour reputation of airships. We must consider that throughout its history, the Graf Zeppelin's achievements proved otherwise. Under German experience and masterful airmanship, the Graf proved conclusively that airships could be safely and comfortably flown anywhere in our world.

Until the Hindenburg tragedy the Graf was always referred to with superlatives. During its nine years of flying it made 650 flights, carried more than 18,000 passengers, traveled over a million miles without incident and landed on five continents. It successfully battled the worst storms and many times safely penetrated severe line squalls. Like her Zeppelin predecessors, the Graf never suffered any structural failure. History records that the only structural failure of any German Zeppelin was on December 7, 1915, when the army airship LZ 57 lost two of its engines due to combat damage but still managed to make it safely back to its base at Luck and then was dismantled.

The actual and ultimate cause of the Hindenburg's explosion must be blamed on the fact that it was filled with highly volatile hydrogen instead of the inert gas, helium. Prior to the outbreak of European hostilities, the German government had repeatedly tried to obtain helium for its airships from the United States. Were history to repeat itself today, it is probable that the humanitariam aura of safety would grant the Germans an allotment of helium. We had the world's sole supply then.

American dirigibles filled with helium faced no such perils as fire and explosion, but all failed in turbulence due to a combination of weak design plus poor airmanship.

On August 8, 1929, the Graf departed Lakehurst for the start of an around-the-world flight, partly sponsored by the Hearst News Services. It flew east, touching down at many

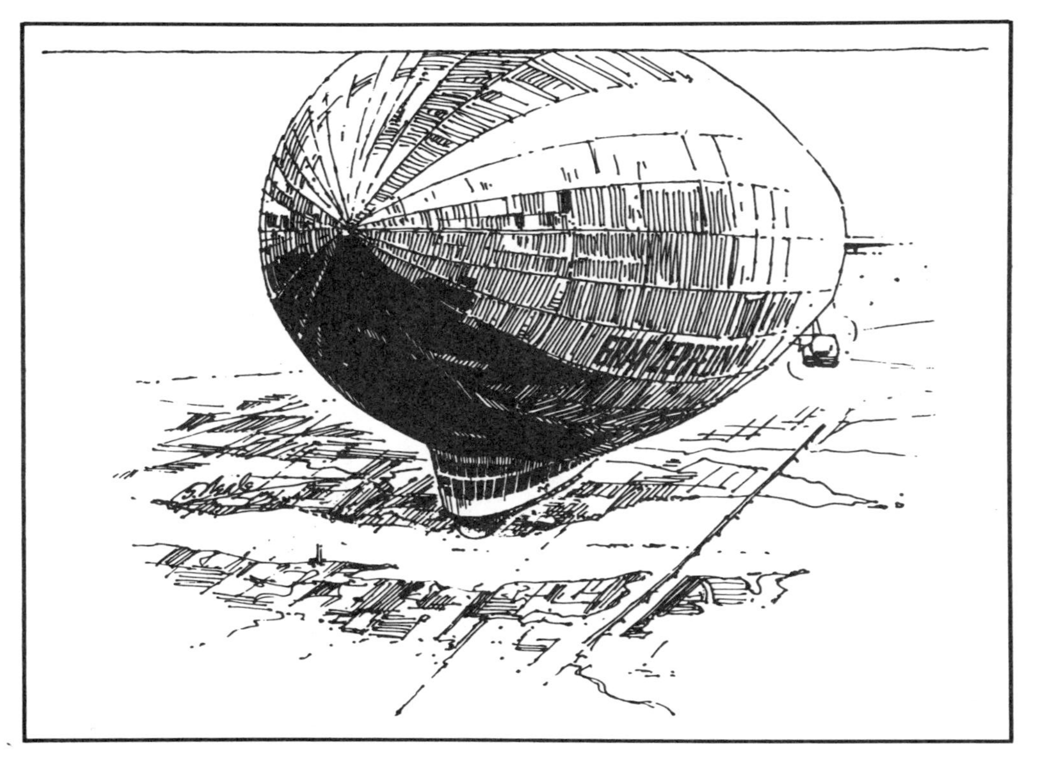

Graf Zeppelin, the airship with a soul. Drawing courtesy of Bill Neale.

ports, including Frederichschafen, Germany, and Tokyo, Japan. Its final destination, Lakehurst, New Jersey, would include a layover in Los Angeles, California. There, its safe record would be threatened seriously.

On August 25th, at 10 P.M. , the Graf was reported over Ventura, California. As an escort, Maddux Airline's chief pilot, D. W. "Tommy" Tomlinson, flew up the coast in a tri-engine Ford and intercepted the giant airship. Both aircraft arrived over Mines Field (now LAX) at midnight. The airship captain elected to cruise along the Pacific coast until daylight before landing.

At 5 A.M. , the Graf descended into the cool, moist air from the hot inversion layer in which it had been flying. As the ship lowered, it became 4000 pounds lighter and was forced to valve off 35,000 cubic feet of precious hydrogen gas to land.

The Graf stayed at Mines Field for two days and had an unexpected takeoff the following evening. The airship's commander, Dr. Hugo Eckener was wise to the ways of weather and planned prudently. He determined that more gas had been lost in ballasting and valving while the ship lay at her mooring. Eckener knew the ship would have to be filled with local "natural stove gas" if a successful takeoff was to be made.

My father took me to Mines Field to see the airship's departure. Nearing dark, the lines were cast off and Eckener ordered full power and up-elevator to clear the high-tension lines ahead. With increasing speed, the Graf raced toward the red obstruction lights atop the electricity poles that bordered the airfield. Immediately, it became apparent to everyone that the ship would not clear the wires.

"It's going to crash!" A hushed cry came from the crowd.

My father gripped my hand tightly and I felt my heart pound as I hoped the ship would make it.

Inside the control car, Eckener watched the nose clear the wires, but with the climb angle of 12°, some 700 feet of hull still hung below. He alerted the helmsman, his son Knut. As the ship drew ever closer to a catastrophe, Eckener dropped his arm and shouted "Now!"

Knut spun the elevator wheel to full down. The nose eased over the great bulk of the hull and tail miraculously lifted. The ship then cleared all obstructions by three feet. A great, audible gasp of relief came from the waiting throng. Had the airship struck the wires, an awesome explosion of the remaining hydrogen would have instantly incinerated all of those aboard and nearby. But it did not, thanks to the skill of its seasoned commander.

On May 6, 1937, the Graf's sister-ship, the mighty Hindenburg, burned and crashed at the Lakehurst Naval Air Station in New Jersey. With a global conflict nearing, the U.S. Government still refused to provide the Germans with nonflammable helium gas. The day of the giant airship was drawing to a close for few passengers would risk flying in such fire-hazards.

On June 8, 1937, Dr. Eckener ordered the Graf Zeppelin to its base at Frankfurt to be laid up and deflated of hydrogen gas. She was then used as a public display charging one mark per visitor to its innards.

Hermann Goering, who hated airships and the people concerned with them, ordered the original Graf and her successor Graf II dismantled for their aluminum salvage value. On May 6, 1940, with the airships now carried away in bales of scrap. Goering ordered the huge hangars dynamited. Coincidentally, the date was the third anniversary of the Hindenburg's disaster.

The remains of the original Graf Zeppelin were shipped to Holland and used for radar towers. But despite such ignominy, the world remembers her as the greatest aircraft to grace the skies.

4 THE SEAPLANE THAT SHOULDN'T

It was late winter in 1936 and a series of "unusual storms," according to Los Angeles' Chamber of Commerce, had pelted the southland for a month.

Despite the attempt to portray southern California as everyone's Mecca, the benign prevaricators had to yield when low-lying areas turned into lakes three- to six-feet deep.

My barnstormer-turned businessman-father was staring through the windows of our home and grumbling as only he could. During his heyday as a member of the Angel's Flying Circus I had heard him vent rage at this or that item of trivia, but today he was in exceptionally rare form.

"Blankety-blank—bleep-bleep, rotten lousy cursed weather! Here I am trying to run a few service stations and my main one is covered with three feet of water. Grrr! Bleep—bleep!" Black hair waving as he roared like some jungle beast with a bellyache, his resonant baritone voice shook the windows. Anyone there could tell this was not time to engage him in any conversation.

Timidly, I said, "I'm going out to the airport, Pop."

"Lotsa luck!" he roared. "If you can find the damned thing in all this water, go!"

It was true. We lived next door to his major business location and it was now the worst low spot in the small town of Compton, California. A solid city block surrounded Pop's property and the land was covered with reddish-hued muddy water between three and four feet deep. Autos were stranded everywhere one looked but my Model-T Ford had been parked two blocks away on higher ground. Besides, I had built a small raft on which I could get to dry ground.

Once on the highway and headed toward Compton's airport (that my father had started ten years back), I saw great puddles of water and slabs of muddy goo everywhere. When I arrived at the airport, I had to park at the edge of the road because all of the airport was such a gooey mess. I had forgotten that the ground was composed of adobe and when it rained, the airport was out of business for some time.

In my pocket were a few dollars that were fast burning a hole in my trousers. Money meant flying time and flying meant life to me. That much was never complicated. Whatever it took, I had to fly and I would use any method to gain that end.

There had to be another airport somewhere that wasn't built on adobe soil.

I drove to Long Beach. It was half-flooded and crews were trying to repair deep holes and ruts all over the airport's landing areas. A sign read: "CLOSED FOR REPAIRS UNTIL FURTHER NOTICE."

The Model-T and I hurried to Mines Field, west of the town of Inglewood where I knew of a small paved runway section. But when I arrived there, I saw that the paved area had between it and the hangar line a lake about a foot deep and as large as a football field. Another airport lay dead.

Sitting on a bench with my chin sunk into my hands, I saw

A seaplane rating was easy to obtain in Ken Baetz' Cub. Photograph courtesy of John Underwood Coll.

a flying friend, Ken, coming toward me.

"Hi Gerry, why the long face?" Ken did not seem affected by the weather problems at the airport. He was smiling and appeared elated.

"Hi Ken. I got some flying money but all the airports are shut down because of the weather." I had to add, "So what makes you look so pleased?"

"I'm going flying—today."

Why did he seem so smug?

"And I'm in no mood for humor," I sarcastically answered.

Tall, skinny, hawkish-looking Ken, laughed and answered, "I'm not putting you down. I'm *really* going to fly today. Want to go with me?"

Ken and I were both ready to take our private pilot's tests and it was illegal to carry a student on our student permits. Still the need to fly obscured all my reason. "You kidding? You don't have your license yet and the airports are still covered with water."

He grinned as if he'd found a pot of gold. "Sure, I know all that. And if you go with me, I promise both of us will get some flying in."

"In what, a seaplane?"

"Exactly."

I knew he had flipped.

He saw my incredulous look and explained his meaning. "Hey, I am renting a seaplane that flies out of the San Pedro bay area. You drive down and meet me and the plane at Belmont Bay and I'll pick you up. You pay half and you get to fly a seaplane—fair enough?"

Though I had difficulty believing his weird plan, flying had been offered and I was driving as fast as I could to Belmont Bay.

Ken taxied the Silver J-2 Cub floatplane towards me and I saw that except for the fact that it was a seaplane, I had been flying one like it without floats. Wise Ken asked for my money as I strapped into the front seat. I gave him my half and we took off. Instantly, I discovered the joy of seaplaning. On the step before takeoff it was as thrilling as the fastest speedboat. Only it flew, and that made it so much superior.

Flying northwesterly, I studied the land below from our 1,000 foot cruising altitude. We crossed over the Compton Airport and I thumbed my nose at it. But the entire area was in bad shape. Lakes replaced the housing tracts and most of the highways were flooded. Drowned autos lined the edges of all the streets and one could see the frustrated motorists waiting for help. Truly, the Los Angeles Basin area was at a standstill.

Soon we were flying over the Western and Rosecrans Avenues and could see the large lake that had been Gus Gotch's thriving airport a few days ago.

Ken tapped me on the shoulder and pointed down. "There, we'll practice on the lake at the airport." He'd eased off the power and glided to a perfect landing across the flooded runways of Gotch's airport. It appeared as if seaplanes were much easier to land than their landplane cousins. "Don't these ever bounce?" I shouted to Ken as he taxied back for my turn at the controls.

"Don't know," he answered. "I've never seen one bounce and all my landings are real slick."

As we turned and Ken showed me how to draw up the water rudder, I asked, "Why do they call them, 'landings'? They are really 'waterings.'"

"Damned if I know that either. Never thought about it. So let's see you fly a seaplane. It's half your money so you can make landings or waterings—I could care less."

I made about five circuits of the field and amused myself

by taxiing across the airport's runways, taxiways and around Gotch's gas pumps barely visible above the top of the water. Autos along the roadway slowed to watch us in amazement as we slowly taxied alongside the road embankment. Then we saw the cop bring his motorcycle to a stop and wave at us.

"We better get outta here!" Ken shouted.

"No, he may be a cop, but look, he's smiling at us."

"Okay, taxi to the edge of the road and I'll shut off the engine at the right time."

We coasted to the road and nudged the float bows against the soft mud embankment. Ken opened the Cub's split doors and respectfully asked the officer, "Yessir?"

"How about a ride?" beamed the uniformed man. "I never been in a seaplane . . . I'll even pay you."

No wonder Ken eventually became a success in business. "So get out and wait for me, Gerry. I'll make it short. Wow! Five bucks!"

Ken and the officer taxied out to fly and I waited on the road but in the short time they were aloft, six motorists pressed money into my hands as they requested "passenger rides."

Then and there, I was certain the gods had brought the rain purely for Ken and my good fortune. I did know what we were doing was illegal but I did not know how to refuse such a bonanza.

In a few minutes Ken had returned and when I showed him the fistful of money I'd collected and explained the reason for it, he said, "I told you we'd have fun. So let's make a million!"

As we were leading the first passenger to the seaplane for his ride, we heard this terrible cursing coming from someone who'd driven up and parked.

I recognized stocky, muscular, black-haired Gus Gotch immediately. Known to most of those in aviation for his skill as a racing pilot and all phases of aviation, he was normally a nice, pleasant person. But not when a seaplane was making money off his airport.

Jabbing his arm toward us menacingly, he trotted to the policeman, leaned into his face and bellowed, "Arrest them! This is my airport. Arrest them!"

"Well now," the officer began to stammer. "It somehow just doesn't look like an airport, sir. It looks like a place for seaplanes and these lads aren't even touching any of your land."

Gus seemed to calm slightly. Pausing a few moments, he spoke again in a deadly tone of voice. "I fly for the sheriff. You arrest these two or I'll tell the sheriff you won't do your public duty."

That statement caught the officer's full attention. He came to us, both standing on the right float, and offered, "Boys, I sure did like the ride but this man is awfully angry and I guess he could make trouble for all of us. I'll turn my back and you get in that thing and just git!"

Ken nodded, leaped into the Cub and I knew enough to start pulling the propeller through as he turned the switch on. It started and Ken applied throttle as I made my way back into the cabin. Luckily it was only a 40 h.p. engine or I'd been blown off the floats. We took off tailwind and as we climbed over the airport to return to Belmont Bay, we could see Gus Gotch looking up at us and wildly shaking his fist in our direction.

It ended peacefully. I did get in some seaplane flying. Ken had his turn too. And I was stimulated enough about seaplane flying to return to the San Pedro area and obtain my seaplane rating.

Several years later, I would rent airplanes from Gus Gotch, who would study me carefully now and then but never connect the fact that I was in the hated seaplane that "shouldn't have."

5 ANNA AND THE ERCOUPE

World War II was still ahead on this clear, warm August day. By noon on this Sunday, I already had flown more than 20 "fly-it-yourself" trips in Monrovia Airport's two-control low wing Ercoupe. At that time our wee airport was noted for being a few miles east of the Pasadena, California, Rose Bowl, for being very short and for running downhill to a railroad embankment. In spite of these shortcomings, it was a busy field full of Civil Pilot Training Program students, personal flying and innumerable passenger hops on Sundays.

Our red and white sign proclaimed:

The Ercoupe was liked by all—except Anna. Drawing courtesy of Bill Neale.

$5 ! FLY IT YOURSELF $5 !
(Or your money refunded)
MONROVIA FLYING SERVICE—NOW!

Waiting to refuel, I saw them as they walked to our ticket window in the tiny office. Laughing, the three of them were silent only long enough to purchase one ticket.

"It's for her," said the young man, beaming. "It's her birthday. Do you really let someone do the flying?"

Having walked to the trio, I answered, "We sure do. I help set up the power and talk our guest-pilot through the flight from takeoff to landing. Everyone in our area is doing it."

They introduced the "birthday girl" to me as Anna. I greeted her warmly and displayed my usual confidence meant to inspire trust in first-timers. Anna was lovely, dressed immaculately in white sharkskin slacks, a blue-gray Angora pullover sweater and an old-fashioned lace shawl to protect her blonde hair. Anyone would find her striking—especially any man. She was slim and moved sprightly. Her manner and her voice told that she was vibrant, youthful and an inveterate lover of life.

She also was obviously very nervous about the coming flight.

"Are you sure this won't scare me?" she asked in a voice too low for the others to hear.

I spent several minutes assuring Anna of the finer points involved in the two-control Ercoupe and its claims for safety. Still beaming, I warmed to the subject about the utter joys of flying. Ending my canned pitch, I described how we held our fist in front of the control wheel when our "student" took off so he or she would not overcontrol the airplane.

"Nothing to it," I finished but my confident tone of voice had disappeared. I was disturbed by her look of suspicion and the nervousness that she could not now hide.

Moving to help her into the airplane, Anna refused my aid and nimbly stepped into the tiny cockpit, seated herself and deftly buckled the seatbelt as if she'd done it for years. You do get fooled, I thought and assured myself that once we were airborne, my passenger-copilot's fears would vanish.

Of course they would. Hadn't every soul I'd taken for first rides in an airplane done so?

Anna, it seemed, had other ideas. First, she refused my offer to let her taxi the airplane. I shrugged my shoulders and slowly taxied to the takeoff point. Anna stared straight ahead—immobile.

I realized that firm action had to be taken to dispel this customer's fears, so I opened the throttle and shouted, "Grab the control wheel. Drive it!"

She did not move and when I looked, I saw that her eyes were shut tightly and that she had a deathlike grip on the bottom of the seat. With the runway end approaching, I pulled the airplane into the air and proceeded through the traffic pattern.

When clear of our pattern, I turned to Anna, still determined that this one person would not spoil my record of never having frightened any passenger. But no, her eyes were still shut tightly and her hands still held the seat edge with white-knuckled determination.

Using my most persuasive tone of voice, I pleaded, "Hey, Anna, look down and see how beautiful everything is!"

Without moving her head or a muscle, she said through clenched teeth, "No!" Then uncertain I'd heard, she screamed, "No. No! Take me down, please!"

Obviously my powers of persuasion were totally out to lunch. Anna remained frozen, still immobilized and her eyes, if anything, were more tightly closed than ever. I felt crushed. My flying ego as a pilot had been battered by this lovely lady. Cutting the flight short, I entered the pattern and landed the plane as lightly as possible.

When I began slowly to taxi back, Anna spoke. "You say it steers like an auto?"

My turn for surprise. She again was calm, friendly and her lovely self. Stunned at the personality switch, I released my hands from the control wheel and watched with disbelief as she confidently steered the Ercoupe back to the flight line without any help or suggestions from me. When we'd stopped and I had opened the hatch, she was pointing at her hand on the control wheel so her friends would think she had made the entire flight. They were waving enthusiastically at her and beaming broadly.

Stepping off the wing, Anna turned to me, "You won't tell, will you?" Her face pleaded for my support.

Of course, until now I've never told anyone of Anna's secret fears. Would you have told on a lovely person's 80th birthday?

6 POP'S LAST FLIGHT

I remember it so well. The date was February 22nd 1965. For several weeks I had not visited my father, Claude Casey, the pioneer aviator. Naturally, I was fretting about his health and welfare because his birthdays were many and he'd retired from aviation some time ago. But, from his present conversation, I could tell the flying disease still coursed through his veins.

Since 1950 he had not flown pilot-in-command, but seemed happy when once a year, I would take him with me on a local flight around the Los Angeles area. On these treks I would let him do all the flying except the takeoffs and landings at congested airports. A true stoic, he never complained and on these local trips I would think about his previous experience. . ..

In 1945, with the help of Pete Sarah, who operated a flying school at the old Central Avenue Airport south of Los Angeles, Pop took a refresher course in a 65-hp Porterfield Collegiate trainer. When I told Pete of my concern about Pop's lack of skill, he snorted. "You're expecting too much from the old bird. Maybe he isn't precise, but he's sure as hell safe! You have forgotten that the old timers manhandled airplanes. So what?"

So, Pop flew with Sarah for several months but had to stop because of his limited retirement income.

My thoughts went back to 1943 when I was giving night transition training to Ferrying Command students in a C-47 (DC-3) at the Long Beach Army Air Base field. I had sneaked Pop aboard as he'd never before even ridden in a twin-engined airplane. As we flew, he stood in the companionway behind the student and me and watched intently everything that was going on. After we landed, I asked how he'd liked the flight. Poker-faced, he replied, "It touches down at exactly 63 miles per hour. I guess I could fly her okay."

Wisely, Pop traded his Aeronca K for a used TV set.

What confidence for someone who had never ridden in a twin.

In 1950 I was stationed in Seattle, working at the Civil Aeronautics Administration as an aviation safety agent at its Boeing Field GADO. When I learned by letter that my father had purchased a much-used and abused Aeronca K, I hurried to Los Angeles to see him. When I saw firsthand the airplane's horrible condition and flew around the field with him, I tried to discourage him, "It's a junk-heap, Pop. And you fly it too heavy-handed to be safe. Get rid of it!"

"Maybe you are right, son. The prices the mechanics charge these days . . . well, I don't know . . .."

"Then you'll sell it?"

"As I said, don't rightly know."

None of my arguments seemed to reach him until I said he was sullying the Casey name and making it embarrassing for me to be a CAA safety agent. That appeared to get to him and after my promise to fly with him as often as I could get down his way, he agreed to sell the airplane.

Back in Seattle, I received a letter from him a month later telling how he'd traded the Aeronca for a television set. He assured me the TV set gave him more pleasure than the airplane simply sitting on a field and costing him precious retirement money. I thought it was an appropriate deal and relaxed over his new lease of longevity.

Time passed and it became 1965. I was living back in Southern California again. For helping a friend get his instrument rating, I had the use of a very fine Beechcraft Travelaire twin, B-95A. My fretting about Pop, the availability of the airplane and a slight residual guilt over causing him to sell the Aeronca all came together into a plan. I asked him if there was any particular flying he would like to do with me.

He answered without hesitation. "Yessir. If it's possible, I'd like to get my hands on one of those small twins the rich guys fly."

Pleased, I told him about the Travelaire and said we could fly that very day. "Where would you like to go?" I asked.

He grinned mischievously, "I heard of a place to get some swell apple pie and coffee." (Slyness runs in our family.)

"Okay, so where is this place?"

"It's in San Diego at Gillespie Field. Is that too far for a big aviator like you?" I could see his enjoyment in trying to bait me.

I laughed. "Why not? Sure, let's go."

We started from the El Monte Airport east of Los Angeles. The day was superfine. Weather was responding to a large lazy high-pressure area, producing light winds. A few stratus clouds caressed the coastlines and smooth air abounded. We flew directly to the coast and as soon as I had the airplane on course toward San Diego, I let Pop fly. He accepted the controls, but diverted his attention every few moments towards the coastline on our left.

"What's bothering you, Pop?"

Frowning, he squinted at me. "I've never flown an airplane this far over the ocean."

We were no more than a mile offshore. I explained that away from land a bit, we would have less chance of unexpected traffic.

"Wouldn't hurt to be a little higher," he said.

"So do it."

I advanced the power and he climbed to 5500 feet and leveled the plane as if it had been his own. I marveled as I watched him fly the unfamiliar wheel-controlled airplane. I saw that old pilots' habits never die. Pop was a classic "stick-nibbler," as were many of his barnstorming ilk. A stick-nibbler for us younger folk is a pilot who wiggles and adjusts the controls even though the airplane he's flying requires no correction.

Foolish me thought I could teach this old bird a new trick he would appreciate. "Say, Pop, look out there at your ailerons and tell me what you see."

"Nuthin, son. Just air."

"Do you notice how you are wiggling your ailerons?"

"Sure! You a dummy or something? I'm flying!"

"Here, watch me a moment." I took the controls and violently moved the wheel to its limits right and left. "If you'll notice," I said with a hint of sarcasm, "the ailerons wiggled but the airplane didn't do anything."

"Aha! Damn but you're one smart pilot, son. Let me try her again."

I returned the controls to him and he proceeded to stick-nibble exactly as before. I shut up, remembering it was his day, not mine.

In San Diego, I had him follow through on the controls into and out of Gillespie Field. I never did learn how he'd discovered the super pie at the airport coffee shop but thought it possible old barnstormers might have developed a sort of ESP about good places to eat.

Enroute back to El Monte, I let Pop make a landing and takeoff at Orange County Airport. His handling of the airplane was perfect. I guessed that ancient skills might have imbedded in the old pilot's psyche.

Over the Norwalk area near El Monte, I spotted several huge open fields and decided it was time to give my father an added thrill. Without warning, I cut both throttles to idle and shouted, "Forced landing!"

And just as suddenly, it was my time to be thrilled. I gritted my teeth as Pop began a series of wild maneuvers intended to set the airplane up for a landing. I vowed I would not touch the controls, no matter what. (But I sure wanted to!) By then the airplane was leaping and cavorting about the sky as if swatted by a giant baseball bat. I saw the horizon go by my vision several times at some very crazy angles. I hung onto whatever was handy. The airspeed swung to extremes because of the wild maneuvering. I looked to see Pop's response to the simulated emergency. His attention was riveted to the field he'd selected and he was paying no attention to anything else.

No, we did not crash. In fact—and I hate to admit this—when the airplane was at a proper point of final approach, the airspeed was exactly as it should be. The glide angle was perfect and stabilized. And when the Travelaire crossed over the fence, it was precisely set up for a proper landing at the closest point.

"I'll take it!" I said, and Pop released the control back to me.

"Damn that was fun!" he shouted.

I admitted amazement that he could do such disgusting things to another pilot's stomach while making a simulated forced landing. Pop grinned broadly. It was a very obscene know-it-all grin. "Why didn't you ask me to do something hard, son? Hell! Ain't anything easier than a forced landing!"

Since then, my father has gone to where all runways are without end. But I remember his last flight very well.

Part 2

Days of the Airmail

7 THE INFAMOUS LIEUTENANT

Retired General Otto Praeger was the assistant postmaster and had ordered the very first United States airmail flights to begin on the morning of May 15, 1918.

The Army's supervisor, Captain Benjamin Lipsner, anxiously studied the sky and was grateful that it was clear. He also hoped that Major Reuben H. Fleet, who would ferry the first airplane to Washington from Philadelphia was already airborne. Time was running very short.

Lipsner was also very concerned about the pilot whom officials had chosen to make the first flight from the Washington field. Lt. George H. Boyle already was late to report. Lipsner frowned deeply as he tried to recall the man. He could not and thought it odd; the Army air service was so small that almost everyone knew each other.

Boyle, extremely ambitious, thought it a stroke of good luck that he'd become engaged to the daughter of Judge Charles McCord, the Interstate Commerce commissioner who had influenced the government to allow Army pilots to start the mail service rather than civilians. But no one, it seemed, knew precisely the actual talents or experience of the dashing, young lieutenant. Lipsner was more concerned when informed that Boyle had only recently won his wings from flying school.

At 10:35 A.M., Major Fleet glided over the trees, landed and taxied to the temporary grandstand. Watching was President Woodrow Wilson and Assistant Secretary of the Navy, Franklin D. Roosevelt.

Lt. Boyle finally arrived resplendent in a new leather jacket, shiny boots and brand new goggles jauntily set upon the forehead of his new helmet. Though he *looked* the perfect aviator, Lipsner and Fleet had a gnawing suspicion about his ability.

After the political speeches ended the mail was loaded. Fleet asked Boyle for his maps so he could check them and was astonished to learn that Boyle had none.

Questioning the smiling pilot further, Fleet discovered that Boyle had done no actual cross-country flights except the 50 mile jaunt near his flying school.

Hurriedly, Fleet prepared a map, explained its points and taped it to the leg of Boyle's flight suit. Boyle took a brief glance at the map, climbed in the Hisso-Powered Jenny and took off.

Fingers crossed, Lipsner and Fleet watched as Boyle climbed away but quickly looked at each other in disbelief—Boyle was flying in the wrong direction.

Their worst fears had been verified but there was nothing to be done except wait until they heard from Boyle.

An hour passed and finally a call from Boyle came. He had become lost and in landing had picked a soft field and nosed over, breaking the Jenny's prop.

Lipsner and Fleet were furious at the brass bypassing seasoned Army pilots for a rank novice. Though they demanded Boyle be replaced, their superiors ordered they give him another chance.

The following morning, with a new propeller installed and Major Fleet to guide him, Boyle took off from the soft field successfully and repeated Fleet's instruction to himself: Keep Chesapeake Bay on your right—on your right. After making sure that Boyle was following his orders, Fleet broke away and turned toward Washington, D.C.

One thing Boyle did very well was follow a direct order. "Keep the bay on your right—keep the bay on your right!" Repeatedly he drummed this into his brain. And he dreamed of the fame he would have by being airmail's *first*.

History shows that both of Boyle's desires failed miserably.

Boyle, it seemed, had concentrated so hard on keeping the "bay on his right," that he'd flown a 360′ circle around it.

Lost again, he landed safely and took on fuel. Again airborne, he pointed the nose of the airplane in the direction of the airmail field in Philadelphia. By keeping the Jenny's nose exactly on the course set by those on the ground, Boyle was sure his troubles were over.

In the Philadelphia area, Boyle saw a polo field and landed. It wasn't the airmail field at all. And it wasn't long enough to land in.

When the dust cleared, it was noted that the Jenny was wrecked and Boyle had slight injuries.

Though the post office officials brazenly asked Lipsner and Fleet to give Boyle another chance, they adamantly refused and demanded that the young lieutenant be returned to flight school for additional training.

Oddly enough, the records show that Lt. Boyle did accomplish these firsts:

—He was the first official airmail pilot;

—He was the first airmail pilot to get lost;

—He was the first airmail pilot to crash;

—And he was the first airmail pilot to be injured while flying.

But history also reveals that Boyle, as far as the budding airmail service was concerned, had made his last sponsored flight.

8 WESLEY L. SMITH: PILOT

To those who reviewed his flying application, it seemed ironic.

Even in early 1918, the man named "Smith" appeared more as an opera singer than a pilot. Ironic or not, he had studied for the opera but had also studied to be an engineer.

Also unusual was the fact that he'd excelled in both subjects. It was apparent he was a study in contrasts.

Though Wesley L. Smith's first dreams were for an operatic career, World War I thwarted his plans. As an engineering student, he was exceptionally talented. Upon graduating with honors, Wes turned to teaching. His students remembered him as a no-nonsense, big, barrel-chested man with piercing dark eyes and straight black hair. One predominant trait was his persistence to achieve. Contrasting this amibition was his desire to avoid personal publicity or any form of public acclaim. This feature of Wesley Smith was to dim his aviation achievements to this day.

Tiring of teaching, he heard from other pilots that the newly formed Air Mail Service was seeking trained pilots. Here at last was his chance to make use of his military aviation training. The air mail people hired him at once.

It was soon evident to Smith that too many pilots were being killed trying to make schedules in poor flying weather. With an infinite faith in aviation's future, this caused him to preach to all who would listen that aviation must develop ways to make its airplanes and engines more reliable, and ways to fly without being grounded by weather.

"W.L." deduced that to master weather, a pilot would have to consider two basic priorities: first, he would have to use instruments to show him the airplane's attitude when flying blind; second, he must know where he was and how to navigate to where he intended to land. Because ships at sea were already using direction finders for navigation, Smith knew that blind flight navigation was possible. And he intended to prove his theories as soon as he could keep an airplane under control in clouds.

It wasn't long before W.L. had developed a crude but effective method of flying blind in relatively stable air. Before entering clouds, Smith would carefully trim his airplane for level flight. Thus the engine sound and the tachometer because his references for level cruise, climbs and descents. He learned too, that if he held the airplane perfectly straight by ruddering a compass heading, he would avoid falling into the dreaded "graveyard spiral."

Always eager to advance aviation's techniques, W.L. shared his experiences with other pilots who would listen and try his discoveries. On May 20, 1920, he checked the fixed loop that had been installed on one of the airmail planes, took off solo and lowered a makeshift hood so he would be flying blind. Aloft for an hour, Smith made a triangular flight from his departure point to his checkpoints and back to his original field.

Once on the ground, Smith enthusiastically told the postal authorities of his success and pleaded with them to support further, extensive blind flying experiments. But when the upper echelon checked with the other line pilots, Smith's peers said the flight was a freakish thing and they wished no part of flying "without seeing the ground."

Nine more years would pass before any pilot would make a successful blind landing.

Persistent, and able to complete more assigned schedules than most of his ilk, Smith was finally able to convince three other line pilots to join him in his flight experiments. When airmail employee and instrument design genius Howard Salisbury joined the four, luck was with them. Salisbury came up with two workable blind flight instruments that actually opened up the entire field of scheduled flying. His turn and bank indicator, adapted from the crude military one, and the altimeter with a barometric adjustment immediately began to save pilot's lives.

It appeared at last as though Wesley L. Smith's dreams were coming true. He now had instruments that would take him safely through clouds and weather, and the Department of Commerce had installed lights along the airways and even had initiated a few low frequency radio range stations for navigation. Ice, it appeared to Smith, was now the urgent mystery to solve.

On February 6, 1929, Smith took off in a Douglas M-4, the Wasp-powered version of the Liberty-engined M-2, from the Cleveland, Ohio, airmail field in search of icing conditions. After an hour's fruitless flight, he started down to land but saw that the clouds below had become a thick, wooly undercast.

Letting down with the radio tuned to the Cleveland radio range, he made an instrument approach to 800 feet above the field but saw nothing so flew back on top of the clouds. Two more attempts took him lower but the clouds remained. What he did not know was that the airport had gone to zero-zero conditions. Without a two-way radio, Smith could only surmise the field conditions. With fuel running out, Smith knew that this third attempt would have to succeed—or else.

This time, when he was over the "cone-of-silence," Smith cut the engine and steered the final approach course to the field closer than he'd ever done before. Moments later, the plane thumped to earth and rolled to a stop in the *center of the airport*. It took the ground personnel an hour of walking over the airport to locate Smith and his plane. But though history has not recorded this event, Smith knew that he had just made the first blind landing, ever, under actual instrument conditions.

History did record that on September 24, 1929, months after Smith's achievement, Jimmie Doolittle made the *second* such landing at Mitchell Field on Long Island.

9 HEROES OF THE AIRMAIL

It was true. After each pilot was born, the mold was thrown away. Individuals all, they avidly protected and nourished their own counsel. They were as varied as could be, yet each was bonded by a sameness, a unity of the soul.

When we consider the 1920's and their chapter in history, these pilots lived in a compression of time and experience. Many would go on to enjoy long, rewarding careers in flying. And too many would die in an instant. Whatever the length of their service in pioneering the airmail, each would leave a legacy of greatness.

One of the first major efforts of aviation pioneers was to turn the haphazard efforts to deliver mail into a solid business. Much that we enjoy in aviation today is a result of the daring attempts of these rare individuals. The promoters, the ground personnel, the pilots, all must be acknowledged as the heroes of the airmail.

In reviewing the history of the airmail in 1918, one immediately finds a stark contrast between the people concerned with the ground efforts and the pilots. Those on the ground worked in concert, blending as a large dedicated team with the mission of keeping a few planes and pilots airborne. But after the ground personnel had turned the DH4's metal props and started the old Liberty engines, the airmail effort was totally dependent upon the skills and courage of one man—the pilot.

Once in the air, each pilot had to understand and embrace nature's fierce duality or he would not survive. Truly, these men lived a stark either-or existence; either the old Liberty engine throbbed away or it quit cold. And when it stopped—as it often did—the pilot solved his urgent problem quickly or he died. The weather followed suit. It was either flyable or totally impossible and the recognition of these two extremes often had to be made in the flash of a microsecond. The pilot, too, was composed of a dual nature: he had to be smart and also had to be lucky, for both the smart and the not-so-smart died in flaming crashes. Some of the lucky ones seemed to possess a mysterious but innate sixth sense. For these few, the odds appeared stacked in their favor.

All the airmail pilots had to deal with many perilous situations in their day-to-day flying. Though these events accumulated with each flying hour, accounts of them are few. True, each of the pilots shared accounts with other pilots. But as a group they were closed-mouthed and reluctant to describe their trials and tribulations. Their heroics of flight—even their impossible odds—still lie buried in the musty past. What accounts remain are as bare as the limbs of a winter tree.

No one today has been told what Jack "Skinny" Knight felt during the long hours he flew in snowstorms one long night across Nebraska through to Chicago. What went through his mind during the tense hours he flew at tree-top level? How many times did Knight decide to give it up and land, but pressed on in a gamble with fate?

Then on an extremely foggy night over the vicious Allegheny Mountains between New Jersey and Bellfonte, Pennsylvania, Charlie Ames flew along under the stratus clouds and faced one more hill beyond which lay the airmail field at Bellfonte. His feet were curled around the control stick of the DH4 for comfort as he eased the plane up into the fog to cross the crest of Hecla Gap and its pale beacon light. What could anyone know of his feelings when the earth suddenly and shockingly caused his death? Did Ames die because Wes Smith and Howard Salisbury had not yet perfected their new "barometric altimeter?" Either man might have given his own life to have saved Charlie Ames. Where lies the guilt but in the lap of fate?

Not much later, Ames's buddy, Wesley Smith was caught in zero-zero fog above Cleveland. With the newly perfected altimeter and his prowess gained through persisting in flying blind, Wes managed to land safely smack-dab in the center of the Cleveland airport. Fate? Skill? Or, dumb luck?

Was it any better for Wes Smith to leave his flying career only to die of diabetes in a New York apartment? Which of us can determine the reward or the penalty of fate?

Today we fly with all that these pioneers paid for in human blood. They flew "without." They did not have instruments in those early days to tell them if their airplanes were straight and level in a cloud. They could not press a microphone button and ask someone on the ground at a station ahead how the weather was. Even with the low-frequency radio ranges and the lighted airways, to fly instruments often meant death somewhere along the line.

All connected with the pioneer airmail service starkly revealed their fantastic abilities when the president of our land ordered them to stop flying. He was advised that the military pilots could deliver the mail and do an even better job than the civilians. But in a few short months, the military had lost 12 pilots in 66 accidents. World War I ace Eddie Rickenbacker made national headlines when he proclaimed, "This is legalized murder!"

In history, the duration of the airmail was brief—ten years. Despite the challenges and the impossible odds they faced, the airmail pilots managed to fly nearly 16 million miles in delivering 302 million airmail letters. And though the odds were against them, these great men managed to make 90% of their assigned schedules. They did this despite the 6,532 forced landings, 200 crashes and the 32 fatalities. They persisted doggedly until they had racked up an incredible 158,000 hours of flying time.

Whatever is classed as defeats for these men had to be tied into their unexpected crashes. They often gambled with fate and lost. The wrecked carcasses of planes came from hitting smokestacks, mountains and the ground when their flimsy biplanes iced up. Many spun in when orientation was lost in a murky black sky.

We must not allow ourselves to think of the heroes of the airmail as having been defeated. For though a passenger in a jet, or a pilot in his sport aircraft cavorting in sheer joy, all of these are there because they stand upon the shoulders of these supposedly ordinary men who so extraordinarily achieved aviation's first account of scheduled flight.

Let none of us ever forget.

10 249—LOST ON CAM 18

The next morning would be December 15, 1922. Airmail pilot Hank Boonstra surveyed the sky. He did not like what he saw. Across the great Salt Lake plain, racing in from the west, a heavy overcast of slate-gray clouds cast a gloomy shadow on the land below. Hank studied the scudding air mass and knew that tomorrow's flight to Rock Springs, Wyoming, would be no picnic.

At 7:30 the following morning, airmail plane 249, a rebuilt DH4 piloted by Henry G. Boonstra, was airborne, climbing east toward the snow-laden Wasatch mountains. Boonstra saw that the overcast would prevent him from flying over the high ridges. Boonstra hunkered down deeper in the windblown cockpit of the DH4. There was no way of telling what the temperature was but it was way below freezing. He saw that he could stay in the clear by skirting Porcupine Peak near Coleville, Utah. Through the snow squalls, he could see that the weather was clearer ahead of the pass. As he was thinking about the storm pressing his tail feathers, the Liberty engine began to show signs of carburetor icing. It backfired and surged and he tried working the throttle but the engine slowed then stopped completely.

Hank started to glide down and saw that there was no way he could escape coming down among the higher peaks of the Wasatch Mountains. There was a small clearing in the snow below him into which he might make a crash landing and stay alive—if it were done just right. There wasn't room to level off for an easy landing. He saw that, to survive, he would have to smack the DH down onto the field of snow hard enough to break off the landing gear. In that way he felt he had a chance to keep from flipping the airplane onto its back.

A quick glance at the altimeter showed him he was at 9,400-foot elevation and a few feet from the snow field. At about twenty feet above the terrain, Hank pressed the control stick sharply ahead and the DH crunched into the snow, immediately breaking off the landing gear. Holding his breath as the plane slid to a stop, Boonstra thought he would be able to "walk away" from this one.

Stopped, he tumbled from the cockpit in case the airplane decided to catch fire. Literally swimming through the deep snow, he managed to get about 50 feet from the plane before he turned to survey the results of the landing. Though steam was spouting from the broken radiator, there was no sign of other vapors, oil or gasoline. Shaking from the bitter cold, he crawled back to the plane.

It took him almost an hour to remove the compass from the instrument panel as he alternately warmed one hand then the other in his armpits. When he had it free, Hank started down the mountainside.

Then began a struggle through snow and treacherous sheer cliffs that went on for 36 hours. Hank knew that if he stopped or rested he would die from freezing. On and on he went, tumbling, sliding, thrashing through soft snow and alternately sliding across frozen patches of ice. Finally, he came to a farmhouse where he was taken in, fed and warmed and put to bed. There was no phone or other means of communicating with his Salt Lake headquarters until he could again travel.

Hank rested for two days at the farmhouse while division superintendent Arlen Nelson led a massive ground and air search for Boonstra. Rested from his ordeal, Boonstra traveled 10 miles to the nearest phone by which he reported his experience to Salt Lake headquarters. Days later, the airmail survey party found the plane and removed the mail sacks. All in this group conceded that the airplane could not be saved due to the impossibility and danger of the terrain and snow.

So for airplane 249 began a 43 year waiting period before its resurrection would begin.

Old 249 had been built in 1918 at a factory in Dayton, Ohio. It was first assigned as a trainer for the aviation section of the U.S. Army Signal Corps. Ferried to Love Field in Dallas, Texas, its pilot was Eddie Stinson, a flight instructor serving under Major Reuben H. Fleet. His famous *Stinson* airplanes were still in the future.

In 1919, with World War I over, the airplane was declared surplus. The following year it was sold to the newly formed airmail division of the Post Office for $1. After its extensive modification as a mailplane at the Maywood, Illinois, shops, it was given the number 249 and assigned to the Central Division as a reserve plane. Ultimately, 249 was reassigned to the Western Division where it flew between Omaha, Nebraska, and San Francisco, California. Famous airmail pilots such as Tex Marshall, Frank Yager, Jack "Skinny" Knight, Jim Murray, Ernie

DH-4 tried to cross the Wasatch Mountains but fate intervened. Photograph from the Jesse Davidson collection.

Allison, "Dinty" Moore, and Dean Smith often flew the plane.

Hearing that the remains of 249 were still on the Utah mountainside, restorer Bill Hackbarth of Santa Paula, California, decided to investigate. In 1964, Bill visited Boonstra, who was retired and living in Salt Lake City, Utah. The story Hank relayed convinced Bill Hackbarth that here was an airplane that deserved to live and fly again.

Another year would pass before Hackbarth reached the airplane's remains in his four-wheel-drive truck into which he loaded its 600 pounds of bits and pieces with great care. Spectators thought he was a junkman.

For the next two years, members of the Airmail Pioneers Association aided Hackbarth in the plane's reconstruction. All appeared to be going well until October, 1967. Without warning, one of California's infamous brush fires roared down the hillside at the rear of Hackbarth's farm workshop. Unfortunately, three wing panels and an almost completed fuselage of old 249 were in the shop and were destroyed.

Undaunted, Bill and the stubborn AMP members waited only five days before beginning work anew at the Santa Paula airport. One of the pioneer mail pilots remarked, "This old bird sure doesn't want to die!"

Cost was a serious problem. The airplane's radiator was not found in the wreckage and had to be built from scratch. When Hackbarth finished, 1,200 feet of copper tubing was used that cost more than $1,000.

For some time, the search for an engine seemed a hopeless quest. But my friend, and owner of the airmail archives, Jesse Davidson, heard of the group's plight and came to the rescue. He knew of a restored and overhauled Liberty engine in Clarion, Pennsylvania, that belonged to John Trunk, a contractor and former World War II B-29 pilot. Jesse convinced Trunk to donate his engine to the great cause. Graciously, United Airlines airfreighted the Liberty to California.

One year later Bill Hackbarth climbed into 249 and flew the restored DH4 across the U.S. in easy stages to what was assumed its last resting place—the Smithsonian Museum. Unwisely, Smithsonian experts termed the airplane a replica instead of a restored, original airmail plane. The Airmail Pioneers were, understandably, unhappy enough about that slap in 249's face that they retracted their offer of the airplane.

Meanwhile, the San Diego Aerospace Museum wanted to

display 249, but the costs of returning the airplane to California appeared insurmountable. Local funds for the airplane had been exhausted and all wondered if 249 would vanish before hidden dreams were realized.

But again, a transfusion of life pumped new energy into 249. Mrs. Reuben H. Fleet, widow of the man who literally had started the airmail service and created the huge Consolidated Aircraft Corporation, generously donated the needed funds. One could almost imagine the old plane heaving a sigh of relief.

Others involved were not as fortunate.

In 1965, John Trunk lost his life in the crash of a J-3 Cub. Then Bill Hackbarth died in 1974. Old 249's pilot, Hank Boonstra, died of natural causes in a Salt Lake City hospital in April, 1984, at 94 years of age. And my friend, Jesse Davidson also died in 1984. But today, old 249 lives.

After 68 birthdays to her credit, the old bird is aging quite gracefully at the San Diego Aerospace Museum.

May she rest in peace, always.

Part 3

Aviation's Famous and Otherwise

11 HE FLEW BACKWARDS

Something in California simply wasn't right that spring day of 1928.

Weathermen watched the barometer fall slightly and noticed that fast-moving alto-cumulus clouds filled the western horizon. As crude as their meteorological know-how was in those days, they knew a muscular storm was coming. But how bad or exactly when was pure speculation.

When it came, it immediately erased all doubt as to its potency. It was a huge winter storm from the mid-Pacific, and it was wet—very wet.

Midstorm in the San Francisquito Canyon, St. Francis damkeeper Tony Harnischfeger looked more solemn than usual as he made his routine inspection of the dam and its facilities. The dam, a subject of controversy since its engineer, William Mulholland, had rushed it to a hasty completion, was leaking badly.

Two minutes before midnight catastrophe struck. With an explosive roar heard 10 miles away, the dam collapsed, sending over 12 billion gallons of water racing towards the sea some 44 miles away.

Four hundred and twenty people perished in the ferocious flood waters.

In nearby Los Angeles, a 22 year-old pilot of considerable

skill had just hung up the phone, completing a deal with a news photographer for a picture-taking mission as soon as the sun had risen.

On the morning after the break, the sun shone with a pallor that revealed the worst of the storm had skidded by the Los Angeles area after doing its damage to the area of the St. Francis dam. In its wake, a strong northwest wind was blowing. Into the teeth of the near-gale, the pilot and the cameraman boarded the pilot's demonstrator, a long-wing Eaglerock biplane powered with an OX5 engine.

Inflight, the photographer asked the pilot to fly high for his first shot, an overview of the damsite and the downstream flood damage. No problem; the pilot easily climbed the silver and blue biplane to 12,000-foot altitude. When the newsman asked him to fly slowly so he could get "good resolution shots" of the dam's remains, the pilot easily flew the biplane at speeds below 35 miles an hour.

Doing his flying professionally, as local newsmen knew he could and would, Jack, the pilot, had something else of importance on his mind that day. He'd invited prospective Eaglerock purchasers to witness a flight demonstration at his Western Avenue Los Angeles Aero Corporation of American Airport. Notwithstanding the pompous name, the airfield was similar to many others of that day: small with rutted runways and with a few dilapidated buildings serving as an office and shop, and rickety-looking hangars.

Though his photographic mission had seemed a success, the pilot's heart sank as he approached his airport and saw the small cluster of prospective airplane buyers waiting below. That he was late was obvious. He knew he'd better figure out something impressive to show them without delay or he would have a very unfriendly group of critics rather than happy prospective airplane purchases. Jack gritted his teeth as he contemplated the grim vision of going broke and seeing expected profits turn to dust.

Approaching his airport from the west, he flew downwind at great speed and crossed the landing area. As my father and I watched, we saw the Eaglerock make a steep climbing turn into the strong headwind as if it were a ballet performance rather than a mechanical thing of flight.

Watching intently, Pop had the same thought. "Looks like a pirouette," he grunted but I saw that his face showed respect

The Long-Wing Eaglerock — you could buy it on credit. Drawing courtesy of Bill Neale.

for the pilot's maneuvering.

Into the wind the biplane continued—slower and slower. Then to everyone's consternation, the forward speed of the airplane halted. Gasps of disbelief came from the assembled group.

"Damn fool! He's gonna stall it," someone shouted.

"Not by a damnsite," Pop muttered.

But there was more to come.

As we watched, we saw the nose creep even higher and heard the 90-horsepower OX-5 increase its revs. My Pop shook his head. "He may just spin it if he isn't careful," he said.

But as we watched, the unbelievable became the unacceptable.

"He's backing up!"—all the voices at once.

Indeed, father's appraisal of this pilot was right on target. Not only did this young aviator know the exact capabilities of his airplane but was well versed and practiced in the technique of "flying behind the power curve." Few pilots knew then that the addition of power at the stall point lowers the stalling speed.

When the biplane had drifted backwards to an exact point of a downwind approach, considering the strong wind, the pilot let the nose drop. In moments, its wheels touched the ground in front of us so gently they would not have torn a cigarette paper underneath them. As it stopped, the widely grinning photographer clambered out and rushed away with his equipment. Then the pilot turned toward his entranced spectators:

"Twenty-five hundred dollars, gentlemen. And you can buy it on credit." There was total confidence in his manner.

Indeed. Pop looked at me and winked. "Son, we are going to buy one of those."

Several other sales were made right on the spot. The new distributor of Eaglerock airplanes for the west coast was making his mark in business.

Later, this young pilot sold his puny Standard Airlines and himself to the budding Western Air Express. In 1931 the firm merged to become TWA.

Not yet 30 years of age, Jack became TWA's president, a position he eventually used to stimulate the design and success of the Douglas transport series of airplanes.

Most aviation types recall the famous photo of him looking out the cockpit window of a DC-2 airliner as it readied for its departure. With the famous Eddie Rickenbacker, a new coast-to-coast record flight was made.

The chubby-faced, youthful appearing pilot went on to even greater accomplishments in aviation. His full name was Jack Frye.

12 "A.E." AND THE TIN GOOSE

Everything had been attended to—all was perfect. The weather out of New York was clear. That in itself was a minor miracle for the month of October in 1930.

Officials of the young Transcontinental and Western Airlines were pleased. Though TWA was a spinoff from its predecessor TAT, the start of the first scheduled coast-to-coast airline flight was going well.

No longer did TWA worry about wooden winged Fokker F-10 tri-motors and wood rot. Now they boasted of a fleet of the latest Ford 5 AT-B tri-motors. All agreed that nothing could ever break off the stalwart "Tin Goose."

Originating at Newark Air Terminal, the flight was planned to cross the Alleghenies to Columbus, Ohio. Three fuel stops were a must in between the two points. After a crew change at Columbus, the next leg to Kansas City was planned as a night flight.

Indeed, to everyone concerned, all appeared to fit neatly in place. Pilot H. G. "Andy" Andrews, TWA's chief line pilot, was assigned this first flight. Few pilots were as experienced as this veteran of the airmail.

To further its PR efforts, TWA had convinced Amelia Earhart to ride along as a passenger. By then Amelia had already flown the Atlantic Ocean as a passenger and had placed third in the previous year's Women's Air Derby. Ahead of her would be marriage to publisher George Putnam, a solo flight from Newfoundland to Ireland, and her untimely death in the Pacific Ocean near Howland Island in 1937.

Amelia had decided being a passenger on this historic

flight would encourage more women to fly. Also, she had participated in a near-copy of this flight for TAT the previous year. Then she'd been a passenger on a Ford Tri-motor with Charles Lindbergh as pilot. Unlike the TWA effort, that flight had started by entraining its New York passengers to Columbus overnight. From there, the actual cross-country flight began.

In Los Angeles, Lindbergh would command the "City of Los Angeles"—the eastbound section—to Winslow, Arizona, await the westbound flight and command it to its final destination at Grand Central Air Terminal in Glendale, California.

For a woman to fly anywhere in those days took a certain amount of bravado and elan. Airliner restrooms were simple bucketlike affairs, open to the rushing wind below. Theory had it that everything discharged would disintegrate before it hit the ground. And perhaps so at great cruising heights, but this flight cruised mostly at a bare 500 feet above the surface. Several years of complaining from the irate earthbound would pass before airline officials would redesign their aerial thundermugs.

Andy Andrews was pleased. The weather was clear. No longer did he have to concern himself with Liberty engines that stopped midway across the Alleghenies. He now had three reliable Pratt & Whitney Wasp engines to depend upon.

The weather stayed as forecast until a hour out of Newark. Then the lumbering Tin Goose began to get banged about like a yo-yo as it crossed the Allegheny ridges. At 8,000-foot initial cruising altitude, Andrews had computed the wind at 80 mph right on the nose. His groundspeed was an outrageous 40 mph. At that rate, he knew the place would exhaust its fuel prior the first planned stop.

Down went the Tri-motor. When the Ford was clearing the mountain crests by 500 feet, the pilot leveled out. Breathing easier, he noted the groundspeed rise to 82 mph. Better, but it still meant battling a 40-mph headwind.

Up and down in wild thumps, bangs and lurches went the shiny metal monster. And so did the stomachs of some of the passengers. Andy peered back at his "load" and noticed that though some faces had green tints, their owners reassured him with a smile. Well, he reasoned, I've got that famous flyer Amelia Earhart back there to comfort them. So, I'll just concentrate on flying this clumsy beast.

Yes, most of his passengers were handling the wild turbulence with a degree of aplomb, but one was having a serious problem trying to keep her stomach from rebelling.

Amelia Earhart was airsick.

Too rough for Andy to leave the cockpit, he was aghast when he saw the famous pilot stagger into the tiny restroom, to return much later with a very ashen face.

Eventually, the mountains were behind and the rough air ended. Even Amelia settled down to endure the remainder of the trip to Columbus. Chagrined, she made Andrews promise not to reveal her unexpected "weakness." Even today, few readers note that early photos of her during this flight show a very uneasy lady pilot sitting in the wicker chair of the Ford tri-motor.

Until the great woman left our planet, Andy kept her secret. And until you read these words, so have I.

That was scheduled airline flying back in 1930.

13 JIMMIE ANGEL'S AIRSHOW

All his life he had been something of an enigma to those who met him. Newsmen to this day persist in spelling his name wrong. He was outwardly brash, and he was a promoter par excellence, but of dubious honor to those who'd dealt with him. One trait about him though brought a uniformity of opinion: Jimmie Angel could damn well fly anything with wings.

Born in Springfield, Missouri, in 1899, Jimmie told the press one story about his exploits and still another, more truthful account to his friends. The public was told that he was a parachutist for a circus at 14 years of age. Through my father I learned he'd soloed when an early barnstormer had paid him a quarter to guard his Curtiss biplane while he spent the day in a nearby town. Always an activist, Jimmie Angel's genes did not tolerate the word "spectator." Within the first hour, and with the help of some friends, Jimmie had started the airplane's engine and was taxiing back and forth across the large field. In another hour, he'd figured out the controls and what they did. Thus it was preordained that he would taxi faster and faster until the airplane left the ground. Before the owner had returned, Jimmie had made numerous circuits of the field without mishap. As a 14 year-old boy, this experience proves the remarkable inherent instinct he had for flight.

Jimmie's brother, Parker, an airplane design genius, told us how Jimmie had served in the British Royal Flying Corps. He said his brother had downed three enemy aircraft before being shot down while ferrying an unarmed FE-2b pusher.

And here it was, a bright and clear April day in 1926 at my father's new airport in Compton, California. Though the morning was calm, our collective mood was electric. Jimmie Angel was flying in.

Eight of us were waiting that day and all tried questioning Jimmie's brother, Eddie, the airport's sole flight instructor.

"What will he be flying? What will he do?"

"He'll be in a Fokker D-VII. He's coming from the National Guard field at Griffith Park." Eddie appeared annoyed at the questions.

One pilot, sneering, asked, "So what will the big eagle be showing us?"

Always cautious, Eddie smiled at the man and spoke with studied deliberation. "Well, Jimmie's often been a kind of showoff. Guess you'll see if you stick around."

A few of us, including me at age 11, were too awed to ask any questions. Somehow we sensed we would witness a worthwhile flying exhibition beyond the realm of the ordinary airport types. None of us had any inkling that this man would one day have the world's tallest waterfall named in his honor.

Most of us waiting had seen photos of the Fokker and knew it as having two cantilevered upper wings plus a small winglike spreader bar between the wheels that doubled as an auxiliary fuel tank. This remarkable airplane was called a "biplane," though technically it was a triplane.

"How will we know it?" I asked, tugging at Eddie's sleeve.

"Easy," Eddie grinned. "It's all silver except for the wings, tail and nose. Those are a bright lipstick red." He paused to reflect a moment, then added, "You'll hear it long before you see it." He winked a promise that we'd not be disappointed.

We knew that Angel would approach our field from the northwest. Eddie dug his watch from his pocket, flipped open the face lid and said, "Pretty soon now."

Talk stopped. Movement was suspended as we faced the expected approach course. Our ears strained to hear the

Jimmie Angel and the fantastic Fokker. Drawing courtesy of Bill Neale.

185-hp BMW engine. Eddie pointed skyward.

Then we heard it.

At first, the sound had an extremely high-pitched whine, something like tiny clock gears winding down. Then as it came within sight the whine became an angry snarl. None of us had heard such an engine sound before. Mouths hung slack as our eyes were riveted toward the plane.

When it was closer the screaming engine sounded as if it might explode. But no, the airplane began a curving arc toward our field without any decrease in power. Then it began a lazy, beautiful slow roll as it turned. When it thundered by a few feet off the ground, I heard an added sound: the airframe was producing a low thrumming roar. Each of us, I'm sure, silently regarded this mechanical thing of flight as a predatory bird about to rip its prey into pieces.

How terrible this airplane must have seemed to the Allied airmen of World War I who witnessed it before taking their final breaths.

Angel finished his slow-roll opposite our small band of spectators, then abruptly yanked the plane into a vertical climb. Up, up, up, it went. We'd never witnessed any airplane doing a sustained vertical climb,

At what appeared to be about 1,000-foot altitude, we saw

the Fokker slow, stall, then fall away into a left wingover (stall-turn). Recovering, this turned into a vicious slipping turn. In the slip, it came down as spectacularly as it had climbed—literally plummeting toward the earth below.

Down and down it fell in the slip, but over the telephone wires bordering the airport, the slipping turn modified enough to align the nose with the landing strip. Then to our complete amazement, the plane was snapped out of its slip with a sound as if a paper bag had burst. For an instant it seemed to hang in a full stall a few feet above the ground. Then "plunk!" It was down and rolling a few feet to where we stood. Angel gave it a sharp burst of power to turn it and the plane and engine stopped a few feet before us.

All except Eddie Angel ran to the Fokker and the pilot, who was waiting patiently. Eddie had seen his brother's tricks before.

As we neared the airplane, the broad-faced flyer was already sitting on the turtleback, unsnapping his helmet and goggles. Smiling grandly, he said, "Not a bad bird, is it?"

Some simply babbled with excitement. Others came close to him but were still too stunned by what they'd seen to talk.

"Impossible," I recall saying. "How did you do it?"

Jimmie winked at me. "Wasn't me, lad. It was the airplane."

Despite Jimmie Angel's sudden, unusual modesty, we knew we had seen the impossible with our own eyes. What's more, during the five days he spent at our small airport, we witnessed even greater examples of Jimmie Angel's superb airmanship.

Once more, Jimmie had proven he could damn well fly anything with wings.

14 ARRIGO BALBONI

In 1934 the Depression was still in full bloom as far as teenagers were concerned. My aviation-minded friends and I had started a flying club and purchased a used secondary glider in which to fly.

Our ship was called the "Tailwind" and had originally been an open primary type but had later been converted into a full fuselage secondary glider. The process was simple: one only had to add stringers to the open framework of the primary and cover to produce the resulting change.

None of us had much experience. None of us really knew anything about the techniques of flying or things aerodynamic. The consequence was predictable: about once every 45 days, one of us would make some bonehead mistake in landing. A wing dragged the ground. A stall banged the bottom of the fuselage structure. Or, our frail towrope might break as the glider lifted off the ground. All of these pilot errors caused damage to our glider.

Then we'd stop flying until all anted up for repairs. Leafing through an aviation magazine one day, I came upon the following advertisement:

ARRIGO BALBONI
AIRPLANE SUPPLIES
1543-45 Riverside Drive
LOS ANGELES, CALIF.

Wrecked airplanes bought and sold. Airplanes and motor parts of all makes. Slightly used Jennies, and OX2, OX3, OX5, OX6, Parts for sale. If it is anything connected with wartime planes, I HAVE IT.

Day and Night Service
Capitol 2823
I Supply When Others Fail

When I asked one of the local pilots about Balboni's advertising claim, he said, "The guy is nuts, but there ain't anything flying that he hasn't got a chunk of in that den of iniquity he calls a 'store.' "

"We need five gallons of dope for our wing repair. Would he sell to us?" I wasn't sure I wanted to venture into this man's place even for the paint-like chemical to tighten and finish our glider fabric that we badly needed.

Arrigo Balboni and a Standard J-1. Drawing courtesy of Bill Neale.

"He'll sell to anybody! You show him your dough and he may even offer you a glass of his wine." The pilot hesitated a moment, recalling something about Balboni. "Come to think of it, if you look down on your luck, old weirdo might give you the dope." He paused again as he looked at me and two of our group and at our glider. "By gawd, if anybody ever looked down on his luck, you sad sacks sure do."

I looked at the others. They shrugged. "Give it a try," said my friend.

Next day we drove my Model-T Ford across hot Los Angeles to Balboni's place at the edge of Glendale. We passed his establishment several times because we could not believe that the ramshackle collection of wire fences, shacks and sheds and leaning buildings was a place of business. The place appeared as if it had been fire-bombed, which is not too much of an exaggeration as he had recently suffered a fire and a flood from the adjacent Los Angeles river.

But we were after dope for our fabric. As we parked and walked into his place, Arrigo Balboni met us at the front door. Standing with arms akimbo, he studied us as we entered the cluttered building. Short and pudgy, with black hair brushed straight back from a receding hairline, he asked, "What do you saps want? Are you lookers or buyers?"

"We got to have five gallons of dope for our glider, sir."

"Yeh," Chet added, "And we aren't even sure we've got the money for that much."

Balboni stiffened his body and then leaned back and roared with belly-shaking laughter. When he was again in control, he wiped the tears from his eyes and said, "I can get you two saps into the movies! I know everybody in the business. You outta get an award. What acting. Mamma-mia, if I could act like these two saps." He studied us somberly. "I think I'll whistle for Anna and Hilda and have them eat you up. How would you like that?" "Nossir," I was quick to reply, and Chet shook his head negatively.

At the mention of his dogs' name, two huge police dogs appeared from somewhere in the gloom of the place. Balboni winked at us and stated that his dogs protected the place all the time, and could read people's minds as well as understand English. "Isn't that right, Anna? . . . Hilda?" We were stunned to see both animals lie down beside his feet and stare into our faces. Balboni chuckled again. "As long as you saps don't steal anything, they won't eat you." Another quick study of us and he added, "I guess you're all right. You both look too dumb to steal, anyway."

With that observation and an understanding between Arrigo Balboni, his dogs and two uneasy teenagers, he turned to a large cask and drew two glasses of pale reddish liquid from it which he offered to us. "If you birds are under 21 years old, I don't know it, see?"

We sipped the offering and I remarked, "It tastes like wine diluted with water."

"Sure," he laughed, "strong customers get my strong wine."

Off he went to "see about the dope," after giving us permission to look his place over but stay out of the warehouse and adding, "The dogs will keep you company."

Chet and I started to investigate his stock of supplies and as if they actually had understood his words, the two dogs followed behind us. When we would stop to discuss some item, both animals would lie down in the aisle and watch us with very somber looks.

We went through Balboni's establishment as if Alice repeating her trek through "Wonderland." Bins were full to overflowing with used airplane parts. Metal turnbuckles of every size covered a wall of bins 20 feet long. Coils of control and rigging cables hung from pegs and nails everywhere. Sound and broken pieces of airplanes leaned against other pieces, hung from wires attached to the ceiling joists or were stacked in his yard in piles higher than a man.

Other customers came and went and a silent, very skinny boy in greasy coveralls served their needs. Most buyers appeared to know exactly what they wanted and where Balboni kept the item. It was the world's first serve-yourself, used airplane department store, in my opinion. Finally, Chet and I arrived back at the place where we'd first encountered this strange man.

"Just a second," said Balboni, as he reached to a Jenny wing wired to the wall and ripped a small piece of fabric from it. "Aha!" he said, as he sat before an ancient typewriter and fed the silver fabric through its rollers. Then, aloud, he typed a message upon it. "From French Ace Charles Nungessor's World War I Spad." Finished, he smiled at me and remarked, "It's for a South American museum."

I burst out, "But you took it from a Jenny wing. I know a Jenny when- - - - -"

"Ha! Just think how happy they'll be. Balboni always delivers!" And with that he disappeared into a small niche of an office in search of mailing envelopes . . ..

Arrigo Balboni's early career and his convoluted start in the airplane parts business was as unique as his establishment and his business methods.

In 1925, he was flying a Jenny from his homebase near Redwood City, California, to the Clover Field, Santa Monica, celebration of the Douglas round-the-world flight. But over the Tehachapi mountains Balboni got stuck in a downdraft and crashed the Jenny against a hillside. Unhurt, he hitch-hiked to Santa Monica where stunt pilot Al Wilson offered him $50 for the wrecked plane if he would deliver it. Borrowing a truck, Balboni retrieved the airplane and started back toward Santa Monica. Enroute he had an idea and stopped at each airport he found to sell parts of the Jenny. When he arrived at Santa Monica he counted a profit of $900 and still had half a truckful of parts remaining.

Arrigo Balboni knew a good thing when he saw it and immediately was in the airplane parts business.

At his original Riverside Drive location, Balboni thrived in business and regaled his customers with wild stories about his life. He'd discovered that in Hollywood and its environs, to play the fool netted an award of healthy profits. But no fool was he, for his stories mostly were true. He was born in Renazzo, Italy, on August 20, 1883. At age 12 he arrived in the United States where he and his family settled in the San Francisco Bay area. In 1916, Balboni was taught to fly by Silas Christoferson at his Redwood City airfield. During the following years, Balboni barnstormed, became a U.S. Treasury prohibition agent—which he found too dangerous—and returned to barnstorming.

Along the path of his busy career as a pilot, Balboni managed to fly for a term in the U.S. Army Air Service and fly a Jenny on a barnstorming tour around South America, up the east coast of the U.S.A. and finally into Alaska. Most of his customers were unaware of his background nor recognized the piloting skill necessary to have made such trips in a day when forced landings and crashes were far more common than a successful trip anywhere.

Gradually, news of Balboni's parts business spread across the land and eventually around the world. True to the ad I'd read, he "supplied when others failed."

His fuel tanks went to Brazil. His propellers and engines were shipped to the northern states to be made into powered snowsleds. Complete airplanes, wrecked or otherwise, were rented at high rates to the infant Hollywood movie business. By 1930 Balboni had an inventory of over 200 airplanes of all descriptions. It was not unusual for him to rent a wreck to a studio for background shots then later, re-rent it to the same studio for more shots from another director.

Picturesque, actually puppy-friendly, and always offering his customers a glass of wine with an invitation to sign his Gold Book, Balboni seldom altered his daily costume of baggy plus-four knickerbockers, two-tone shoes without socks, a Tee-shirt and a wristwatch always worn above his left elbow. When California grew cold, he would wear white socks, casually rolled to his ankles. That was his only amendment to his apparel, winter or summer.

Shortly before World War II, Arrigo Balboni retired to make his long-standing dream come true. Irked by the constant pressure from local authorities who wanted his untidy business moved elsewhere—anywhere—Balboni decided he needed his own town to insure him his freedom of choice. He then purchased some acreage west of March Field, California, with the intention of incorporating a town which he planned to name Balboni, California.

For a time it appeared as if he might succeed but fate interrupted his dreams. Arrigo Balboni was killed in an auto accident. Always having dealt in cash, no liquid assets or records were ever found.

While Balboni was successful in creating the image he considered best for his career: that of the jovial buffoon, during the Depression years Balboni had the only telephone in his area and his neighbors, who lived on or near his Riverside Drive location would use his phone as an answering service. When a person or a family got an incoming call. Balboni would run to the corner of Cabot Street and Riverside Drive and call as loudly as he could. "Hey Sap so-and-so, telephone!" And he would continue until the persons responded. No one ever though to take umbrage over his use of "Sap" as a substitute for a given name.

To this day, his true history, character and background remain obscured. Sadly, his precious Gold Book that had in it the signatures of most of the world's famous in aviation, has never been located.

But though Arrigo Balboni's dogs frightened me equally opposite as his gift of wine warmed me, I can easily recall that he would always ask how much money we had for our purchase and then settle for half that amount. Most times, it was also half the going price for the items we needed. I am proud to remember that he was my friend.

15 CLARENCE CHAMBERLAIN AND THE STUBBORN BULL PUP

We humans seem to be fascinated by anything mysterious. Throughout history this fact has enabled the pitchmen to sell snake-oil to the guileless. Though he claimed it would cure most anything, its alcoholic content simply made one feel a little better about life in general.

In the summer of 1937, I had already accumulated a fair amount of pilot-in-command hours in airplanes and gliders and had helped Harland Ross build the RS-1 sailplane for actor Harvey Stephens. To offset my low pay, I was offered a free ride to and from the site of the upcoming international soaring contest at Harris Hill in Elmira, New York.

At that time, I thought I was urbanized and of some sophistication about presumed mysteries. How wrong I was . . .

At Elmira I had planned on meeting many new friends who were into soaring and mooch, if possible, all the rides I could in sailplanes. Also in my plans was the idea of renting a local airplane to take air photos of the soaring machines in action.

Seeing the tiny Buhl "Bull Pup" tied down on the runway's edge made me drool. Someone with the same likes as I had undoubtably flown this thing to the contest. I saw an opportunity to rent the airplane very cheaply or maybe gratis.

It wasn't long after that I met Fred as he tightened the tiedown ropes of the Bull Pup. Here was a dark-haired, intense young man of may age who was a draftsman with the Wright Engine Company in New Jersey. The selling of myself should be easy. But when I began to tell him how much of a favor he would be doing to rent me his airplane cheap—very cheap—

The recalcitrant Bull Pup took them all on and kayo'ed the author and its owner.

he offered its use to me gratis. Right then I should have been cautious and realized that little in life of value is ever free. While I examined the single-place shoulder wing monoplane and wondered about the tiny three-cylinder Szekely 45-hp engine Fred assured me that the airplane flew like a dream and had no bad habits.

"It's a pussycat," he said; "You'll love it!"

As I gave the airplane as thorough a preflight as I knew how to, I missed somewhere in Fred's conversation, his remark about a "little problem taking off of rough ground."

It started easily and I taxied to the takeoff point of Harris Hill's gliderport runway. As the plane had a single magneto and no brakes, there was no point in hesitating. So, pedal to the metal and go.

Maybe the throttle did move to its limit and maybe the airplane did start rolling smartly across the rough ground. But takeoff? No way. Each time it struck a mound of dirt and leaped into the air, the engine would misfire and nearly stop. We went through a series of drunken lurches from mound to mound but the result was always less than adequate flying speed. With the end of the field coming up, I had to abandon my efforts.

Taxiing to where Fred awaited I could see his frown and obviously guilty expression. When I was out of the airplane, Fred admitted, "I was afraid it might do that. It barely got off the paved runway at Paterson Field in New Jersey, where I left from."

"How did you get it here?" I asked.

A lump of tongue appeared in his cheek. "Oh, the paved runway was right into a good wind and I kept the stick all the way back. There was a little bit of room remaining when it got off."

"And no problems flying here once it got off?"

"A few . . ." He hesitated before admitting, "The rough air over the alleghenies bothered me a bit when the engine would miss."

"So why don't we fix it? I'm not too shabby a mechanic."

"Thank you. I sure would appreciate your help."

Five days later, after trying everything either of us could devise, the engine reacted the same as it did on my failed takeoff attempt. We were helped by mechanics at the Chemung Valley airport who serviced American Airlines DC-3's. They tried for two more days and finally stated that whatever the engine needed to cure its problem was not in their bag of professional tricks. A few days later, I told Fred goodbye and returned to California.

Through letters, Fred told me the rest of the story.

The ignominious Bull Pup was trailered back to his home field in New Jersey. Fred told his plight to the best mechanics at Wright Aeronautical and they spent many, many fruitless hours trying to mend the recalcitrant engine. The stubborn Szekely thwarted the best of them.

Watching the unfolding fiasco with amused interest, renowned pioneer aviator Clarence Chamberlain offered his help. Fred thanked him but added, "Nothing will help."

Chamberlain retorted, "Won't do any harm then to try my system, eh?"

In his letters to me, Fred hinted that the great pilot had even threatened the airplane under his breath as Fred propped its engine. Chamberlain's approach to a cure was decidedly different. He would fly the plane and determine its ailments by actual test.

Poised against a brisk wind, Chamberlain opened the Bull Pup's throttle and held its tail on the pavement until it lifted off the runway. Fred and the others watched as it steadily climbed above the field. When it was but a speck against the sky, Clarence Chamberlain engaged in a series of violent snap rolls right and left. These were followed by spins, dives and pull-outs that had the wee engine shrieking. Finally, he glided into the pattern, landed and taxied to the waiting group.

Chamberlain climbed out of the Bull Pup and gave all a confident grin. "It's fixed now!" he announced.

Indeed it was. Fred made several test flights and the engine continued to run perfectly on smooth or rough surfaces. No fool, Fred sold the airplane a few days later. History records that the engine continued to function perfectly for its new owner.

I would have liked to have asked Clarence Chamberlain his secret formula for sick engines. But he took this mystery to his grave. It was and still is, the unexplained.

16 GENERAL PATTON AND THE "BLUES"

My log book entry shows the date of November 19, 1941. World War II was coming soon but I, like most citizens, did not expect it or the surprising way it made its debut.

As chief pilot of a Civil Pilot Training Program at Monrovia, California's airport, I had mailed a letter of complaint to Interstate Aircraft's chief engineer, Walter Hite. In it I had complained about the manner in which the Interstate Cadet S-1 floated when flown solo and when a landing was attempted. I had sent along my suggestion for adding a pair of lift-spoilers to the top of its wings. With that suggestion, I included drawings of how they could be operated by attachment to a throttle-arm that would bend downward to open the spoilers. During that period much of my spare time was spent often writing to anyone I could reach in my zeal to advance the ease and safety of flying.

I had not expected an answer. To my surprise, I received a phone call about ten days after I'd mailed my letter of complaint. It was Mr. Walter Hite and he invited me to fly the Interstate we were using in our program to Mines Field and discuss my proposal with him.

The next day I did as he'd suggested and met with him in his office. Hite thanked me for my interest and listened as I half-apologized for my complaint but added that my reason for it was that I considered the S-1 such a fine airplane in all other respects. He then added that my idea for a throttle-operated device was very clever. I had to blush as I revealed I'd "lifted" it from the Waco Aircraft Company design of the throttle-brake on our Waco F biplane. He appreciated my honesty.

It was a pleasant experience to talk to Mr. Hite as he was courteous, respectful of my ideas and listened with interest.

"Why don't we fly your airplane and you show me what you mean?" Hite asked.

So we did just that and he watched as I flew and explained that with two in the plane, the float was diminished.

Back in his office, he sprang his surprise on me.

"Gerry, your ideas are sound but conflict with our intention to compete in this lightplane market. Adding the spoilers would raise the retail price considerably. I don't think we'd entertain that risk but I am very interested in your awareness of the slight problem and how you approached an answer with good rationale."

"Thank you . . . I didn't mean to degrade the airplane."

"I realize that. What we would like from you is your services as our test-pilot."

For some moments I couldn't say anything. Here I was a complainer about his product and he had offered me a job as a test pilot. My brilliant response was, "How come?"

"In a few weeks we will enter a secret competition of observation type airplanes for the U.S. Army. They are developing a unit called the 'Grasshopper Corps,' and some manufacturer will get a nice fat contract for the design they settle on."

I had to interrupt. "How would that concern me?"

Hite smiled and continued. "I like the way you approach a problem. You fly well and I think you would make a fine dmeo pilot for us in the upcoming Carolina War maneuvers."

You guesssed it. How could any young pilot refuse such an exciting offer?

In a couple of weeks, A. H. Lowell, their other pilot, and I departed for the Carolinas.

As factory demo pilots we were to be an official part of the war maneuvers. Thus, we became Grasshopper Corps pilots, flying missions as required during the active military maneuvers.

The type of flying in which we engaged must be termed "brutal." Planes and pilots were from four major lightplane manufacturers. As most were situated in the eastern sections of the U.S., they were well-equipped with spare parts and even spare pilots. It was obvious that the competitive nature of trying to earn a new airplane production order was very serious to all involved.

We followed the command posts from point to point. Every few days the command post would relocate due to a change in the military situation between the Red and the Blue forces. At each relocation, the various factory pilots would choose fields as close as possible to the command post to impress the military brass about the superior qualities of their planes. In truth, this became a battle of pilot skills rather than a contest between machines.

Each move we flew off a smaller, rougher field than the previous. Piper's pilots sought fields as soft as possible, knowing our wheels had narrower and higher pressure tires. In a few more days, the fields became so dangerous that except for our airplanes and those of one other manufacturer, the competition had dropped out.

Accidents eliminated several airplanes. Trees were struck on takeoff. I ran off a road in a strong crosswind and ruined a right landing gear in a weed covered ditch. All these incidents—luckily—were minor and no one was injured. The officers who flew with us on observation missions soon looked at us with a jaundiced eye. It was apparent that this challenge was no place for the faint-hearted or the unskilled pilot. Luckily, we had a trunk full of spares with us.

At the command post near Waxhaw, North Carolina, the Army brass was facing the crucial problem: a major maneuver to determine which Army won the mythical war.

When I was alerted to fly a mission with General George S. Patton, I confessed I had never heard of him and did not know why his comrades called him "iron pants."

The hour came and I watched as the General swaggered to my plane and barked, "Let's go. No need to stall around!"

We went. When Patton gave an order, one moved. Each time I would try and check the airplane or engine, he'd bark, "Let's go! There's a war on!"

No warmup or magneto checks or decision about any wind direction or force. I was thankful it was calm. It was immediately apparent to me that this man knew very little about airplanes and cared less.

About ten minutes of flying time and we were over the area in question where a combat problem was in progress. We watched as a Red Army Sergeant stepped in front of a long column of the Blue Army's mechanized equipment, waved a large frying pan, and (we learned later) shouted "Chow! Turn in here."

Instantly General Patton understood that the clever enlisted man had duped and captured the Blue Army regiment with his bogus lure of food.

Patton exploded like an atom bomb. I was sure the cabin windows bulged from his expletives. From his scrambling to unfasten the seat belt, I thought he might leap from my airplane before we'd landed. When he saw a number of his tanks apparently parked and his men talking instead of fighting the war his ranting and raving was louder than the engine noise.

"Land! Land this bleep-bleep thing!" No question about the windows now; they were being severely strained by the volume of his voice.

I studied the terrain below us and noted the only possible landing spot was on a curving, narrow dirt road with low brush, ditches and fences on either side.

As cautiously as possible, considering the bellowing coming from behind me, I made my landing. It was next to impossible to shut out the terrible curses blasting my ears. We landed as I struggled to keep the airplane on the curving section of road.

Suddenly I heard an explosive rush of wind and turned my head in time to see my passenger bail out of his seat through the plane was still moving about 20 mph. Unceremoniously, Gen. Patton rolled head-over-rear into the ditch, picked himself up and raced to the tank commander. I watched in awe as Patton berated the man for a steady 10 minutes.

Unaware of his torn and dirty uniform, his face glowing red with anger, he returned to the plane and ordered me to fly back to the command post. Gen. Patton ranted and raved and shouted about the dubious ancestry of his tank commander all the way back. I wondered if I were flying with a madman or a genius.

Before we landed, I suggested to the general he might wait a bit on the landing rollout before exiting the plane to give me time to slow down. At his glowering look of censure I added, "Sir, you might break the door by rolling out before we stop."

His reply is not printable.

Despite my misgivings about this weird mission, our company received a contract and manufactured many of the Interstate L-6's for the U.S. Army.

In retrospect, I decided that if this experience was only a mock war, I wanted no part of the real thing. And as the real war evolved and I read accounts of General George S. Patton, I could only shake my head in wonder.

17 OPERATION "CAPTAIN"

This episode in the early history of scheduled airline flights is true. Some of those involved are still around so names have been changed. But no one can stop you from guessing who or where these souls are. It is possible you could have ridden in a modern jet transport quite recently with one of their sons in command . . . .

Albuquerque in January is usually cold and this day was no exception. "Jim," we'll call our copilot, was trying to firm up his flight plan to Burbank, California. To prevent his toes from feeling numb, he alternately stamped his feet on the broken, red asphalt tiles of the floor of his airline's Flight Operations offices. Like many anxious copilots yearning to someday fly in the left seat, he was early. As he set down the various factors of wind, fuel and distances to fly, he heard the battered wall speaker announce that his incoming flight had reported abeam Cline's Corners, a navigational fix between Tucumcari, New Mexico, and Albuquerque.

Jim decided that he must concentrate on the flight plan and try to untangle the chicken-scratches that company meteorologists called a weather map.

Grudgingly and by closer scrutiny of the station models penned on the weather map, he managed to decipher its secrets. A grunt escaped him as he mentally decided that weather maps were some antediluvian throwback to man's first alchemists.

Though he'd flown with Captain Max many times, it always amazed him that this god of the cockpit could spend a few seconds looking at such a map and immediately come up with a fully developed and accurate depiction of what the weather would hold for their flight.

Totalling a column on his log, he computed that the point to point air time to Burbank, California, would be four hours and 10 minutes.

As Jim finished his task, Captain Max burst into the small room, stamped loose snow off the tops of his cowboy boots then broadly smiled at his copilot.

"Hi!" he said, giving Jim a resounding thump on the back. "So what do you make of it, lad?" That this man was a seasoned veteran of flying was obvious. How else could he have such a perpetual squint to his eyes and the gnarled bony hands that so surely took command over the ungainly airplanes of the day?

"From the map, I'd say the weather is O.K.," the younger man offered his captain. "There are layers of stratus and we'll

Boeing 247D airliner. No matter what, the Captain was right! Drawing courtesy of Bill Neale.

be on the gauges most of the way but no turb is reported."

Max squinted a bit more and leaned toward Jim. "What about the wind?"

"I make our flight time to be four hours and 10 minutes, sir."

"That so?" One of Max's eyebrows arched upwards as if to challenge his copilot's findings. Then he peered a few seconds at the weather map. Turning, he gave Jim another backslap and said, "A dollar to five says four hours and 50 minutes." A silver dollar appeared in his outstretched hand.

"Here." Without hesitation, the copilot handed his captain one of his few badly soiled and crumpled dollar bills. He knew that it was an unwritten rule during these early days of airline flying for copilots do almost anything to keep the approval of their captains. He was also aware that his alternative to being a copilot was near-starvation at some backwoods airport.

Captain Max smiled broadly and pocketed Jim's money in a silver money clip as if it were already his own.

Jim wondered: how could this air-veteran take no more than a three second peek at a weather map and forecast a trip's enroute conditions and total flight time? Secretly, he felt this night would make him $5 richer.

Away at last, Captain Max took the airplane off the icy runway without seeming to notice the very strong left crosswind. They climbed on instruments to 12,000 feet and picked up a trace of granular rime ice on the wing leading edge but found the air smooth as predicted. When they were in level flight, Max gave Jim the controls.

Time droned on and it appeared that Jim's captain would busy himself catching up on all of his late correspondence. His writing was complete with sporadic chuckling as he penned his thoughts. Being so engrossed, Jim was certain the captain hadn't noticed his heading and altitude drifts from their prescribed paths.

Two checkpoints were crossed. The copilot's computer verified that his flight plan was on the nose. He planned to use the captain's $5 for a nice steak dinner.

Somewhat later, Captain Max shifted in his seat and stared abstractedly into the frost-covered windshield. He asked, "Winslow?"

Hurriedly the other checked his flight log. "Nope, got about six more minutes." Jim emphasized his point with a negative head-shake.

The captain turned back to his writing. "Winslow now," he said and pointed to the earth below.

Confident the captain has erred, Jim again shook his head. And at that instant the automatic direction finder needle started to swing madly to and from, finally settling on the 180 degree reading. They were over Winslow.

So much for copilots' flight plans and so much for all captains very brief glances at weather maps. Jim had to amend his flight plan to show a strong quartering tailwind. Captain Max's fiver seemed more of a sure thing for a dinner. "Be in much sooner, Captain," Jim suggested.

Max vigorously shook his head. "Huh-uh. Pretty soon we'll catch a strong southwest flow. Bound to make us slow."

You know what happened, don't you?

True, they landed at their Burbank destination but as they strode into their Flight Operations office, Captain Max studied his wristwatch before thrusting in front of his copilot's face.

"See that? What does it read, lad?"

Mr. Copilot, Jim, hung his head searching for some logic. How would he tell any other soul of a pilot who wins wagers without any scientific input? Finding no logic, Jim answered, "Sir, your watch says four hours and 50 minutes and one dollar of my money." He felt the red flush rising from his collar.

Max was generous though. He slapped his copilot on the back with a mighty thump. "Thanks for the buck, lad. You might make that left seat yet." Whistling off key, the aging captain walked ahead with a very confident stride.

That is the way airline things were that cold wintry night back in 1936.

18 MILO BURCHAM: TEST PILOT'S PILOT

I became aware of the remarkable pilot in the fall of 1933. Our country was still deep in a depression and I was struggling to build flying hours.

Walking to the hangar at Long Beach, California's municipal airport, where I rented the puny E-2 Taylor Cub, I would pass the headquarters of the Burcham Air Service. Owner/pilot Milo Burcham was starkly evident, for adjacent to his Bird biplane he would be suspended upside-down in a chair roped to the ceiling rafters. Often early for my flight, I would spend time chatting with this unusual but highly respected pilot. Talking with an inverted human being took some getting used to but I understood that he was preparing for an attempt at the inverted flight record. Also, I would bleed the brains of any experienced pilot whom I had the pleasure to meet.

As time unfolded Milo Burcham would enjoy a meteoric rise in the field of aviation. But at that point he was trying to become known as a leading aerobatic pilot. Wisely, he knew that an inverted flight record would earn him a needed reputation.

Burcham was barely 30 years of age when he was running his own fixed base flight operation at Long Beach. Born in May, 1903, in Indiana, his family migrated to California when he was nine years old. In 1924, then 21, he was selling burglar alarms and planning a family. As all of us who have caught the disease called "flying" know, it is incurable.

Milo, too, had caught the disease. Gradually, his time was being spent more on airplanes and flying lessons than on selling his product. Inevitably, he soloed at the original Fullerton, California, airport in 1928. Before that year ended, he'd accumulated over 200 solo hours, obtained Transport License #5274 and a job as a flight instructor with Lloyd O'Donnell's Air Service at the Long Beach airport. From that point onward, his flying ability and fame would steadily rise.

Also, during the aforementioned period, he experienced the first of a series of accidents that would eventually end his brilliant career. Flying O'Donnell's Fokker Universal with several students into Mexico, he crashed while taking off from a short, dirt runway. At the most critical point during takeoff, the engine had quit. Later, operating his own flight service, he would become involved in his second accident.

Teaching an overweight student the fine points of spins in a Bird biplane, Milo discovered too late that the center of gravity was excessively aft. On entering a spin, the craft immediately spun like a top in a nose-high flat attitude. No control input affected the recovery attempts by Burcham. The airplane fell much like a dry maple leaf into a plowed field. Though it needed extensive repairing, neither occupant was injured. Luck was with them but Milo's fate was being pressed.

In 1934 at the age of 31, Milo began his inverted flying. It was evident to all who watched him practice that he was a pilot with a natural flair for aerobatics.

During this formative period, Burcham acquired a Boeing 100 biplane with a Wasp engine. With this airplane his acrobatic routines became more impressive. Also during this period his inverted flying duals with Italian Air Force pilot Tito Falconi were making international headlines. When either pilot would set a new inverted record, the other would quickly better it.

The day after Milo flew inverted from San Diego to Mines Field, Los Angeles, in one hour and 47 minutes, Falconi flew inverted from St. Louis, Missouri to Joliet, Illinois for a period of three hours and six minutes. It appeared as if Milo Burcham had been summarily trounced. But for those who knew him personally, it was understood that "giving up" was not in his vocabulary.

It took Milo four months of practice in his Bird biplane and

Milo Burcham, the test pilot's pilot. Photograph from the Marian Burcham-Anderson Collection.

long hours in his torturous upside-down chair before he notified the press and the Federal Aeronatiques Internationale timers that he was ready to reclaim the inverted flight record. Before nightfall on December 28, 1933, he had set a world record by flying upside-down for four hours, five minutes, and 22 seconds. Tito Falconi took the hint and returned to Italy to heal his wounded ambitions.

By this time Milo's renown was such that he was a crowd-pleasing addition to the events at the National Air Races and readily acknowledged as one of the world's best aerobatic pilots. He and the Boeing 100 gave an electrifying performance.

What he considered a pinnacle in his career at that time was being asked by the French government to participate in their major airshow at Paris, France. He accepted and dismantled his Boeing and shipped it to France, accompanied by his wife, Peggy. After the Paris event, he toured Europe giving exhibition flights.

Returning to the United States, Burcham then accepted a job with Lockheed Aircraft company as a test pilot. His major contributions to aviation were soon evident.

Much of the initial flight-testing of the radical-appearing XP-38 twin-boomed, twin-engined fighter was accomplished by Burcham. It was then 1939 and very little was known about the effects of altitudes in excess of 30,000 feet upon airplanes or their pilots. Typically, coordinating his efforts with the Mayo Clinic, Milo applied himself to high-altitude chamber effects and long hours flying the P-38 in the rarified air.

When that research task had been completed, Lockheed dispatched him to England to oversee the reassembling of the Lockheed Hudson bombers arriving in ship convoys from the U.S.A.

Returning stateside in 1943 at age 40, and with the second world war in full bloom, Milo gave demonstration flights to the newly trained pursuit pilots flying the P-38. Along with this activity, he still found time to do the original flight testing of the new Constellation transport. His accomplishments were growing but his personal runway was shortening.

After a futile attempt to check out the testy Howard Hughes in the "Connie," Milo was relieved to turn the task over to other pilots and get on with testing the secret turbojet fighter, the P-80.

On October 20, 1944, Milo was due to give the military brass a demonstration of the P-80 at Burbank. Within moments after liftoff, its engine failed and Milo Burcham was dead. His wife and children witnessed the flaming crash.

At 41 years of age, his brilliant aviation career was ended. Posthumously, he was awarded the coveted Air Medal which had been recommended by the President, Franklin D. Roosevelt. Few civilians had ever been so honored.

As are many others to whom he had demonstrated or explained the finer points of flying the P-38 and staying alive, I am personally indebted to him. I know his explanations saved my life on two occasions.

Milo Burcham—the test-pilot's pilot.

19 ENTREPRENEUR CLARENCE PREST

Entrepreneur: Someone who organizes and manages an enterprise, usually with considerable initiative and risk . . .

The dictionary implies that to succeed in most any effort, one must: a. Take a risk; b. Have much volition; and, c. Display a degree of command ability.

When considering a man named Clarence O. Prest regarding these attributes, I ask your opinion of someone who:

—flew a Jenny out of a tennis court;
—tried to barnstorm Alaska in 1921 and 1922;
—could and did shoot a caribou with a pistol in the center of its eye;
—managed a good living selling World War I surplus airplanes in the face of massive competition;
—designed a sportplane considered far ahead of its time; and,
—when employed later in his life by a major airplane manufacturer, talked the company into sharing five complicated patents with him.

I trust you are impressed with this man and want to know more.

In 1926, he inspired enough confidence in my normally suspicious father to pay more for a Prest Jenny above market value. However, let's turn back the pages of history and see what made Clarence Prest "tick" . . . .

Apparently his aviation career started in 1910. For the next nine years Prest would gradually transition from being a trick motorcycle rider for a circus into a pilot. Eventually, he was barnstorming airplanes full time.

A hint of the future appeared when Prest moved next door to the LeViers, a family with whom he became good friends. The Leviers had a son named Tony. Here we introduce an oddity about Clarence Prest's life: subtle influences abounded during the year 1920. Can anyone confirm or deny that the association of the LeViers and the Prests, did not influence Tony to become Lockheed Aircraft's most illustrious test-pilot?

More such unexplained influences were coming in Prest's life.

Whether or not Prest chose Venice, California, as a point from which to start an aviation career, or that it was a matter of luck is unknown. But if one wished to witness aviation's action, the Venice airport was the place to be.

In 1919, B. H. DeLay purchased the small triangular airport from Harry Crawford. Crawford was too busy to spread his time and energy into an airport when his airplane parts business was burgeoning. DeLay operated the airport from September 1919 until February 1920, when it was taken over by Gil Budwig and Fred Hoyt. From then onward the field bustled with movie flying, flight instruction, day and night passenger rides, and a variety of airplanes manufactured and test-flown. Historical photos show that most of the wing-walking and plane-change stunts were performed by pilots and stuntmen operating from Venice airport. One wonders if the exotic atmosphere might have influenced Donald Douglas to settle his factory nearby.

In 1920, Clarence Prest, employed by the Crawford Airplane and Supply Company, located on Washington Boulevard, probably used his business connection to acquire an odd assortment of parts from Crawford's supplies. From them he constructed a biplane which he named "Poison."

No doubt, Poison was a phenomenon of its time. Most airplanes of the day were war surplus Jennies, TM Scouts, Standards and Canucks. All looked similar and flew about the same, but Poison had a 50-hp rotary engine which apologized for its short wingspan of a mere 18 feet. It flew as if it might kill the pilot at any moment—Poison. Aptly named, it took off at 45 mph, cruised better than 100 mph and through its design, assured an extremely fast landing speed. Each flight Prest made caused spectators to watch as he struggled to land the small beast without crashing.

In September, Prest landed Poison on a windless day with such speed that he was unable to stop. Trying to miss obstructions, Prest turned and groundlooped the airplane. Poison promptly flipped onto its nose few hundred feet from the hangars. To the crusty clan of aviators watching, the mishap was a delight. Seeing a photographer rush towards the airplane before Prest had emberged, the pilots followed suit. When Prest climbed out of Poison, the assembled group posed around him for the benefit of the photographer. It was a wonder a photo was possible for pilots were chiding and razzing Prest about his "wonderful landing."

In the above group were: R.E. Goldsworthy, Frank Clarke, Jimmie Hester, Waldo Waterman, Wally and Otto Timm, Swede Meyerhoffer, Harry Sperl, Al Wilson, George Stephenson, Joe Hoff and Mark Campbell. To a lesser man than the determined Prest, this derisive jury could have discouraged his flying career. The event only seemed to spur on Clarence Prest. However, there is no further historical mention of Poison.

Trying to assess Prest's character is complicated for he was unpredictable in many ways, but firm in his utter determination to succeed—at something, anything!

Another question about the area's mystique was wondering how much influence these pioneer aviators spread. Many of the group that surrounded Prest for his infamous photo went on to greater things. Frank Clarke gained international renown as a movie pilot. Otto and Wally Timm astonished all by successfully designing, building and flying fine airplanes. Waldo Waterman captured media attention by building and flying an automobile with wings—the "Arrowbile." Al Wilson would be known over the land for flying his restored Curtiss Pusher biplane in airshows throughout the U.S.A.

In 1921, Prest's plans had smouldered long enough. In the local press, accounts appeared detailing how he and budding plane designer Morton Bach planned to fly a Jenny from Mexico to Siberia for a movie company. After accompanying Prest as far as Canada, Bach wisely withdrew from the flight.

On his own, Prest substituted Alaska for Siberia and continued his flight. That the flying was tough is verified by historical photos showed Prest landing and taking off from a Canadian tennis court because other fields were inundated by rain.

Near Circle, Alaska, his engine failed and Prest made a crash landing. It earned him lasting fame as the frozen north's first air-crash victim. Captain Gilbert Cook, an Alaskan-born riverboat operator rescued Prest and carried him to Tenana. Eventually, the battered Jenny was hauled to Fairbanks.

Perhaps intrigued through his association with Prest, Captain Cook later became a partner in Washington Aircraft Corporation of Seattle, Washington.

Returning to the states in 1922, the tenacious Clarence Prest may have been delayed by his failed Alaska venture but not beaten. Soon he'd promoted a Standard biplane and re-announced his intention to "develop aviation in Alaska."

Evidently, his entrepreneurial talents began to ripen. Banking odds against a similar failure, Prest had the Standard—which he'd named the "Polar Bear"—shipped by steamboat to Juneau, Alaska's capital. There, he took off from a beach and headed northeast. Enroute, the plane's engine quite four times. On each failure, Prest had to crash-land in the Alaska bush, make temporary repairs, then renew his flight. Finally he made it to Dawson where he gave Alaskans their first impromptu airshow.

Pleased, the viewing miners passed a hat and gave Prest the money they'd collected plus a pistol and shells for his protection in the primitive land.

His enthusiasm renewed, Prest flew on toward Fairbanks. However, over the Seventy-Five Mile river his engine failed again. Prest landed in the only possible spot, a swamp. Though he was uninjured, The Polar Bear was demolished.

Walking out, he saw a herd of caribou, carefully aimed his pistol and killed one with a single shot through its eye. With meat to insure his survival, Prest stumbled downriver in heavy rain for four days. Search parties ultimately discovered him. His first words to the party were: "I'll try again next year."

Doubting his abilities after two failed attempts, the *News-Miner* press wrote: "Next time his airship will probably knock off the top of Mt. McKinley and create a flat spot for a summer resort!"

Perhaps recalling his ribbing after crashing Poison, Prest did not return. Recovering from his ordeal, he reasoned that adventure did not guarantee meat on the table. He decided he'd better involve himself in something more stable and predictable. "Business," he concluded, was where he belonged.

In 1926, I went with my father, Eddie and Jimmie Angel, to the small town of Arlington, California. We'd been drawn there by the following advertisement:

PREST VALUES

are

BEST VALUES

First find out what your money will buy here. Wire or write today.

Here is some of our large stock ready for prompt shipment:

Orioles		$2500.00
Sea Gull, without motor		1050.00
Boeing		1000.00
Jennies		750.00
Wing Sets complete		275.00
OX5 Motors		200.00
165 HP Gnome motors		50.00
80 HP LeRhone		65.00
K6		500.00
Mercedes 180 HP		500.00
Honeycomb Radiators		5.00
OX5 Props		15.00
AC plugs		.25
Intake rockers		.50
Exhaust yokes		.50
Exhaust manifolds, pair		10.00
Exhaust stacks, each		.25
Dope, gal.		2.50
Cosmolac varnish, gal.		6.50
Green enamel, gal.		3.50
Linen, yard		.75
Tape, frayed edge cotton, 60 yds		2.40
Resistal goggles	3.50	6.00
Fine Helmets		6.50
Flying Suits		10.00

Fada Radio.

K6, OX5 and JN parts at reasonable prices.

We occupy our own building of 60,000 sq. ft. floor space, are equipped with wood and metal working machinery and with 15 years experience are prepared to build any special ship to your requirements.

PREST AIRPLANES & MOTORS

ARLINGTON, CALIFORNIA

As I recall, the four of us were entranced by the huge Clarence Prest warehouse of airplanes. One block east of mid-town Arlington, it sat alongside a railroad track and was shaded by immense pepper trees. My father remarked it looked like a balloon hangar. With 60,000 square feet of space, there was every kind of airplane, engine and stocks of parts imaginable.

Pop negotiated with Prest and wrote out his check for one Jenny, brand new and in the crate, one spare engine and four new radiators. Jimmie Angel reminded him about tires and he ordered twelve new ones.

We stayed in Riverside for two days while the three men assembled, rigged and test-flew the Jenny. It was during this process that I learned how barnstormers check for missing wires: "You let a bird loose in the front cockpit," said Jimmie, "and if he gets away, you look for a missing wire!" Jimmie made the first test hop, Eddie and my Pop made the second and I got a ride with Eddie for a third flight to recheck the rigging changes. Pop and Eddie flew back to our new airport in Compton, California, while I rode in the car with Jimmie Angel, who regaled me with wild aviation stories all the way home.

In the coming year, my father would purchase several more airplanes and extra parts from Clarence Prest. I heard him often tell others that Prest was a man of his word and money alone could not buy that character trait.

Prest remained in Arlington for many years doing business out of his warehouse and also managing the local airport. During that period he designed and sold four of his famous Prest Baby Pursuits. For its time, it was a remarkable design. It boasted a diamond-shaped fuselage of welded steel tubing, a small wing area and was powered by a three-cylinder Szekely engine. It was fast and tricky to fly and Prest seemed unable to find orders for its sale.

Later, he joined Lockheed Aircraft Corporation in Burbank, California, as a technical consultant. There he developed a photo-template process through which photos of a part could be transferred directly onto a metal template. He was so valued by Lockheed that they shared equally with him the five patents involved.

Whatever Clarence O. Prest tried was always a step above the mundane and involved a dedicated struggle. In my book, he is a classical entrepreneur.

20 SUPERWOMAN PILOT HANNA REITSCH

There are people, things and events that cannot adequately be explained or described through language.

Humans use rationale, seeking causes to forecast an event. Then in the natural order of our world, the inexorably slow process of evolution is suddenly and shockingly upset by what modern man calls "mutation." So much has been said of this action that the word connotates an immediate negative image.

We must caution ourselves not to fall into such a trap. A mutation may be a drastic change to a *higher* form. "Metamorphose" is a word that better describes the lady we next investigate.

Changing from one form to an incredibly beautiful and greater form of life expression is what one tiny female child with typical Aryan blond hair, bright blue eyes and a wide, generous smile managed to do with her life.

Hanna Reitsch was born on March 29, 1912 in Poland. When she was a child, her parents assumed she would mature to be as large as the others in the family—normal. But Hanna did not conform to molded images—remember? Fooling all, she grew into a well-formed woman who weighed only 90 pounds on her 18th birthday.

Though tiny, she was very strong and appeared to have avoided most of the childhood illnesses experienced by other children. When her parents tried to persuade her to aim for career as a wife and mother, she balked.

You see, Hanna had this serious problem: she wanted to fly.

As a very young child she began to watch and study the soaring birds in flight. The more she watched them, the more she identified with the freedom and the sensuous expression of riding the wind.

When anyone asked Hanna what she wanted to be, her answer never varied. "I want to soar like the buzzards!"

Arguments trying to urge her into a different profession she ignored as if she had not heard the words. Try as they would, her parents could not understand how their child had become so obsessed with the desire to fly. True, she'd often watched the awkward primary aircraft at the nearby glider school glide down the grassy hills. Though these contraptions were not as graceful as any of nature's soaring creatures, the simple act of a person being airborne appeared to capture her attention so profoundly she could blot out everything else.

At 14 years of age, her father, himself a successful eye surgeon, asked her for the umpteenth time about choosing her life's work. He'd hoped Hanna would follow in his footsteps. Both parents had reasoned that the environment of the medical profession would insure greater protection for their undersized daughter. Respectfully, she'd listen to their suggestions, but when they asked, "Does that not make more sense, Hanna? Wouldn't you rather be a fine doctor in Papa's hospital?" Hanna would then answer, "Maybe I could be a doctor who flies to his sick ones. That's it! I will become a missionary doctor."

History later proved this was as close as her parents ever came to making a doctor of Hanna. Her father, perhaps overprotectively, still thought he could persuade her to study medicine and that in time, she'd forget her silly ideas about flying machines. After all arguments failed to sway Hanna, her father offered a proposition: "If you will shut up about flying until you get your high school diploma, Hanna, I'll buy you a glider training course at the Grunau School for glider pilots."

Papa Reitsch had struck a responsive chord in Hanna's psyche. But in her mind, she twisted the offer into a successful culmination of her dreams. Her father thought the years of study and schooling would crowd out her "irrational" desire to fly.

Answering, Hanna's eyes flashed with delight. "All right, I'll make you and Mamma happy. I'll shut up about flying and do what you wish."

Determination was as much a part of Hanna's character as her own heartbeat. For a long time her mind had been made up that she would fly and nothing in heaven or on earth would stop her ambition.

Though she continued with her education and no longer discussed flying with her parents, her mind raced with imagery of birds and flying machines, and the physical sensations she imagined flight to be. Away from everyone, Hanna read books about gliding and aerodynamics as often as time would allow.

In 1930, true to her promise, Hanna graduated from high school. Delighted that she'd stayed with the course of a formal education, her father offered Hanna a valuable gold watch as a graduation present. In his mind he was certain his child had forgotten about flying.

"Papa! I will not accept this gift. You promised you'd pay for a glider course if I kept my word. Now, won't you please keep yours!" Hanna had glared at her father. It was the first time he'd ever heard his daughter border upon impertinence.

Reluctantly, her father made good his previous offer and Hanna was introduced to the head of the glider school, the famous Wolf Hirth, and to those who would be her classmates—all boys, older, bigger, and decidely unapproving of "girls wanting to fly."

For Hanna, her entry into the glider school was a mixed blessing. Touching, fondling the cloth-covered gliders, and helping construct them was for her as water to a thirsty person. However, the male students kept up a barrage of insults and nasty predictions about her future in flying. For one who'd been totally sheltered as a child, this was a brutal introduction to society.

In working with wood, wire and cloth, she excelled. In the ground classes, whenever a question was asked—no matter the subject—Hanna's hand was raised first. Her grades were always higher than her fellow students which caused their resentment of her to grow.

Finally the day came when her class was to take turns sliding down the Wasserkuppe Hills in the clumsy primary gliders. The routine was to shock-cord launch the glider with barely enough speed to slide it down the hill let alone fast enough for it to fly. In that way, the student had sufficient wind flowing over the machine so the controls were responsive but not enough to sustain flying lift over the wings.

Hanna's turn was last—being a girl—and it seemed her instructor forgot that she weighed a mere 90 pounds. Before her turn, she'd made up her mind that if her weight permitted, she would urge the glider into the air and impress everyone watching.

Too late her instructor realized that the lightly loaded machine *could* become airborne with Hanna's weight. He crossed his fingers and hoped real hard . . . but it didn't work for even as he watched, he saw that Hanna was tugging the control stick back, trying to unstick the glider from the hill. Never having flown, she hadn't the slightest skill needed to operate the controls. Up and down went the nose in wild leaps and dives. It was inevitable that she would come to grief. On one exaggerated swoop upwards, the glider stalled and fell heavily to earth. Luckily, neither Hanna nor the glider was hurt.

Her initial ride to impress the other students worked well enough to impress her instructors too. She was grounded for three days for disobeying orders. Ever the activist, Hanna spent the time studying the slides of the other students down the hill and evaluating the advanced glider-pilots soaring on the wind.

Soon Hanna's concentration paid dividends for she easily surpassed her classmates in flying skills and technical knowledge. Her brilliance was so obvious that Wolf Hirth personally guided her through the remainder of her glider training.

A launching of more than a sailplane occurred to Hanna shortly after passing her final tests at the Grunau school.

Hirth generously allowed Hanna to fly their newest high-performance sailplane, a gull-winged Rhonsperber. Not realizing the possible consequence of his words, Hirth told Hanna, "Enjoy yourself. Stay up as long as you wish."

The wind was perfect for the slope that day and the soaring was excellent. Once aloft and riding the brisk updrafts for the first time in her life, Hanna realized her dreams had become fact. Revelling in the experience, she shouted with glee and sang songs at the top of her lungs. The ecstasy was fierce and she unashamedly cried with her release of emotion.

Later in the flight the weather turned stormy, causing the other sailplanes to land. But not Hanna; eagerly she pressed the glider's nose into the sharp rain squalls that soon turned to snow showers. As long as there was lift and visibility enough to see Hanna did not intend to land. To Hanna, the coming darkness appeared all too soon and she landed, expecting to be criticized for remaining aloft too long.

Hirth was waiting, as were the other students. As she coasted to a stop before them, all cheered. Hanna, in her five hour flight had set a new endurance record for women. Her career was launched.

From that day on, Hanna Reitsch advanced herself in the field of aviation with the relentless passion of a zealous field marshal. She never looked back and never once retreated from her avowed adoration of flight.

In May of 1933 while flight-testing Hirth's new Grunau Baby secondary sailplane, Hanna flew under the swollen belly of a forming thunderstorm. Her rate of climb in the storm's violent updrafts were phenomenal and she was determined to ride out the lift. But at 10,000-foot altitude, the brutish storm took control of the wee glider and flung Hanna and the machine over the sky as though a dog would toss a rage doll. She could only hang on and await the consequences. Thousands of feet higher, the storm spewed glider and woman out of its flanks and Hanna saw the ground—upside down. She quickly recovered control of the glider and landed in a pasture many miles form her starting point. Another record was hers: the official new German glider altitude mark.

Hanna Reitsch was moving through her flying career with rocketlike speed.

Publicity about this remarkable woman-pilot reached the attention of 44 year-old professor, Walter Georgii, head of the German Institute for Glider Research. Hanna jointed them and stayed for 11 years, earning world recognition for her remarkable flying in South America and for flying across the Argentine Pampas.

Leaving the Institute for still greater flying opportunities, Hanna attended the Civil Airways Training School at Stettin, Germany. There she performed as a test pilot in twin-engined planes, did advanced aerobatics and complicated cross-country flying. More laurels came from her successful testing program of dive brakes for military planes. The year was then 1927.

Adolph Hitler and his military leads had been eyeing the progress of this astonishing woman. Famed German pilot, Ernst Udet was dispatched to offer Hanna a position as a senior test pilot at the Luftwaffe's Rechlin, Germany, test facility. While there, she gained more worldwide laurels flying the new helicopter inside a huge German stadium.

With her career moving at full speed, Hanna traveled to the U.S. in 1938 to participate in the Cleveland National Air Races. Easily, it seemed, she captured the hearts of all Americans. To the press, she admitted she found American men pleasant for their chivalry and lack of pompousness.

World War II accelerated Hanna's prominence as a German test pilot. Eagerly, she tackled each new test assignment. The V-1 buzz bomb was test-flown by her, as was the unpredictable rocket-powered ME-163. But this was an airplane that Hanna could not tame, despite all her skill, and on an uncontrolled descent, Hanna crashed. Her face smashed into the forward gunsight and literally tore away her nose. She was hospitalized over five months before she could return to flying.

Her career climaxed when she was dispatched to fly General von Greim to Hitler's bunker near the Brandenburg gate. Under massive air and ground attack, she managed to land her plane on a street and wait under rifle fire until her passenger was ready to fly to safety. Her flight to a distant airbase involved being attacked by Russian fighter aircraft, anti-aircraft shells and constant ground fire. Flying evasively and through cloud layers, she managed to reach her goal.

With the German war effort collapsing, Hanna became one of the few people who ever scathingly attacked Gestapo head Heinrich Himmler and live to tell about it. Hanna, a devoted Nazi to the end and totally loyal to Hitler's cause, faced Himmler and demanded, "Is it true you have contacted the enemy with peace proposals?"

Himmler nodded it was true.

Hanna screamed at him, "Traitor! You have betrayed the Fatherland and your Fuhrer!" With that, she strode from his office.

With all the publicity this remarkable woman received in her life, it seems odd that there never was mentioned any romantic involvement. Whatever her private life, the public didn't hear of it. In writing her biography, no mention of any love-interests was made.

At war's end, Hanna was taken prisoner by the Americans. In 1946, she was released and returned to her first and greatest love, soaring. She wrote that only in a sailplane, alone on the heights, had she found a new and enduring sense of peace.

In retrospect, her career etched her character traits in stone. Never was it apparent that Hanna had vacillated from her love of flying. "Restless" and "capable," were her words and her life.

21 ARCHIE FERGUSON, ALASKA'S ANTIHERO

A common raw material in Alaska's early aviation history was an abundance of heroes. Merely to fly any airplane from point-to-point was a herculean effort, and one pregnant with risk.

For any aviator to disregard these real-world threats to life and limb was either an exercise in supreme bravado, or a damn fool needlessly taking chances.

Looking back, history has recorded that most of the pioneer pilots certainly were heroic. Men such as Noel Wein, Ben Eilson, Joe Crosson, Harold Gillam and Bob Reeve fit the hero mold.

But as it sometimes does, history hiccuped in producing an Alaskan aviator who was the antithesis of the accepted model of a hero.

Those pilots previously mentioned were handsome men who showed mature personalities, thoughtful aims, determination and superb flying skills. In making any Alaskan flight, all faced great odds of weather and terrain. However, when one flips the hero coin and reads the back side, there appears the contrast.

From his deeds, Archie Ferguson must be acknowledged as a heroic pilot. But none who knew or heard of him would ever describe him as a "hero."

Everyone, it appeared, had an opinion about Ferguson and would vocalize it at the slightest invitation:

—one sourdough offered, "He's as crazy as a loon;

—a veteran airline pilot remarked, "The more I see him fly, the less I fear an airplane."

A businessman who had dealt with Archie admitted, "In any deal, Archie will come out ahead. Really, he's no dummy!" A miner who regularly used Ferguson Airways claimed, "He's generous. Archie would give you the shirt off his back—only it would be so raggedy you couldn't use it."

Was Ferguson a study in contrasts? Yes. Was he predictable? Never. One admired by all? Most certainly not. Honest and moral? The last is not a question to ask about Archie. Indeed, he was filled with the old-fashioned virtues of integrity.

Why then, can Archie be classified as an "anti-hero?" Simple, In his flying, his schemes and pranks, the way he always appeared and his manner, he was the opposite of the classic hero.

Duality followed Archie as a swarm of gnats. Most who met him instantly felt a mixture of fascination and repulsion. Though of average height, he was dumpy with an out-of-proportion torso. His skin was wrinkled even as a youngster and looked to all as if he'd been born an old man. In contrast, his face tended toward chubbiness and his cheeks had huge dimples showing whenever he smiled or laughed—which was all of his awakened hours. His ears leaned slightly forward as if fighting a wind and his sandy-colored hair was unruly, brush-like, with a spur of it sticking up from his scalp.

Our anti-hero's clothes were a disaster. He wore baggy pants that did not fit his short legs and extra-long torso. He reminded some of an ancient court-jester. His shirts were usually of the sport variety and he wore them open at the neck in some of Alaska's fiercest weather.

A greater shock to those meeting Archie the first time came when he spoke. Few would agree with you that he "spoke." His voice was much like Donald Duck's and it came out as a cackle. Worse than his tone of voice was his language. Archie used epithets and curses rather than nouns and adjectives. In every sentence and constantly in his overall conversations, Archie used four-letter words. Almost illiterate, he scrambled new words to where they totally lost meaning. When a C.A.A. inspector told Archie he should study meteorology, Ferguson asked, "Metrinology? What in hell is that?"

A consensus of opinions about him from his friends and associates found that he didn't bear too well. He was always talking. Most thought him funny but added that Archie could grate with his cackling babble going on incessantly. A little of Archie, they said, went a long way.

When asked what were the most important things in his life, Archie grew more verbal. He'd quickly admit that Hadley, his natural-born Eskimo wife topped his list, flying an airplane came next and then a good laugh followed.

Ask other pilots about him and they'll say, "He's a performance. The Archie Ferguson show never stops." They often grow pensive for a moment before adding, "He's worth the price of anyone's admission."

Few people appeared to take Archie seriously. But solid facts built for him a reputation of courage, good business acumen, constant unflagging energy and a staunch loyalty to his friends and loved ones.

Hero or anti-hero?

Impressions created him as a comic-opera figure. Truth revealed to the searcher of facts that the real Archie Ferguson was an extremely capable man in many areas.

What was the seed? What soil did he mature from? How

Archie Ferguson: "I luvs tuh fly!" Photograph from the CAA via Burleigh Putnam.

did Archie come to be a famous Alaskan aviator?

Investigation into Ferguson's life must begin in 1917 when the Ferguson parents brought Archie and his brother, Warren, to Alaska. From Nome, they went deep into the Artic Circle prospecting for gold. Later, they successfully operated a mine in Alaska's California Creek area. During this period, Archie showed his enterprising nature by constructing a homemade scow and starting a freight business along the Kobuk River. At the same time, he trapped for furs in the Colville River region.

In 1919, with the family's income stabilizing and a favorable Alaskan future assured, Archie and Warren each took an Eskimo woman as brides. The clan then built and operated a successful sawmill, opened several trading posts and ran a mink farm. Innovators all, they started the first civilian movie house north of the Artic Circle, imported the first auto—an International pickup truck, and even a motorcycle. To the delight of all, Archie put skis on the motorcycle and he and Hadley would race around the area throwing snow in all directions.

It was natural for more civilized assets to come for the energetic family. A few were surprised though, when they imported the first dairy cow at a great price.

Watching the painful progress of transportation, largely by dog sleds, Archie gradually became convinced that airplanes were the only hope of opening up Alaska's potentials. It was then 1926 and there were few planes operating in the frozen north. Those that were had a backlog of business. Air transportation brought premium prices to the aviation entrepreneurs.

Archie decided he had to investigate airplanes and paid Noel Wein for a passenger ride in a Standard biplane. Wein, trying to please all his customers, did not realize that Archie had never before flown and was fearful about being off the ground. Wein executed several tight loops that terrified Archie. Though he took no more passenger rides, his conversations included airplanes—airplanes—and airplanes.

At a family meeting in 1931, they decided one must learn to fly and that it was only logical for Archie to become a pilot as he was the one who had flown in an airplane, albeit as a passenger. Archie agreed. A dominant trait of the Ferguson clan was to observe everything, tell no one and then act upon their own counsel. Without telling anyone the family placed an order stateside for a new Great Lakes biplane trainer. The plane cost $4,000 and another $1,000 to have it shipped to them at Kotzebue. From the state of Colorado they hired pilot/instructor Chet Browne to teach Archie how to fly. It seemed a fitting climax to their achievement of now having three stores: one each in Kotzebue, Kiana, and Selwik.

Poor Chet Browne, locked into his job by contract and saddled with a student whose aptitude was probably the worst he'd ever experienced, plodded along day by day trying to solo Archie. Both instructor and student were becoming more and more impatient with the passage of time. Browne was certain Archie would kill himself if he ever did manage to solo. Apparently, this conclusion was being shared by others who gathered at the airfield each day to witness Archie's flopping about in the sky. In time, bets were placed upon when Archie would kill himself. No one had doubt about "if."

Indignant about the derisive remarks, and frustrated, Archie demanded Chet solo him without further delay. Having given the near-impossible student a full 60 hours of dual instruction. Browne yielded and saw the solo as a possibility of returning to Colorado. The next time Archie asked about his solo, Browne answered, "Go ahead and kill yourself. I give up." Turning his back on Archie, Browne walked away from the field.

Archie managed to get the airplane off the ground and stagger around drunkenly on his solo. But being alone in an airplane after all the hours with Chet so unnerved Archie that he landed several miles from the home field. But from that day on, Archie's tenacity gradually won out. He was constantly in the air, trying new things, experimenting, and often making landings that damaged the airplane. Though he never seemed to have any real skill, he got to where he could fly anywhere in the area and "get the job done."

By 1936, the Ferguson Airways was in full swing and turning a healthy profit despite the bones of 10 airplanes litering the area behind the hangar. Once in the crash of a Cessna, Archie was badly injured. He'd fractured his back and bitten a chunk out of his tongue. But in time, durable Archie recovered and the crash failed to hinder his ability to screech at everyone, cackle as loudly as ever, or talk endlessly.

At 45 years of age Archie, and his brother Warren were solidly established as major businessmen in the area. All seemed at peace with the Ferguson clan. However, in 1939, disaster struck the family. Warren, driving over the frozen sea in an auto dropped through the ice and was drowned. This increased Archie's responsibilities in the family business.

One year later, in 1940, people realized Archie was not the fool he pretended. The family business prospered more than ever and the airline grossed over $200,000 annually—27 percent of their total income.

Archie had grown to love and trust flying, and was considered to be airborne most of the time. During one summer month, other pilots kept track of his flying and learned that Archie Ferguson had flown an astonishing 185 hours. A hundred hours of flying was considered a very full month.

Many Alaskan pilots who at that time worked for Archie went on to greater fame and fortune. Known as a fussy boss and constant heckler, Archie kept pressure on all who worked for him to surpass their own efforts. Though his people complained, they stayed with Archie because he was paying twice the going rate for pilots. No one who worked for Archie smoked, drank other than beer, or had immoral character traits.

When a CAA inspector once asked to see Archie's pilot log books, Ferguson snorted, "Don't keep no log books—only when I crackup cause then you guys want to see all the details."

In 1946, with World War II ended and a new breed of Alaskans invading the far north, Archie expressed his disillusionment about the trend of events. Sig Wein, already operating his own successful airline, heard of Archie's comments and offered to buy him out. Surprisingly to all, Archie closed the deal almost immediately. He was 52 years of age.

In 1967 at age 72, Archie Ferguson died.

Everyone who'd known him had been convinced he was a clown—an anti-hero as his outgoing personality had suggested. History in a land that gave no quarter to the fainthearted left doubts about Archie's achievements.

Now at last, it can be said that Archie Ferguson was quite a man.

Part 4

Airplanes I've Known (and a Few I Wish I Hadn't)

22 THE HEATH ENIGMA

In the final days of his flying career my father had been doing an aerobatic routine in a World War I Thomas Morse Scout biplane.

Eventually, family pressures caused him to leave active flying and enter the boring world of business. Despite his disinterest, he became successful as the owner/operator of a few small service stations.

With his nouveau respectability, he decided to overhaul my dreams of flying.

"I'll not have you become an airport bum, son."

So the next day—after he forbade me to fly anymore—I began to build a primary glider in our high school woodshop. When my father heard this, he was undecided as to what his next move to thwart me would be. He threatened dire consequences if I continued.

I threatened to run away.

He said, "Fine, that'll save me lots of money!"

I stayed.

When months went by and I was adamant about making aviation my career, he yielded. Though I'd recently celebrated my 13th birthday, he decided upon a plan to delay my fervent ambitions. Without telling me until the first package arrived from Chicago, he had purchased a Heath Parasol builder's kit.

I protested. "This is just boxes of junk!"

He smiled at me with a victorious leer. "You want to fly? All those boxes will make an airplane. Build it and you'll fly—maybe. I've done my part, so now you're on your own."

For some time I wondered how he got so smart so suddenly.

As each box arrived, it was like another Christmas. My young friends helped me unpack the boxes and orient the parts to the well-detailed plans and instructions. Kit builders gradually appreciated the genius of Ed Heath.

Heath had correctly assumed that if his product was to be successful, his directions dare not leave anything to chance. Further, he correctly forecast that the unskilled do-it-yourselfers—like me—needed this fool-proof guidance. Inevitably, the result of faithfully following Heath's directions assured the builder of a sound, accurate airplane.

Before long I had received all the parts except the engine. Ed Heath, a very smart entrepreneur, did not push the sale of his $300 engine when his kit was priced under $200.

Protectively, my father had asked a mechanic friend to check my progress at regular intervals. In all of the parts and plans, only one thing disturbed the mechanic: the two 3/16-inch diameter bolts attaching the wing spars to the cabane struts. With their wee castellated nuts under full tension instead of shear, he urged we substitute 1/4-inch aircraft bolts and nuts, and we did.

When the parts began to look more like an airplane than an assortment of junk, my father began to worry about the engine Heath had suggested for the airplane. The engine recommended was a Henderson 4-cylinder, in-line motorcycle engine. In checking with other Heath Parasol owners and pilots, Pop had discovered innumerable engine failures due to crankshaft breakage.

Frowning, he'd told me, "That Henderson has only three main bearings for its crankshaft, son. We've got to find us a better powerplant. You keep on building and I'll look around for a better engine."

Always searching for bargains, my father had yielded to an advertisement touting the wonders of the Lawrance two-cylinder, war-surplus engine that had been used in a Penguin trainer during the war. It was designed to teach pilots to fly as the airplane flopped about the ground due to a wing area

The Heath Parasol came in an easy-to-build kit. Making it fly was a serious question. Drawing courtesy of Bill Neale.

too small to support flight. The engine sales company promised great, reliable performance from the two-cylinder affair and stressed that owners of kit-built Heaths were flying everywhere with their engine.

By then I was concerned over the many modifications my father and his mechanic friend had insisted we build into the structure. The first weigh-in proved we were nearing 100 pounds overweight.

Eventually the engine arrived and we had it installed. Neither I nor my friends thought its strong vibrations odd. We did not understand the negative consequences of a single-throw crankshaft in a two-cylinder opposed engine.

The day for the test flight arrived. I'd waited until my father was out of town on business and looked at my meager logbook for the hundredth time. Sure, it still showed I'd soloed the Standard J-1 a year ago when I was then only 12 years of age. But it also showed few entries since that time.

So, what the heck . . . I gave the signals for the chocks to be pulled and away we went. The airplane seemed to leap ahead with the power of the Lawrance at full throttle.

It also seemed to leap sideways from wheel to wheel as the single-throw crankshaft did its number. Approaching takeoff speed, the tiny parasol monoplane began leaping sideways and forward in huge, drunken, rabbit-like lurches.

Back to the drawing board!

My enraged letters reached my father, still in the Midwest. After some delay, he found a Mid-western machine shop that would convert the single-throw Lawrance into a double-throw crankshaft, eliminating the terrible imbalance.

Two months later, my friends and I were ready for the second test flight. This time the ship made its takeoff run as straight as an arrow and as smoothly as silk. Too smoothly, it appeared, for though it climbed slowly to 25-foot altitude when I attempted a turn back toward our airport, it settled into the alfalfa field below.

So we towed the thing from the alfalfa patch to our cow-pasture airport a mile away behind my friend's Model T Ford.

Relenting from his hard-nosed stance, my father enlisted help. Obviously, each engine fiasco had dug deeply into his pockets. Though late in deciding, he made a deal with a man considered the leading expert in high-performance engines. When Pop relayed to "Winnie" his concerns about the Henderson, the man offered his solution: he would convert the five-main bearing Indian Four and then "our troubles would be over."

In less than a month, he called us to examine his handiwork.

When we drove to his shop, Pop and I were excited at seeing the engine mounted on a test stand, complete with propeller and apparently ready to run.

Immediately walking to the prop, Pop tugged one blade and appeared astonished by the engine's unusually high compression ratio. Looking at Winnie, he asked, "Wow! What did you do to this thing?"

Winnie smiled with pride. "Oh, I fixed a few little things. Ground the cam for better valving, ported it out a bit, and used one of my downdraft carbs on each cylinder. Wait'll you hear it run, you'll both love it!"

Pop swung the prop while Winnie operated the switch and throttle. As soon as it started, I realized I'd never before heard such an engine sound. Most airplanes engines with which I was familiar purred when healthy. This engine, when throttle was applied, snapped, growled and barked. When I moved the throttle, it responded like a machinegun.

When Pop worked the throttle, I suddenly realized no wind was flowing back from the propeller. But when I stood near the prop's edge, I found the wind that should have been flowing back over the engine.

The horrible truth came to the three of us at the same instant: the engine revolutions were so high that the small wooden propeller was simply cavitating the air outward from its tips. The powerplant was not developing any thrust. Even I knew "no thrust—no fly."

Apologizing, Winnie told us to return in ten days and all would be fixed.

True to his word, when we returned, Winnie had removed and replaced the cam for one that developed greater low-end power. Also, he'd settled on only two downdraft carburetors. His genius solution for added horsepower but a slower-turning propeller was arrived at with a reduction drive between the engine and prop made from an automobile timing gear. Now, the engine turned 2,600 revs at full throttle but the prop was turning nearer to 1,600 revs. I checked, no tip slippage. At last we had an engine.

Later, I was to experience many engine failures due to magneto problems, but the work done by Winnie remained both functional and reliable. The Indian-Four engine provided me with a usable airplane.

Though its service ceiling was a maximum of 2,000 feet, I loved this dinky little bird and flew it regularly for almost a year. Each weekday morning I would fly it five miles to school. I never missed a day despite the atrocious fogs, wind and rain. After track practice on Friday nights, I would fly my airplane 60 miles to the farm my father had purchased. During these sojourns, I accumulated 13 night forced landings without mishap, and in doing so became a believer in my rabbit's foot charm. As I look back to that period and remember, I shudder and wonder what kept so many of us tyros alive.

Often, those who survived the ignorance of flight find it a miracle that "those days" allowed us to live to enjoy "these days."

23 JENNY, THAT FEMME FATALE

Jenny was no lady.

Factually, she was a 1915 Curtiss-built biplane weighing some 1,900 pounds and lofted by wings spanning 44 feet.

Dubiously powered by many different types of engines, the OX-5 was considered her standard powerplant. It was a classic vee-type, eight-cylinder, water-cooled design intended to deliver 90 horsepower.

On the pilot's panel were only four instruments: a Stewart/Warner tachometer; a Creagh/Osborne compass; an oil pressure gauge; and, a ball-level limited to 10 degrees of bank.

About one foot ahead of the front cockpit coaming was a gasoline quantity gauge. Centered in line with your passenger's head, it was often impossible to read.

But you know that you can depend upon two hours of flying. That is, if the camshaft didn't break, which was often.

Her original design started in the U.S.A. made a slight de-

Curtiss JN-4D. She was not a lady! Drawing courtesy of Bill Neale.

tour to England, and then was firmed up again at her American birthplace.

In February 1914, the U.S. Army issued a ban on purchasing any new airplanes of pusher design. Their records had shown that the pusher was killing pilots as fast as they could be trained.

Glen Curtiss was invited to submit a proposal and he offered a radically new tractor-powered biplane he named the "N" model. While visiting airplane designers and factories in Great Britain, he was impressed with the design ability of B. Douglas Thomas, who would later gain his own fame from the famous "Tommy Morse" line of airplanes. Willing to help Curtiss, Thomas drew up many design improvements of the "N" model.

The design of the two men was the newly designated Model "J.CQ Hence, the design, in succession, became the JN-1, 2, 3, and ultimately the standard model JN-4D. Thus the nickname, "Jenny."

Pilots of that day may have started the fad of calling all airplanes "she." Sentimental and loaded with male chauvinism, their reasoning might be excused for in reality, Jenny was a very fickle creature capable of thrilling the blase or killing the ignorant. Pilots felt justified in proclaiming her a symbiotic thing of love and hate.

While she reigned, I knew her as well as any teenager of that time, I suppose. Most of my initial flying had been as a passenger in her drafty front cockpit while my father barnstormed. Much of the old girl's character is etched in my memory.

In her day she was considered somewhat complicated as to her structure.

The nearly 44-foot wingspan boasted an Eiffel #36 airfoil section. No one to this day can explain why it was chosen. Lightly loaded, its wing carried five pounds per square foot of area. But she suffered agonies from a power-loading of 21 pounds per horsepower. That the OX-5 engine produced 90 hp was positive thinking at its best. If in perfect condition and operated at sea level on a cold day, it might make it. Otherwise, forget it!

The absence of carburetor heat accounted for scores of dead pilots and folded Jennies. Total weight was calculated at 1,900 pounds. Every pound in excess of that figure meant a drop in altitude.

Jenny's maximum airspeed, if new and flying low, might reach 75 mph but never more. Ordinarily, she cruised at 60 to 65 mph.

With power off, she stalled at 43 mph but by carrying a slight amount of power, the stall speed could be lowered to about 37 mph. Facing a headwind on a forced landing, pilots walked away from wrecked Jennies that appeared to be miraculous escapes. Old-timers admit that if it was a matter of life or death, simply slide it between two hefty trees on landing and when the wings tear off, all the dangerous energy of a crash is dissipated. Then you could walk away laughing.

Jenny's most frustrating figure was her rate of climb. Computed at 200 feet per minute at sea level, any altitude or heated air could bring it to zero. Her service ceiling was listed as 6,500 feet and considered very debatable.

With best climb speed at 50 mph and the stalling speed of 43 mph, the margin of only 7 mph between flying and spinning caused most of the Jenny fatalities. She could climb only in straight flight with wings level. Any attempt at a climbing turn and the airplane would fall into a spin.

Considered fairly large for her time, Jenny's fuselage was 27 feet, 4 inches long. She was rigged for one degree of dihedral, and topped nearly 10 feet in height.

With no brakes or steerable tailwheel, like all her contemporaries, she was difficult and dangerous to taxi. The landing gear on Jenny was secured by loops of rubber shock cord as was the tailskid stub of ash. If she was not landed just right, the combination of the two shock-loaded items would cause her to buck like a bronco. More Jennies were wrecked taxiing with a tailwind than were crashed from flying mistakes.

To power the airplane, one would consult his pocketbook. Selling surplus after World War I for as little as $300, the engine installed was an OX-5. Dig a bit more deeply in your pocket and you could get the engine "Millerized." Leslie G. Miller, assured one of getting at least 10 additional horsepower from his modified version of the OX. One of his engines beat out a Wright Whirlwind-powered airplane in the famous New York to Spokane economy race. The prize money put Miller in business.

His modifications included: roller-bearing rocker arms, silver-bronze rod and crankshaft bearings, high-compression pistons, perfect circle rings, replaceable valve guides and seats and Rich valves.

Spend some more and one could choose a Hisso. With a 150- or 200-hp Hisso, the Jenny became a pleasure to fly.

Shall we take a spin? . . .

The line inspection is simple and quick. With a stepladder, we check the water and oil quantity and the radiator cap tightness. A bit more than two inches from the propeller, if the radiator cap comes off, it's goodbye prop. Fuel is okay for a short flight, so we get in and buckle up.

After a ground helper pulls the prop through for several blades to prime the engine, he stops and yells, "Contact!"

In the rear cockpit, I reach for the magneto switch near my left knee—it reads On or Off—and answer the man with "Contact" as I turn the switch to "ON." The throttle of most Jennies is on the right side which forces one to fly the heavy-controlled beast with the left hand.

"Pop—CHOKE—wheeze—gasp—gasp—"

Finally a rumbling gurgle develops as the engine begins to smooth. The vibrating tachometer reads 400 rpms. The engine is assumed to be in good health.

Chocks are pulled, power is added and a mechanic holds the right wing as we pivot for a downwind taxi. We now must taxi fast enough for the propwash to reach the rudder surface, yet not so fast that it groundloops. We have no brakes or steerable tailwheel—remember?

A few more blasts of power precisely timed and we rapidly wheel into the wind. There is no point in making a pre-takeoff check. There's nothing to check. With only one magneto, it's working or it isn't. If the water isn't boiling and the revs are correct, we go.

The throttle is opened wide. Speed gathers and I sneak a look at the tachometer. It's wildly vibrating between 1,100 and 1,200 revs. Good, that means it will turn 1,400 revs once the airplane is in the air.

On Jenny's takeoff roll, the transition to flight stems from a miracle of cooperation between wires, wood, fabric and human determination. The lurching gives way to a more pronounced rocking motion as speed gathers. Bracing wires begin to hum a low note, and the airplane hops from rise to rise with a new nimbleness. The stick transmits lift into the pilots hands. He can *feel* the airplane readying itself for flight. The hopping smooths, and the wires increase in pitch to a low thrumming. With one last bump the airplane lifts away.

Airborne, it seems the question of flight has passed from the airplane to that of the pilot. Gaining speed but still perilously close to the stalling point, the controls take a great amount of movement to pin the airplane at the proper attitude.

Speed and climb increase more and the wings send a firm feeling to the pilot. Gone now is the awkwardness of the airplane when locked to the ground. Gone is the alien world of things that do not fly. This airplane has soared into its element. It has broken free of the chains of earth and has become a bird. With all its mechanical parts clattering and clanking, the flight is majestic. The wonder is that it ever got off the ground at all. But it did and we are climbing higher.

You think our climb is slow? Let me assure you it is okay. Our tach is steady on 1,400 revs and the wires sing a 50-mph song. Relax, my friend, we are climbing a good 200 feet per minute.

While we are reaching for altitude, we can consider a few more facts about the Curtiss JN-4D Jenny.

Jenny was the first American plane to fly in anger. In the early months of 1917, Farnum Fish was a pilot for the legendary Pancho Villa. Returning from a flight to observe the Mexican Government troop movements, Fish inadvertantly flew over some of Villa's forces who were unaware they had an airplane flying for them. All quickly aimed their rifles and fired into the Jenny. One bullet hit Fish where he sat down. Turning, he flew the Jenny wide open and made it back to his original takeoff point. As he rolled to a stop from his downwind landing, he fainted.

When Fish had healed enough to travel, he resigned from Villa's airforce of one plane and one pilot and returned to his home in Los Angeles, California.

All things considered, Fish was lucky. Earlier, in 1913, a Lieutenant Taliaferro of the Army Signal Corps was flying Jenny Number 30 at San Diego's North Island Air Field. When over Mission Bay he tried a loop but stalled inverted and spun into the water. He was the first pilot to die in a Jenny crash.

So here we are at 3,000 feet. Let's try a loop. We dive until the wires shriek and then pull back hard on the stick. As the plane climbs into the loop, the stick is pulled back more. We must be careful not to get any negative "G" loads in our maneuvers lest the radiator overlow scald us. (Most barnstormers had very bad complexions.)

At the top of the loop, it gets quieter and everything on the airplane shakes madly. But it goes on around and we use the excess recovery speed to climb toward a stall.

It shudders and shakes as the speed decays. When the stall is at hand, a touch of rudder and it drops into a spin. One turn—one and a half—two! Reverse the rudder, press forward on the stick and the nose stops whirling.

Two more spins and we end by making a steep left spiral toward the airport. Wires protest the steep angle but we must keep the nose pointed acutely down. With all the drag on the airplane, a dive must be maintained on the approach to prevent a stall. But listen . . . there's no sweeter music than wind through the wires.

From about 20-feet high, we pull back steadily as long as the plane does not balloon. It drops like a rock, but the landing is fine as we were a mere six inches off the ground. It was a perfect three-point landing.

Taxiing back upwind is easy. When we are stopped and out of the airplane you ask, "Are you an experienced pilot?"

I bow politely, "Yes, indeed. I have flown about 30 hours solo. I hope you enjoyed your ride."

24 THE CYCLOPLANE SAGA

The 1930 glider craze was winding down. After all, how many times can one be thrilled by coasting down a hill a few feet above the ground?

A few who started flying the cumbersome primary gliders later discovered the joys of soaring and migrated into further motorless flight. But soaring in the '30's was mostly accomplished above the brow of a hill or over steep cliffs facing the wind. Sites were rare and too often only marginally successful for sustained flight. Sailplanes and soaring, it turned out, was a bundle of hard work.

While it seemed American men wanted to be in the action rather than be a spectator, erecting and dismantling a glider before and after a day's flying was considered too much work for the small amount of fun involved. Color the American male lazy, but businesses have been built or lost upon adherance to this fact.

Then there was always the problem of: "How does one learn to fly alone?" (As contemporary ultralites have done, so was training during this early period.) With care and close supervision, it worked enough to get most people in the air without mishap. This phase of the glider movement had the experience of the Germans to bolster it. However, all these solutions involved risk, excessive toil and little pure fun.

Two men at that time knew all the above facts and still were searching for an aviation opportunity in business. Money had been made through the glider movement, they knew. They were also aware that with the right combination of a sound product coupled with a popular lure, more money was a possibility. They realized if any business idea "clicked" with the public, profit was assured.

The pair were well—suited to the challenge: O. L. Woodson was a respected airplane designer employed by others. Dick Myhres was a well-known test pilot. Both men were ambitious and had been seeking their own business opportunities.

The Cycloplanes. Good idea—bad timing. Drawing courtesy of Bill Neale.

Let's imagine we are sitting in on their discussion before they embarked upon one of the most unique aviation promotional approaches seen during that period.

"So, O.L., we design and sell a powered glider, but with a 22-hp engine, it won't carry two people."

Woodson puffed on his pipe, nodded his head in agreement, and suggested, "So we make it a single-place job."

"Then how will an owner learn to fly it?"

"Good question."

"Bad question, maybe."

Both paused to consider this vital aspect of their attempt to capture the everyman's airplane-market. It appeared to them that solutions would have to come through experiments.

"Guess the owners would have to buy a cheap glider first, learn in it, and then transition to our powered-glider," said Dick.

Feeling uneasy about this, O.L. replied, "So we miss a sale or two."

Another pause, much longer this time.

"I got it!"

"Shoot."

"First we sell them a powered ground-trainer and later they buy the flying version."

"A package deal?"

"Maybe, maybe not. People just starting could buy the Penguin and move up to the more expensive model later."

This opened up a new thought. "Suppose they had so much fun learning to fly on the ground in the Penguin, they wouldn't *want* our powered glider?"

"Never!"

"Right, we're too talented a pair to let that happen, eh?"

Both nodded, realizing the positive-thinker might make money but the pessimist was forever doomed to failure.

Both: "Let's get on with it!"

Though the dialogue is imagined, historical facts have proven that the reasoning process the two promoters went through followed the above line of thought.

As the pair began to design the powered-glider version, they came up with a totally new concept of teaching people to fly, and one that could enrich them and their investors.

They fashioned a package deal with three types of trainers contemplated: a dual-controlled Penguin, a solo Penguin, and finally, the flyable machine.

From the fast-fading glider movement, they proposed a scheme of instruction: whenever a purchaser had graduated into the flyable model, he would be restricted to very short, straight-ahead hops until proficiency was gained. Then the student would graduate to doing "S" turns around markers while flying upwind. As skill increased, turns to downwind and finally a full circle would be perfected. This was only a variation of what the Germans had been using for many years with success. The difference would be the addition of the engine to a glider. Result: the end of drudgery and beginning of fun.

Advertising this program, the two men hoped to attract flying schools as customers for their package deal to sell three machines at once. The idea was sound, and Myhres and Woodson gave their machines the name of "Cycloplanes."

By August of 1931, they had built two experimental trainer models, one Penguin and one flying model. Remarkably, they had acquired a C.A.A., Approved Type Certificate Number 445 for their flying model, the C-1.

It was early in 1932 when I first saw their machines.

Driving to the local airfield, I saw a contraption skittering about the airport trailing a cloud of dust and slewing around corners as if it were a midget race car.

Parking, I saw it was the Cycloplane Penguin, and that whoever was in it was having loads of pure fun.

With its short wing-like stubs, the Penguin would not fly under any circumstances. Its appearance was as any powered-glider of that day. In the open, ahead of the wing and under the engine, sat the pilot. The unique quality of the design was that the machine was slung below an A-frame type of tubing structure. This allowed the tricycle gear to stay flat on the ground but the bulk of the machine to bank, lift or drop its nose, and make banked turns on the ground the same as any other airplane in flight. Truly, it was flying on the ground.

The 22-hp Cleone engine would be identical in all three of their designs. Unconcerned with air-drag as a ground-trainer, the thing would scoot along wide-open at better than 60 mph. Sitting a scant 10 inches above the ground, the operator had an enhanced feeling of speed.

Some said it was like a race car; others likened it to an airplane at takeoff, while some others compared it to a motorcycle cavorting on a dirt race track. All agreed it was about as much fun as any person could legally have. In short, it was a hit with those who rented it.

Airport operators were pleased to have the Penguin operating at their field as it drew large crowds of people. Even in that day, a crowd at an airport meant many passenger flight revenues.

Sales prices were established and advertised but buyers were few. With the Penguin selling at $895, those interested were afraid their investment would be lost when they moved into the flyable machine, priced at $1400. A threat to the enterprise at the time was the appearance of the new sleek-looking Buhl "Bull Pup," a true airplane being offered for only $1,250. The handwriting on the wall implied that the two promoters of the Cycloplanes could be in serious difficulties when competing with large manufacturing facilities.

Another serious threat appeared when a "Mr. Taylor," offered a conventional airplane with a 40-hp engine and two-place capacity for $1325. The machine carried the name of "Cub." The Cycloplane promoters were becoming very nervous.

Meanwhile, the dodo-bird Penguin was unique enough to have customers for rides waiting in line. For my turn at it, I had to wait three hours. But once in it and slithering about the loose dirt at Compton, Californias airport, I felt it a bargain. It did take about two baths to get the dirt off after the dusty ride though.

The Cycloplane Penguin had a 25-foot wingspan, weighed empty at 250 pounds, with a fuselage of open-framework-welded tubing. Wing and tail surfaces were conventional wood and wire and covered with fabric and dope. It lacked both vertical and horizontal stabilizers, neither being required for a ground machine.

The dual model offered was the solo Penguin with a crude seat attached to tubing and located under the high wing. Its appearance reminded one of Alberto Santos-Dumont's "Demoiselle." To have called it a "dual-trainer" was a wild stretch of anyone's imagination. Without any controls, all the instructor could do was to scream orders in the student's ears.

The Penguin wings offered a unique solution to the problem of sufficient aileron control. They were two slab-like affairs appearing as a wing but with huge, diagonal ailerons.

The idea of using the Penguin for preliminary flight training was tested by Woodson and Myhres. When they followed up with several students who had started in the Penguin and moved on into conventional airplanes, it was discovered the Penguin experience shortened the time needed to solo.

Constrasting the Penguin's popularity, the full-sized powered and flyable Cycloplane was a total flop.

Published specifications for the powered-glider did not relate to the machine's actual performance. At first, the designers listed the service ceiling at 12,000-foot altitude. After flight tests it was changed to 10,000 feet, and those who tried to reach 3,000 feet were discovering the machine would exhaust its fuel before it reached any figure near the claimed ceiling.

The specs offered a rate of climb of 450 feet for the first minute. Flight tests by others learned it climbed nearer to 150 feet per minute, and that only if the day was cold and the airport near sea-level.

One plus feature of the C-1 production model was that the pilot had an enclosed pod and a small plastic windshield. With generous wing area, it spanned 40 feet with a chord of five feet. Copying the German gliders, it used the Gottengen 398 airfoil. It might have cruised at 50 mph and it assuredly stalled at 20 mph. Its empty weight was 430 pounds, much of that being the over-heavy, under-powered Cleone 22-hp engine. Only six Cycloplanes were ever built.

My experience flying the Cycloplane taught me the critical nature of its engine.

In 1938 one Cycloplane was still flying, owned by an individual with whom I was acquainted. I mooched a flight. Immediately after taking off the aircraft felt as though it would stall at any moment. So I scooted around the field at 10 foot altitude, landed and complained the engine must not be running properly. With the owner in the cockpit operating the throttle for a test run, I stood by the engine carburetor adjustment. At his signal, I tweaked the setting leaner until the engine rpm's maxed.

When I tried flying it, the climb was positive, though slow, and I presumed I would have an enjoyable flight. As I thought this, the engine quit. At 200-foot altitude over the center of an airport is about the worst place to be for a forced landing in a strange airplane. Luck was mine for I managed a sloppy 360 degree turn and a landing without denting me or the machine.

On the ground, we removed a cylinder and found a neat, round hole in the top of the piston. So we learned about learning two-cycle engines the hard way. The dilemma of the Cleone engine was that if it were set slightly rich on the ground, it might still lean out excessively with any altitude. Also, the "slightly-rich" setting dropped the needed horsepower amazingly.

That aborted experience with the flying version of a Cycloplane was in direct contrast to the fun of handling the Penguin. Though the C-1 did get airborne, its low power made it dangerous except for a highly skilled pilot.

The idea nurtured by the two promoters was good. Their integrity was above question. They had almost everything right.

The Cycloplane died blameless. For all involved, dreams of a successful business fell in flames. An accident brought everything down—the accident of wrong timing.

R.I.P.

25 THE ALBATROSS LAYS AN EGG

Airplane designers from yesteryears of aviation often named their creations after birds. Curtiss set the pace with his names running from the fish hawk Osprey to his utilitarian Robin series. Most manufacturers sought terms that implied strength, speed or the grace and beauty of flight.

To have named an airplane an Albatross in defiance of the cliche "an albatross around my neck," would have seemed unwise to the superstitious. When one considers the flight characteristics of the sea bird, there are plusses and minuses. It's true the albatross can soar all day long without a wingbeat. But in takeoff and landings it is so ridiculously inept as to appear bizarre.

Omens or not, in 1927 an aviation company named their product "Albatross." It was the Zenith Airplane Company, consisting of a group of former naval aviators and a wealthy Californian rancher.

She christened it "Albatross" and it promptly laid a lead egg. Drawing courtesy of Bill Neale.

For a time, all appeared rosy. The original group had managed to complete its first design, the largest landplane in the world at that time. Former navy pilot, Charles Rocheville, one of the original investors, flight-tested the tri-engined craft in early 1928.

Its dimensions were impressive. The high wing spanned 90 feet and the fuselage was 47-feet long. It boasted an unheard of fuel capacity of 1,300 gallons with an expected gross weight of 6,000 pounds. Powered by three 140-hp Seimen-Halske German-built engines, it cruised an even 87 knots with a top speed of 109 knots. Its fuel endurance was expected to be 90 flight hours.

Needing additional capital, it seemed logical to all that an endurance record set by the plane would attract more investors. Logical and reasonable, but the mythical albatross was ready to strike.

Pilot Charles Rocheville's first attempt failed due to a broken fuel line. That repaired, he tried again, and this time managed to circle the Imperial Valley east of San Diego, California, for 47 hours. Gradually, though, an engine insidiously over heated and caused a premature landing. Undaunted, Rocheville tried a third time, but a broken pushrod in the engine ended that effort. The hoped-for publicity was only negative. Worse, their funds were rapidly drying up.

Early in 1929 the original group sold out to a company of Guatemalan investors who claimed to represent the "Guatemala Air Service." No one in California appeared able to learn any details of this purported airline. Renamed the "Albatross Airplane Company," the new owners promptly hired famed Jimmie Angel as their chief pilot. A few days later, my father and I enjoyed an hour-and-a-half ride in the huge monoplane.

After a few flights, Angel complained the ship was loggy and needed more powerful engines. Thus the German engines were swapped for three 150-hp Axelson engines. The amazing result of adding more horsepower was an unbelievable decline of airspeed. It now flew 8.7 knots slower!

The mythical albatross was in motion. The date was October 29, 1929, when the stock market spun in.

Angel assembled a crew of five others in addition to himself for another try at the endurance record. They were: George Schleppey, Sam Hopkins, Ed Frame, Bob Perlick, and Paul

Wiser as the radio operator. Angel was unaware that Schleppey was member Number 42 of the infamous Caterpillar Club for parachuting at Kelly Field, Texas, in January of 1927, An omen?

On Monday, December 16, 1929, the airplane and crew were ready. Amid much fanfare Jimmie Angel opened the throttles for their takeoff from Grand Central Air Terminal in Glendale, California. Odd, with all its weight and low power, the airplane jumped into the air—too quickly.

The mythical Albatross had now fastened itself around their necks.

In the air, both pilots had to push against the control-wheel with all their strength to prevent the ship from stalling. Obviously, something terrible had happened to the center of gravity. Angel shouted for those in the rear to check it out.

One of the crew quickly went through the cabin but found nothing amiss until he happened to look through a rear bulkhead door. Near the tailskid braces, he saw a young woman clinging in terror to the cross-bracing. Just what they needed—a stowaway. On the edge of a stall, Angel wisely ordered the young lady to be left alone while the remainder of the crew went as far forward as possible. As if walking on eggs, the two pilots made a wide circle and landed. With the center aft of gravity the plane thumped heavily down and broke its tailskid assembly. Miss Billie Brown, the publicity-hungry stowaway, was unhurt. The duration attempt had ended in 28 total minutes.

During the repair time, Angel apparently tried to sell several pilots on being the new copilot for the next and "successful" endurance record flight. That was what he promised, and painted such a glowing picture to my father that he easily and without resistance, parted with a healthy check.

It was soon apparent the proposed flight was dubious at best and the turkey'd new copilots were becoming more furious daily. Several secret attempts were then made to fly the ship to Guatemala City, but all failed as mechanical breakdowns plagued the trials.

The Albatross sat in storage for many years, then reappeared shortly before World War II as a gasoline service station in California's San Fernando Valley. Ultimately it was hauled off as scrap.

The legend had finally became fact—fait accompli. The myth of the onerous Albatross had come true.

26 BIG IS NOT ALWAYS BETTER

In 1924 Norwegian explorer Roald Amundsen was firming up his plans to fly to the North Pole. When he asked his two pilots, Hjalmar Riser-Larsen and Lief Dietrichson, to recommend the most suitable airplanes, their answer came as a surprise.

"We buy two Whales!"

"No doubt about it," echoed the other.

Unimpressed by the connotation of an airplane called a "Whale," Amundsen's confidence in his pilots was further shaken upon learning that Germany's Aviation Entente-Commission had banned the airplane's manufacture. That the designer was one of the Fatherland's most famous did not alter the Commission's opinion.

Amundsen's doubts increased when he studied a photograph of the twin-engined flying boat. In the photo, the "Wal," (A German name for "Whale,") was about the ugliest airplane Amundsen could imagine. With a huge slab-sided single-float hull sitting astride a large sponson, it appeared as if a twin-floatplane had lost a float somewhere in the design process. As the explorer studied the craft further, he noted that little effort had been made to alleviate wind resistance from the many appurtenances protruding from the wings and hull. The two sponsons appeared as if they'd been sawed off with a dull saw by some inept carpenter.

But as Amundsen evaluated the awkward-appearing flying machine, it began to make sense. He realized his pilots had wisely selected the best machine available for the intended polar flight.

Above the hull, atop an assortment of cabane braces, sat a squared-off rectangular wing, firmly secured to the hull with brutish-looking metal struts.

Good, the wing will be above the rough ice, Amundsen thought as he continued to evaluate the plane. Gradually, his appreciation of the ungainly flying boat increased. Above the center of the wing, where it attached to the cabane bracing, sat two 600-hp BMW-VI engines. To avoid the adverse and often fatal yaw of ordinary twin-engined planes with powerplants far out on each wing, these operated in tandem—one pushing, the other pulling, and both in the ship's centerline of thrust.

Using what at first glance appeared to be four-bladed propellers Amundsen noted with a new respect for the plane and its designer, that the four blades were made up of two, two-blade propellers fastened at right angles to the other. So, no special props would be needed as spares. Amundsen must have nodded his head with increased approval.

Studying further, the explorer and his crew discovered with delight a host of other features which appeared as though the designer had just their particular type of flying in mind. Designed and built of thick aluminum plates, the boat was tough, albeit beautiful. Its hull was so strong it could operate off rough fields of snow and ice by sliding along on its bare hull.

Even its numbers spoke of muscular substance. A large craft over 57-feet long, its wing spanned nearly 74 feet, and it reached 18 feet high. Best of all to any explorer was the fact that the flying boat could lift its own weight. Fully loaded, it would fly at 76,000 pounds.

Later, Amundsen would unhesitently claim that his survival and exploration success in the Arctic was due in large part to the Wal flying boats.

Though the Wal had made its first test-flight on November 6, 1922, and Amundsen's trek started in 1925, a long lineage preceded the airplane's design.

Created by Claudius Dornier of Germany, the Wal's development represented seven previously successful seaplane designs.

Dornier had designed and built three-engined and four-engined, military and civilian craft, and by the year 1932 could show sales of over 300 Wals. This type racked up an impressive record of flying and safety statistics during their operating years. In airline service, Wals had flown over six million miles. Further, the airline version had remained structurally unchanged for a period of 15 years—an unheard of record for that time. Old newsreels still show the Wal J-Model being catapulted from ships at sea several days in advance of their port arrivals to deliver foreign mail.

One wonders if the expression, "If it ain't broke, don't fix it!" did not originate with some mechanic who serviced the Dornier Wal.

With Dornier's established reputation as an airplane designer, it is difficult to understand why the German commission banned his planes. Unable to change their ruling, Dornier moved his plant to Italy where the bulk of his designs first saw light.

Equally impressive to any student of history was the life and career of Claudius Dornier. No doubt his expertise with aluminum fabrication stemmed from his initial employment as a designer engineer with the Zeppelin group. Ugly though his line of flying boats may have been, "do the job" became their true description.

A study of the evolution of his planes shows a gradual empirical movement through the years. His first flying boat designed in 1916, the DoR-II, would set the designs that followed. It had the same tandem-engine configuration as later models, plus the single hull with the stabilizing sponson. His planes sold from their inception until the early 1930's.

Secretive, Dornier told no one of his big dream: he wanted to design and build the world's largest airplane.

This dream of Germany's famed airplane designer was not a flight of fancy. Serious and knowledgeable, his intentions were based upon sound data. His airplanes had gained a reputation for stalwart performance. He'd proven to the world his engineering ability. And deep within, he felt the Zeppelins were much too slow for crossing oceans. What the world needed at this time, Dornier decided, was an ocean-crossing seaplane large enough to carry 100 passengers. Though his reasoning was based upon his wide experience and he saw no sign this plan could not be realized, time and public opinion would later prove him wrong.

Preceding his plans for a "DOX," were five airplanes by other designers that at one time or another vied for the title of World's Largest.

In 1912 Russian designer Igor Sikorsky flew a four-engined mammoth he called "Le Grande." It had a wing span of 92 feet, a gross weight of 9,000 pounds, and carried eight persons as crew. It was a hint of his future ability as a designer to have 70 more built and flown up to 1917.

Count von Zeppelin, in 1915 before he embarked upon the construction of lighter-than-air crafts bearing his name, produced the "Staaken." Claimed the world's largest at the time, it boasted of four engines, had a wing span of 138 feet, grossed out at 26,066 pounds and carried a crew of seven. Twenty-two were produced for the German government.

Four years later, there appeared the Siemen's RV-III,

powered by six engines with a wing spanning 157 feet. It carried 10 passengers and grossed at 34,980 pounds. Of five under construction, only one was completed.

Concurrent with the Siemen's airplane was the ill-fated Tarrant Tabor. Clearly the world's largest flying machine at that time, it had an awkward grouping of six engines, most set so high on its thrust line that it upended on its initial test flight and killed its crew. Its primary design intention was to fly from Berlin and bomb Great Britain. Its wing span was 131 feet and it had a gross weight of 44,672 pounds.

Judging from the trend during that era, it appeared to the eyes of the world that airplane designers had gone slightly mad. If the "Tabor" wasn't unconventional enough, there was another about to hatch which would outdo it.

A year later, 1920, on an Italian lake, a monstrous triplane tandem consisting of nine wings spanning 98 feet was unveiled. To the press, it claimed an ability to carry more than 100 passengers in safety and luxury. At 57,200 pounds weight, it resisted flight to the extent that it crashed on its second trial run.

Except for the genius of Igor Sikorsky, most of the giants were abysmal failures. Still in the future in the year 1926 were such craft as Great Britain's Handley-Page HP-42, Hugo Junker's batwinged G-38, and the Russian's Maxim Gorky.

Having watched the failures come and go, Claudius Dornier clearly believed the time was ripe to sound out his dreams. Thus, on Lake Constance in Switzerland, the DOX was born.

In December of 1926, Dornier astonished the world when he unveiled plans for the "World's Biggest Airplane." When questioned by the press, he stated he would call his flying boat the "DOX." The "DO" would designate *Dornier* and the "X" would signify a design of unknown quantity. However, in the unfolding years the public thought the "X" denoted the number of engines as 10.

Again touting the claim of "world's largest," Dornier's numbers were impressive: 157-foot wing span, 123,000 pounds gross weight, a capacity to haul 160 passengers and an ability to cross oceans. As with Dornier's former airplanes, it was a flying boat. It had the same slab-sided hull as its forerunners, a sponson for water stability, and its 12 engines sat atop the main wing on an auxiliary wing. Following the success of his Wal, six engines were tractors and six were pushers.

To the date of this writing, no other airplane has ever boasted of more than 12 engines.

Without doubt, the DOX was impressive. Its hull was 131 feet long, and it was designed to lift and fly with double its empty weight of 65,040 pounds. The influence of Hugo Junkers, a German professor and Dornier's helper, was evident in the use of corrugated metal on the wing leading edge and the huge stabilizer.

Selecting engines for the behemoth became an ongoing problem that was never satisfactorily solved. Its original Siemen's-built, Bristol-Jupiter, air-cooled radial engines were replaced with the American Curtiss Conquerer, liquid-cooled engines of 600 hp each.

Always thinking of transporting paying passengers across the world's oceans, Dornier designed such features as octagon crawl tubes through which engineers could service the engines in flight.

As plush as it was possible to concieve, the plane was outfitted with bathrooms, a huge passenger compartment, and a salon 23 feet long carpeted with Oriental rugs.

On the crew deck, the flight engineer's station handled all the engine and propeller settings for the 12 engines.

Finally, on the 25th day of July in 1929, the great flying boat was ready for its first test flight. Not only did the seaplane fly, it lifted from the water surface in just a few hundred feet—much to the astonishment of its pilot. Otherwise, the test flight proved what the world expected: Claudius Dornier did, indeed, know how to design and build successful flying boats.

The DOX flew well and handled as expected. The only hint of a design flaw was its reluctance to climb above 2,000 feet altitude even when nearly empty.

Several more test flights were made to fix the usual assortment of glitches. On October 21 of the same year, it flew with 150 passengers, 10 crew and nine stowaways. However, its lifting ability outside of the ground/water surface effect was unquestionably poor. Though each takeoff run used less than 1,000 feet, the service ceiling remained very low. It was able to rise to 1,377 feet but no more. Dornier was perturbed but concluded that no higher altitude was needed to cross a flat ocean. However, with its American engines, the service ceiling was raised to 1,640 feet.

The year 1930 arrived and with it Dornier finalized his plans to display his flying boat to its best advantage. He informed the public the DOX would fly from Europe to New York City via Holland, Lisbon, the Canary Islands and Rio de Janiero. The departure was planned for an early November date.

Problems arose as soon as he'd made his momentous announcement. First, there were swarms of curious visitors to the berthing dock that seriously interrupted the preparatory work. Then test flights encountered a series of minor mishaps. Meanwhile, Dornier had selected the crew. German World War ace, Fredrich Christiansen would captain the flight, and an American, C. H. Schildhauer, was chosen as 2nd pilot/navigator.

Despite the setbacks encountered, the giant DOX made its departure from Friedrichshafen for the U.S.A. on the morning of November 2, 1930.

Enroute, small problems almost immediately surrendered to major tangles. Upon reaching Lisbon, a fire seriously damaged one wing. The ship was beached in the Tagus River and repaired.

It crossed the Atlantic Ocean via the Canary Islands where the hull was punctured and repaired.

Finally, it reached Natal, Brazil, and then flew on to Rio de Janiero.

From Rio, the DOX flew via the West Indies to New York harbor where it arrived on August 27, 1931, 10 months after it had departed from Germany.

At once the world press made it the butt of jokes.

Though Dornier and his crew made the return trip from New York City to Germany in only six days, to the public and the press, the effort was considered a waste of time. No one would ever discover the true potentials of Dornier's dreams, for the airplane had made its last flight.

Donated to the Berlin Aircraft Museum, it was on display until the midst of World War II, when it and the museum were destroyed by Allied bombs.

When questioned later, Dornier stated, "The purpose of the DOX was to prove that as airplanes grow bigger, their problems are not insurmountable." His dreams and his huge airplane had flown 20,505 miles before dying with the DOX's final flight.

History records that two more of the giants were built in Italy and powered with 600-hp Fiat engines. But records and data are scarce (or non-existent) as to their accomplishments or disposition.

Bordering upon the bizarre was Dornier's death. In 1925, his DOB, "Merkur 1," (Mercury 1), a highly successful single-engined seaplane carrying eight with a design that persisted trouble-free for many years crashed with its designer aboard.

Behemoths following Claudius Dornier's DOX were few. In 1934, the Russian Maxim Gorky, wing span 206 feet, flew but was destroyed in a mid-air collision with a military fighter plane.

Until Howard Hughes flew his Hughes H-4 on a single test flight, there were no more claimants to the "world's biggest airplane" title.

In recent times, the Boeing 747 transport must be classified as the heavyweight champion of the big numbers. With a wing span of 195 feet and a growing record of service by flying everywhere in the world, it is proving to be the most successful effort in mammoth planes.

Now, in looking back through time, we know that while "big" may be impressive, it is not always better.

27 THE FIRST ATC

For civil aviation in the United States during the period between 1922 and 1925, the air was decidely bumpy.

To an aviator flying a rickety biplane purchased from war surplus for $300, a bump in the air was of little consequence. The nose rose or fell and a quick press of the control stick against the up- or down-draft kept the airplane under control.

For aviation itself, "control" was not in place. The air of aviation-commerce was becoming turbulent. Looking at aviation from one view, there were indicators suggesting the casual attitude of the barnstormer had reached its zenith. From another view, signals said commerce could come from the proper application of flight.

Throughout our land, the spirit of 1926 was one in which the citizens were intoxicated with a booming economy. Automobiles were being produced so fast that every person in the land could be carried in them.

"Contrast" was a thread insidiously weaving itself through people, commerce and politics.

The creativity of some would prove the period generated the genius as easily as it came to produce the Model-T Ford. Great writing appeared in this age: Fitzgerald, Hemingway, Anderson, and Sinclair Lewis were barely beginning to feel their literary oats.

At Kitty Hawk, North Carolina, flight had outgrown its short pants suit. Twenty-three years had passed since the Wright Brothers had fumbled their way aloft in a contraption so ludicrous it took some time for the public to believe it existed. Yet, in 1925 a small company named Huff-Deland had 20 of its airplanes applying chemicals to agricultural fields. Commerce in aviation was brewing.

Other forms of transportation were given Federal subsidies. Aviation was given nothing but a jaundiced eye by the bureaucrats. In 1924, respected William P. McCracken, Jr., said, "For the most part, people think of flying as somewhere between a sport and a sideshow."

Nevertheless, sideshows were not ordinarily in the habit of killing its actors or spectators. For a solid, single week in the New York City area, the worst of aviation made headlines. One flyer buzzed an automobile and caused the driver to lose control and crash to his death. Another pilot, stunting over Rockaway Beach, went out of control and nearly injured a host of bathers. Still another plane lost control over the Hudson River and almost collided with a steamship and an express train before crashing. In Washington, D.C., a former Army reserve officer crashed his plane and killed his passenger.

The above events erased former public indifference and gave way to a closer scrutiny of the antics of barnstormers and careless aviators. *Aero Digest*, a flying magazine of that era, wrote: "Lives and property can be saved by a national law regulating the movement of aircraft."

The dim handwriting upon the wall was now emblazoned in neon lights.

By March of 1926, no fewer than 26 Congressional probes had been conducted into both civil and military aviation. Subsequent events quickly moved the law makers to enact Federal regulations for all of aviation.

On April 12, 1926, the Air Commerce Act was passed by

the House. Soon thereafter aviation interests were legally concerned with aircraft and airman certification, air-traffic rules, and the establishment of airports. The feeling among all concerned was that aviation must be promoted and controlled. Severe penalties were imposed for violations of the new laws.

Thus the Approved Type Certificate was born (ATC). Now, if anyone wished to design, build and market an airplane, or one of its components, he would have to gain Federal Certification.

For the small aviation industry, the race was on.

One of the more secure airplane manufacturers was the Boeing Company of Seattle, Washington. Financially sound, they eyed the acquisition of the very first ATC as a coveted jewel. Their new Boeing 40-A, Wasp-powered mailplane was almost ready to market. Begun in 1925, the plane now faced the added delay of such items as: stress analysis, load-testing and proven flight characteristics. Boeing, however, had an impediment not faced by smaller firms: bigger than others, they were also more inflexible. As so many businesses, Boeing was suffering from acute growing pains.

Across the continent in Detroit, Michigan, unfettered by the reins of big business, two men were furiously at work. Lawrence D. Buhl wanted more than anything else to manufacture his own airplanes. Another capable designer of that day, Alfred Verville, suffered from the same itch that neither had heretofore been able to scratch.

Their association was a natural outgrowth of ambitions. Both opened their personal throttles and happily went to work designing a new airplane under the banner Buhl-Verville Aircraft Company.

First, these two produced the CW-3 biplane powered by the aging but famous OX-5 engine. Though it performed well, it did not excite customers who wanted more performance than the 90 hp engine could deliver. Thus the J-4 Airster metamorphosed from the underpowered CW-3.

The Airster began a long line of popular airplanes produced by the efforts of these two men. Not only did the Airster impress the public, but while in the process of earning its approved type certificate, the new Department of Commerce people ordered two for their own use. In March of 1927, Buhl-Verville was granted the very first ATC.

Subtle though it may have been, when the government

people decided to purchase these planes, it caught the attention of magnate Henry B. DuPont, who quickly added his name to the growing list of Airster owners.

Soon, events for the small company accelerated. In far off Spokane, Washington, pilot and fixed base operator, Nick Mamer had captured third place in the New York to Spokane Air Derby.

Priced at $9300, the Airster was considered a "class" airplane. Five-thousand dollars of its price was imbedded in the cost of its Wright engine.

Tough-looking, the big biplane had its wings stacked atop each other without forward or rearward stagger. Reminiscent of the DH-4, its wings spanned 35 feet and carried a five-foot chord. As others of its day, it used the Clark-Y airfoil. Twenty-six feet long, it carried a gross weight of 3,069 pounds. Easily, it seemed, it cruised at 108 mph with a top speed of 125 mph. Ceiling was claimed as 12,000 feet with a cross-country range of 700 miles.

The Airster was one of the first airplanes to offer a folding wing. As extras, brakes and dual controls were available. One of its most accepted sales features was the split-axle landing gear with Oleo struts and large rubber shock absorbers. The combination yielded a predictable, docile ground handling in a day when most airplanes offered marginal control during takeoffs or landings.

The two men beat Boeing by four months in acquiring the first ATC.

In time, they split their partnership under compatible circumstances and proceeded to build greater personal reputations. Buhl produced a long string of his "Airsedan" sesquiplanes, one of which was lost at sea in the infamous Dole Derby from Oakland, California, to Hawaii. Another brought more fame to its designer by earning the world's endurance record of 246 hours aloft in July of 1929.

In 1931, Buhl designed and sold the famous lightplane, the "Bull Pup." A success as a popular plane, but offered in a declining airplane market, it was the final design effort of Lawrence Buhl.

Alfred Verville for a time tried to develop a low-wing fighter-plane for the military but later gave up the quest and re-entered the civilian airplane market with his new design, the Verville Air Coach. Ultimately, the shrinking airplane market caught Verville in its undertow and he too, had to find other means of earning a living.

For a time, Verville designed and built house trailers but that too folded in 1932. Seeing a more permanent job in aviation, Verville joined the Bureau of Air Commerce and soon was in charge of their ATC section—a twist of fate. This proved a wise move as the depression years caused the majority of small aviation entrepreneurs to fail.

However, both Buhl and Verville left a monument to themselves when they successfully acquired the first Approved Type Certificate granted by the United States Government agency, The Bureau of Air Commerce.

28 THE BEAUTY OF THE "K" WAS SKIN DEEP

The Aeronca Model "K" looked like a fine airplane. It wasn't. No doubt the designers anticipated a leap forward in their technology. Reasonable idea, for the new K was a spinoff from the popular C-3 series. Those who'd flown the Collegiate enjoyed easy handling, gentle stalls, fair climb ability and acceptable cruising speeds.

Regretfully, the K was none of the above. Retained was the 42 hp, E-113-CB engine, dubious at best. And something dreadful had happened to its stability. While the C-3 was docile throughout its stall, the K would snap viciously when it ran out of airspeed. Loggy in climb, it sat so high in three-point attitude that any landing not on-the-button in the stiff-legged beast would assure undignified leaps.

When the Aeronca K first appeared on the aviation scene, expectations ran high. Before it was a vast potential market of pilots who'd done much happy flying—cheaply.

Following a formal debut in a New York aircraft show the previous January, the Aeronca K was issued Approved Type Certificate Number 634 on April 30, 1937. With an apparent seller's market, the factory was producing three airplanes per day. The factory serial number of the one this story is about was No. six.

A year later, Aeronca assessed the airplane's shortcom-

It was an Aeronca K. And the "K" was short for "Kouldn't!" Drawing courtesy of Bill Neale.

ings and offered several improvements: wheel brakes, a tail-wheel in lieu of a skid, navigation lights and a more plush interior. It was priced at $1,745, fly-away, at Lunken Airport in Cincinnati, Ohio.

Its specifications were similar to its predecessors. The K carried a wing-span of 36 feet with a 50-inch chord. As many other lightplanes, it used the popular Clark-Y airfoil. Empty it weighed 590 pounds, and it promised a useful load of 450 pounds. With about 80 pounds for full fuel and oil, and pilot and passenger at 170 pounds apiece, there were still 30 pounds available for baggage. There was an "if" to these numbers, however: one assumed it could carry such a load. Again, the figures *seemed* good. The factory had listed its service ceiling as 12,000 feet. Expecting a 255 mile range, buyers were lining up to become owners. First offered at $1,480, factory expectations were rosy. In time 350 Ks would be sold.

I was familiar with the K in the early summer of 1939 as I'd been flying one to build up time. At four dollars an hour, wet, it was kept busy flying off the old Telegraph and Atlantic airport in East Los Angeles, California.

When I heard from my eastern friend who'd owned a very recalcitrant Buhl Bull Pup, I was offered a proposition difficult to refuse. Good old Fred. With the money he'd made selling the Bull Pup, he had bought a nearly new, shiny yellow Aeronca Model K. After warning him of the poor stall characteristics of the plane, I wished him well and tried to dismiss the airplane from my mind. Then he dangled the bait before me. Seems he'd secured a job with Lockheed Aircraft Company in Burbank, California, and intended to fly the K to his new home. Fred wanted me to go with him and he painted glowing pictures of all the fun we'd have on the trip. Good old Fred! Free flying time and fun too—how could any budding airman resist?

After resting from the long bus ride from my home in California, Fred and I drove to Paterson Field to see his new K. When I inspected the airplane, I had to agree with him—it looked great. Wasn't even any dirt on the floor mat.

Two days later, after we'd installed a surplus navy wobble pump for transferring a five-gallon can of fuel into the main tank while airborne, we took off for the West Coast.

It wasn't long before my worst fears surfaced. Our ground speed between New Jersey and Birmingham, Alabama was a sizzling 51 mph.

By leg No. four, I was considering another hobby; we flew the 608 miles from Birmingham to Dallas, Texas, in the incredible time of 12 hours and 25 minutes. The sun slid over the horizon as we landed for the night at Love Field.

From then on, it got worse.

Dallas to Midland, we thumped along without any problem other than slow—slow-slow.

We thought Midland to El Paso would be uneventful because we'd taken off at dawn. But near Guadalupe Pass, our ground speed deteriorated to 21.3 mph. Believe it, you are reading it correctly.

Over the pass, we descended into the hot valley below and landed at the Salt Flat emergency airfield for fuel. It was Fred's turn to fly. After taking off with no apparent problem, the airplane began to settle in a three-point attitude. "It won't climb!" Fred said. I watched horror-stricken as the Aeronca settled back onto the airport with wide-open throttle. We both spent the night in our sleeping bags under the wing while we contemplated about what hot weather does to the climb of an airplane already underpowered. (Later, I computed our density-altitude as over 7,000 feet high.)

Neither of us at that point in our flying careers could understand why we'd had such a problem when the Salt Flat airport's elevation was listed at 4,800 feet. Also both of us recently had read an article in which a pilot claimed downdrafts never reach the ground. Still uneasy, the true meanings of our experience had escaped us.

Next morning at dawn Fred suggested I fly that leg to El Paso. Using full power and every inch of the airfield, the Aeronca protestingly took off. A mile later, it was still flying in ground-effect at the same perilous three-point attitude.

Seeming suspended in time but not in space, we chugged along in a straight line hoping for altitude. But when the plane's wheels began to touch the sagebrush, I opted for lower ground on our left and cautiously banked toward it.

By twisting and turning, holding our breath and alternately cursing and begging the airplane to climb, we made it to El Paso. From the river to the airport we bucked a head wind with such ferocity that we nearly ran out of fuel a few hundred feet south of the runway. Landing in a 55-knot wind had the airport personnel running to grab the airplane and manhandle it into a hangar. Safely inside, none could believe we'd managed to get to El Paso under the conditions present.

We tossed and turned in the sleeping bags that night in the hangar. Both of us had to know what the other was thinking and feeling without asking.

Again at dawn under a clear sky, we were off to our next refueling point, Lordsburg, New Mexico. Fred flew the airplane while I sat and chewed my fingernails dangerously close to my elbows. In my mind were my father's story about his experiences barnstorming that area. "Ha!," he'd said about our impending trip: "You two weak-feathered chickens will learn something about western flying."

When I had asked, "Why?" he laughed sadistically. "You'll see. You will pray for every foot of altitude and you'll offer the gods whatever you own for every inch toward the west. Ha!"

Fred followed the highway and as the ground rose in elevation, it appeared as if our altitude was dropping. He tapped his finger against the glass face of the altimeter and said, "We are losing altitude!" Looking out, I saw the highway coming closer. A few miles later the airport came in view and our wheels were lightly touching asphalt pavement with each small downdraft. A gust of wind generously carried us over the airport's fence and we landed and taxied to the fuel pumps.

As the crusty middle-aged airport operator fueled the Aeronca, he alternately whistled with disbelief and chuckled at some secret of his own.

"What's so funny?" I demanded.

"You two, that's what. You birds and your silly airplane."

Now Fred was insulted. "It looks a lot better than that dumpy Taylorcraft of yours over there!"

Putting the fuel hose away, he nodded. "Sure right about that. But when you two open the throttle to get off this airport, you ain't going anywhere! That T-Craft will carry anything you can shove in it and leap off the ground like a homesick frog."

You know we had to give it a try, right?

Using all the runway again, I opened the throttle and watched the end of the airport approach while it seemed we were only crawling. With barely enough room to stop, I had to close the throttle and taxi back to the hangar area. Our friendly operator was standing alongside his T-Craft now and was humming a tune.

We were abashed. "So, what do you suggest?" Fred asked.

"Don't suggest. What I *tell* you is the only way you're going to leave here."

"Only?" Fred's voice was so sad.

"That's right—only. You birds pay me five bucks and we'll load everything you got except one man to fly your airplane into my T-Craft. One of you fly your airplane to a dry lake about ten miles west of here. I take the other and all your junk. When we get there, you two get back in that apple-knocker and make a run of about two miles and when you take off, wait for an updraft before you turn . . . You do know how to turn, don't you?"

I could have hit him if he'd been smaller.

He went on. "After you take off, fly until you feel a good solid updraft. Fly through it before making a turn. Then keep circling as long as you are climbing. When you have about seven or 8,000 feet on the altimeter, point the nose toward Tuscon and hi-tail it out of this high-country. Got it?"

As he said, this did seem our only chance. Fred and I discussed his offer. We agreed that he was full of fertilizer and believed his airplane would stay ground-bound the same as the K. Our alternative was to wait until dawn and one of us would have to take the bus to Tuscon until the other flew there in the K.

Cautious, Fred made a counter-offer. "Okay, we try your plan but if your airplane won't do what you say, the deal's off."

The other shrugged. We then unloaded all our luggage, the five-gallon empty fuel can, the heavy navy wobble pump, the Aeronca's wheel hub covers and prop spinner and my shoes. Fred propped the Aeronca and then the man's airplane. I was already taxiing to the far end of the field. When I saw the wind sock turn from a gust of wind, I gave the K power and in about 1,000 feet, it lifted and climbed about two hundred feet high, As I could see the dry lakes ahead, I steered straight for them and landed at their eastern edge. When I crawled from the K, I saw the T-Craft coming from about 2,000 feet above the terrain. The old aviator swooped down and then zoomed upwards as if the T-Craft had a rocket for power. I couldn't believe what I'd seen.

We did as the man suggested, and with Fred flying, his plan worked exactly as he'd promised. We were now five dollars poorer but we had the enjoyment of hating him soundly. From Tuscon into Blythe, California, that was our script: find a thermal, ride it up and then point the nose toward the west.

Other than what I've related, we had no trouble. "Standard stuff," said my ex-barnstorming father. But when I review my logbooks and note the entries of that trip, the skin on my back does a bit of crawling.

So we two tyros learned about "density altitude" the hard way.

Caveat emptor.

29 CATALINA FLYING BOATS

Military pilots called her a P-Boat. Others spoke of her bulky appearance with derision.

A few heartless soles likened her to an ugly insect with bug-eyes set far back on her thorax. Pilot's feelings about the PBY often started with frustration but ended in a love affair.

From my experience in flying the PBY, she earned these varied remarks.

PBY's were slow—terribly so. The plane's ailerons acted as if they had been hooked up backwards. Flying this airplane in turbulence would reduce the ablest of pilots to a quivering mess.

To fly a range of 4,000 miles, the PBY carried her weight in fuel. Most would term this a great feature, and it was when traversing continents or oceans. But when the tanks were near empty in the PBY-5A amphibian, her light weight could allow her to float across an airfield much like the wee Taylorcraft of yesteryears. So why not use flaps for a landing? Sorry, no flaps on any PBYs.

With all the annoyances of her design the PBY series of airplanes were undoubtably the most versatile flying machines of the World War II period. When the newness of flying this airplane gave way to an understanding, pilots learned to love her.

How I came to checkout and make deliveries of PBYs to domestic and foreign points in this strange bird was as ludicrous as her appearance . . . .

PBY in the open-sea, full-stall landing. Photograph courtesy of the U.S. Coast Guard.

It was a warm, balmy November day in 1943 at the Long Beach, California, Ferrying Command base. When awaiting orders, we pilots would loll around a grassy area behind Operations. We passed time, as all others of our ilk, telling great whopping lies.

When personnel needed a pilot to ferry a military version of a former civilian airplane, it was habit to ask for someone with experience in that airplane type. This method was crude but usually worked, for among the gathering, often such a pilot could be found.

When Operations Officer Captain Larry Schwartzell opened the door and shouted, "Anyone here with a seaplane rating?" Not one hand was raised in response. As I had obtained a sea rating in a 40 hp J-2 Taylor Cub in the backwaters of Los Angeles harbor, I shouted back and raised my hand. Schwartzell nodded to me and went back inside. I left to pack for an expected delivery trip wondering what kind of seaplane I would be ferrying.

Orders were finally cut and handed out. I was astonished to learn that I had been directed to the North Island Naval Air Station at San Diego, California, with my friend Captain Archie Bray to get qualified in an OA-10.

Apparently my brain was grid-locked for I could make no sense of the orders and wondered what in hell was an "OA-10." I had thought I would be delivering something like a single-engined Stinson seaplane. When Bray appeared, I asked what was what.

He said, "An OA-10 is an Army Air Force version of the PBY. We're going to San Diego to check you out and pickup your delivery airplane." He further explained that he'd been checked out during the previous week and that he would be qualifying many others scheduled for delivery flights.

"Why is our Air Force getting seaplanes?" I asked.

"For search and rescue operations, dummy. The 'AO' designation means 'Army Observation.'"

So much for my failed brain. Off we went to San Diego.

Other than that everything I learned was new and strange, I thought Bray's checkout of me went well. Outwardly, I maintained the brash appearance of an air force pilot but inwardly, I was jelly. All about this bird was weird. To save time, Bray had decided to check me out in sea operations only at San Diego and then finish up with a landplane or amphibian checkout at our base in Long Beach.

During our flying at San Diego, Bray cautioned me that the P-Boats had no differential in their ailerons and at any speed nearing a stall, the aileron controls operated in reverse. (Thanks a lot!) When I watched him demonstrate a stall, I couldn't believe my eyes. Nearing a stall, the slightest attempt to raise a wing resulted in a sudden drop of that wing into an incipient spin mode. Captain Bray added that this faux paus during a water landing would result in ripping off the lowered wing. Hearing this was a great confidence-builder.

Though quite heavy on the controls, I managed to learn the intricacies of getting it on and off the placid waters of San Diego Bay. When Bray was satisfied with my flying of the PBY, we returned to North Island for my demo flight with a veteran navy airman who had thousands of hours in PBYs.

Enroute to the open sea practice area, I watched how the wrinkle-faced vet handled the ungainly bird in the light turbulence we were going through. I saw that he was using mostly rudder to lift a wing and accompanying this with reverse aileron. So that was the secret of flying the P-Boat.

"Lieutenant, keep alert while I show you how to get this crate down in an open sea. Things happen kinda quickly." And with that he approached the sea crosswind but aligned with the large, running swells. Slower and slower he flew until the PBY was shuddering on the edge of a stall but still about eight feet above the sea surface.

It stalled suddenly and dramatically. I had thought we were 10 feet or better above the water but the drop into the green surface showed we were much less. As it hit the water, he yelled, "Hang on!"

I clutched at something and it was the control wheel. Nothing else was within reach and I was unprepared for the suddeness or the brutality of the drop following the full power stall. When the nose hit the water, it went under the sea surface. All this happened so fast that my pucker-factor rose to great heights.

Green, foaming sea water rushed over the cabin and the windshield. I had the impression that the plane had sunk to wing-level; they had broken off and now the fuselage was heading to the sea bottom. The other man saw my terror and laughed loud and long. "Hey! Look through the windshield."

I did and what a wonderful, happy sight it was. Daylight

was coming through the glass as the water cascaded off the structure.

"You can breathe again, Lieutenant!"

I took his advice and noted that I was shaking all over.

"That's a mild version, Lieutenant. But there is no other way to land in an open sea without wrecking the bird."

I decided that if at all possible, I had ridden through my first and last open sea landing—certainly enough for any chicken landlubber.

For those of you who've flown the PBYs, I suspect you are laughing with masochistic glee at my account. And I realize that for anyone who hasn't actually gone through such an experience, he couldn't imagine how horrifying it was.

Compared to my open sea experience, the rest of my checkout was a piece of cake. Once again at Long Beach, Bray and I spent two hours making touch and goes on the lovely concrete runways. When I complained about its floating, Bray told me to slip the next landing approach. On base leg to final, I yanked the PBY into a steep slipping turn. It did the trick of spilling off unneeded altitude perfectly. But in the middle of the maneuver, we heard an agonized shriek come from the apprentice flight engineer who was stationed in the wing pedestal. I looked back and saw him tumble onto the deck in a heap. When he came forward, he told us of the huge skin wrinkling that had appeared in the neck/pedestal skin during the slipping turn.

The following morning, with my own crew, we took off to deliver the airplane to Roosevelt Field, Long Island, New York. As we'd flight-planned from Long Beach direct to Albuquerque nonstop, I computed about five hours of flying time. I recalled that this was about the same as I had spent flying a 65-hp Luscombe over the same route a year past. All of us figured the PBY would beat the Luscombe flight time. We were wrong.

Airborne and heading east at a flight level of 11,000 feet in smooth air, we had time to reflect upon the airplane's history and specifications.

The genré of our OA-10 (PBY-5A), extended far back in years. The P-Boat's basic design appeared in Consolidated Aircraft Company's PY-1, a design submitted at the request of the U.S. Navy. Douglas was the only other serious competitor, but lost out on the production contract with a higher unit price.

Though the design of the P-Boats was first issued from the Bureau of Naval Air, the final design must be acknowledged by Consolidated design genius, Isaac M. Laddon. It was 1933 when production finally started.

By 1939 the PBY series had metamorphosed through many design improvements and ultimately emerged as the highly touted PBY-5 series aircraft. The Royal Air Force of Great Britain purchased the first batch of flying boats, 106 in all. Our U.S. Navy then followed with an order for 200 airplanes, their largest single order for airplanes since the end of World War I.

In this series, the airplane's design stabilized. It's length stayed at 63 ft., 6 inches long. The strut braced wing spanned 104 feet. From hull bottom to top of rudder measured 18 ft., 6 inches. Claiming a top speed of near 200 mph, PBYs were powered by two Pratt & Whitney 1830-82 engines, delivering 1,200 hp each.

With their first order, the British named the PBY "Catalina." They admitted a fondness for the nice island off the coast near Los Angeles. It took our navy until 1941 to accept the name. If one considers the small Briggs & Stratton type engine used for the Auxiliary Power Unit, the PBY was a three-engined airplane.

As WW II neared, other seaplane designs emerged that bore striking similarities to the PBY. One only has to see a photo of the German Do 18 to note this influence.

Refueling at Albuquerque, my computer reinforced the definition of "slow." For the 568-sm flight, our time was five hours and 45 minutes. We had averaged a mere 98 mph. Indeed, the lowly Luscombe was as fast.

As a pilot became more familiar with the ungainly P-Boat, he would bow to the temptations of sadistic delights. My crew thought it great sport when we would carry a newly graduated air cadet and then allow him to fly the PBY in rough air. As soon as a wing dropped, the shinning-winged new lieutenant would do as he was taught to do: apply aileron. But friend, this was a PBY, remember? Without the generous use of rudder, the down aileron would only cause the wing to sag lower. In seconds, the perplexed tyro's muscles would be quivering. Then I would take the controls and say, "I got it." With a bit of reverse aileron and a healthy input of rudder, the wing would raise smartly. A mean trick, yes, but all who flew the PBY paid their dues.

A love relationship came gradually to most pilots who were assigned to fly her. I made several deliveries from the West Coast to Casablanca on the African mainland. On one flight from Natal, Brazil, that was supposed to cross over Ascension Island and then continue to Dakar, we decided the inter-tropical front was too muscular for our liking. No problem. We simply made a left turn and outflew it with a small 1,000-mile detour.

PBY flights of over 20 hours were commonplace. On such extended journeys it was usual to look from the cockpit aft and see two crewmen lolling on sleeping bags they had placed in the two fuselage blisters. Reading dime novels, they would be as any seashore sunbather enjoying an outing. For total comfort they would be dressed in shorts and have generous globs of sunburn lotion spread across noses and foreheads. So it was a slow airplane? Who cared?

Savvy PBY pilots made good use of the automatic pilots. We discovered that in water takeoffs, as soon as the boat was on its step we could engage the autopilot and continue in comfort. On one flight to Africa we tallied up our hand-flown time and discovered it to be only 14 minutes out of the 70 plus hours flown.

Most noted for its rescue operations, perhaps the most amazing rescue effort happened to involve one of our Long Beach pilots.

Captain Armand Monteverde and a combat crew he was to ferry to England in a Boeing B-17 were off Blui West One (BW 1) and headed for their next stop, Rekavic, Iceland. It was a slightly hazy day as they climbed out of the deep, starkly shadowed fiord and leveled off to cross a section of the Greenland icecap. On autopilot, he and the others were abruptly awakened from their reverie when they heard all four propellers striking the field of snow. Without knowing of it, they had been flying in an increasingly dense whiteout. In seconds, they were down on the icecap. In those early days of WW II, rescues from the expanse of snow hovered between unlikely and impossible. Usually, those who were saved came down through the efforts of the local Eskimos and their dogteams, and consumed days and sometimes weeks in the effort.

A new Colonel had been stationed at BW 1 and he had a different idea about Arctic rescues. The famous exploration pilot, Bernt Balchen took off in a PBY to rescue Monteverde and his men, but weather closed in and for 10 days he was grounded. Finally, the downed men were understandably shocked to see a cumbersome PBY descend toward their downed B-17. At first they tried waving it off but then realized that the pilot had a determined plan to actually land beside their craft.

Balchen landed but instead of stopping the PBY, he had landed on the bare hull and now was using power to taxi in circles around the B-17. In moments, the downed airmen understood Balchen's signals to jump into the PBY through its side blisters on each lap he made. Several managed to clamber aboard Balchen's PBY each time he circled. When all were in the flying boat, Balchen straightened it out and made a staggering takeoff from the icecap. He deserved and received another medal for his heroic deed.

After that, Monteverde and his men swore they would stop whatever they were doing any time they saw a PBY and offer it a grateful salute.

By 1939 all PBYs were considered obsolete, but with Europe already in a war and no comparable craft with which to replace, it, production orders continued to be filled.

Looking back in time, we note that 3272 PBYs were built. Even Canada built PBYs.

Although it was considered ugly and as slow as a turtle, the PBY was the most successful flying boat ever built. During WW II it sunk many enemy subs and protected our coastlines and shipping lanes. Hundreds of combat pilots were rescued by PBYs when their missions went awry and they crashed into the sea.

Since WW II, over 100 PBYs in various conditions and modifications are still in use. One of the most unique mods came about when Dr. Forrest Bird, of Bird Oxygen products, added two Lycoming engines to his PBY and turned it into a four-engined seaplane capable of operating in and out of tropical rivers.

Other P-Boats are used in the amphibian mode as aerial tankers. Still others are pressed into service in places most of us have never heard of, to haul cargo in and out of fields and lakes too small for other makes of aircraft.

Looking back, how do I feel about the PBY? Well, I love her—of course! She's beautiful.

30 INDOMITABLE FLYING FORTRESS

During World War II, Ferrying Command pilots did more than fly airplanes from point to point. As they were the first to put any extended time on a new production airplane, they were also first to discover its problems or benefits. I was fortunate to be attached to the Long Beach, California, 6th Ferrying Group and lucky, too, to have flown many joyful hours delivering the B-17, Flying Fortress.

When the global conflict was at its height, a newsman asked salty U.S. Air Force chief of staff, General "Toohey" Spatz what was his most important weapon. He answered without hesitation. "The B-17 is the greatest weapon man has ever built. I'd rather have it than any other."

It was no accident that news people who watched the first public flight display at Boeing Field in Seattle, Washington, tagged the huge bomber *Flying Fortress*. Though dramatic, the name stuck and time proved it an apt description. Much has been written about this famed bomber and undoubtably, more words will come. I offer this as one pilot's personal experience. My views come through many hours of domestic and over-ocean ferrying, as an instrument instructor and line-check pilot, and an inverterate lover of fine machinery.

What was the secret ingredient that caused our government to order 12,726 B-17's built?

If a secret there was, it was the essence of old-fashioned Yankee ingenuity vested in the long history of Boeing Aircraft Company. Each airplane they built was carefully analyzed during its service and improved accordingly. From the monstrous XB-15 came much of the Clipper Flying Boat designs. From the sum knowledge of building four-engined airplanes came the pre-World War state-of-the-art airplane, the pressurized Boeing Stratoliner. And from much of that airplane's design came the components of the B-17, named by Boeing as their *Model 299*.

A quick study of the comparison chart showing these airplanes' specifications clearly proves the sibling relationship of the B-17 to the Model 307 Stratoliner. Wingspan, areas, gross weights and speeds are similar. From the summer of 1935 to the fall of 1941—six short years—the B-17 climbed from its generic crib to full-blown adulthood as a fighting machine *par excellence*.

Flying the B-17 left one with many detailed remembrances. I wondered about the belly turret design that in a wheels-up landing could trap the occupant and cause him a very bad day. It seemed odd that the passageway into the nose compartment caused such a wide separation between pilot and copilot. But where else could it have been? War economy dictated that the flight instruments be centered on the wide panel without duplication. I wondered if the designers had ever flown IFR and had to contend with the excessive parallax.

Questions were asked by some pilots why Boeing permitted the airspeed decay with each model improvement. These queries would go on until an older, wiser pilot would point out that the phenomenal increases in gross weight and subsequent bomb-carrying capacity did not come free.

In the Ferrying Command, the big docile plane was often used to carry personnel to our various bases and for instrument flight training checks. When the C-47s (DC-3s) were not available, the B-17 was pressed into duty. It amazed me to see how many of the final test applicants became full of colds-in-the-noses about the same time their date for a flight test in the C-47 approached and they knew a B-17 would be used the following day. No dummies these pilots; they were aware of the beautiful stability that the mass of four engines gave while IFR compared to the lighter C-47.

Frankly, from my viewpoint, I thought the B-17 flew like a dream. It was as stable and forgiving as a Piper Cub Cruiser. You set it where you wished and it stayed. The huge fin area prevented yaw, and turbulence gave the airplane a soft up and down bounce that was never uncomfortable. It flexed in flight and that was appreciated by all pilots who had flown such stiff beasts as the Martin B-26 that vibrated like a tuning fork after each bout with turbulence.

The B-17 came over the fence between 80 to 90 mph and was landed three-point with power-off from a glide at under 80 mph. If one wished to land impressively short, it took the coordination of more than a pilot. The pilot had to flare and three-point the airplane with both hands pulling the yoke to its stop. The copilot had to idle the throttles and prevent them creeping forward. The flight engineer would ready the tail-wheel lock for the pilot's command to release it to swivel. If all worked in harmony, the B-17 could be turned off and stopped in less than 2,000 feet of runway.

For those who had flown IFR in DC-3s and experienced long worrisome spells when ice built on wings and structure, the turbo-powered B-17 was a joy. My first experience in rapidly climbing through an icing level to VFR at 21,000 feet caused an instant love affair with the airplane.

But as all man's mechanical creations, it had its limitations.

Delivering the airplane across the North Atlantic caused many of my gray hairs. I could not count the agonizing hours flying at under 300 feet above the wave tops while carrying a huge load of ice *under* the wings. With the excess weight of full ferrying tanks and the subsequent high angle of attack, the ice built from the rear of the rubber leading edge boots to the trailing edge. But still it flew. I can recall sitting in the pilot's seat wondering how high icebergs were and how high were ship's antennas. To this day I do not know. (And please, if any of you readers do, don't tell me!)

The B-17's ruggedness was proven repeatedly in World War II when so many were literally torn apart in combat yet managed to fly home. Many aviation readers have seen the photos of huge holes in wings, fuselages nearly torn in half and engines completely missing. But these derelicts still made it back to their bases with their aircrews getting medical attention and the airplane consigned to the scrap heap.

To me, this airplane was easier to fly than most light twins of today. It predictability and large slow-reacting mass brought no surprises. Any of you reading this who've flown a light twin could easily and safely checkout in a B-17 within an hour's time. Let us not forget that during WWII, the lady WASP pilots flew it everywhere and did it well. Why not?

As the venerable DC-3, it was impossible to wear out a B-17. A few of these planes still exist and are being used in a wide variety of flying tasks. After the close of WW II, the Danish airline DDL converted B-17's into airliners and flew them on scheduled runs. Our U.S. Coast Guard used them in search and rescue and for dropping belly-mounted lifeboats to imperiled sailors at sea. Many were converted into target drones and shot down, ironically, often by Boeing built BOMARC missles.

You can see them at some airfields today. Chino airport has one on display. Castle AFB in California's San Joaquin Valley has a beautifully preserved static B-17G in full fighting regalia. The Confederate Air Force has at least one that I know of, and the Forestry Departments of many states use them as aerial fire-fighting tankers.

31 BATTLING THE YP-61

As I review that page from my logbook No. five, it appeared as if everything had gone well. But, in fact, things did not work out that way.

During those eight days recorded on said page in September 1943, I'd conducted 12 passing instrument flight checks, and had the pleasure of a renewal check in the P-51B with its new bubble canopy. After finishing the renewal check and landing, I was called into the operations office. Another bit of good luck, I assumed, then wondered why I'd been chosen to ferry a YP-61.

Captain Larry Swartzell answered, "Because you're on staff. You've a senior star above your wings and you look tired, so we're giving you a few days away from the base." His smile was too saccharin, especially when he added, "You'll have a nice time overnight in New Orleans. It's a 'R' month, the great oysters are back in season."

"Oysters? New Orleans? What's the catch?"

"Nothing. By the way, you'll be delivering a YP-61."

A Northrup Aircraft Company's test pilot already had delivered the production prototype (Y designation) to our base for ferrying to the advanced flight test center at Orlando, Florida. But he had returned to the factory and no one at our base knew anything technical about the airplane. My boss, Captain Dick Morgan told me, "Just another airplane, Gerry. Go jump in it and fly it away."

I crawled in, got it started and into the air. When the wheels retracted, they whacked the stops with a loud bang, sounding as if the fuselage had broken in two. By the time I arrived in Phoenix, Arizona, my nerves had calmed and I had sorted out most of my thoughts about the airplane. That's when things began to go awry.

The YP-61 was fueled as I lunched. Back at the airplane I

signed for the fuel, said "adios" to the lineman and reached for the folding steps to enter. One of the rungs was painted a bright red so dumb pilots would know the correct one to pull. I pulled it and the top half of the folding steps snapped down and hit my head a resounding whack. Seems the people at Northrup had painted the wrong rung. So an hour was wasted while they sewed my scalp.

An hour and 50 minutes later, I managed to make El Paso, Texas, where I intended a night's stop to easy my throbbin' noggin.

During the full day's flight, from El Paso to New Orleans, Louisiana, I found the air-handling of the YP-61 a total delight. With its large spoilers in lieu of ailerons, the roll-rate was fantastic. Here at last was sound brainwork by engineers. With spoilers, the bank is established by decreasing the lift on the down wing. Therefore, no yaw is possible. (It would take at least ten more years before airplane designers would come to that conclusion.) I thought how surprised enemy pilots would be when it flicked away from their gunsights. With its two 2,100-hp Wasp engines, it took off and climbed smartly. Painted all dead-black, it didn't resemble any of our other military aircraft.

As I signed out of the New Orleans flight operations, I was advised that all the anti-aircraft batteries along my route had been notified that the YP-61 was a friendly airplane. I thanked them but wondered why this was necessary.

Halfway to my next planned landing at Tallahassee, Florida, I saw some puffs of black clouds suddenly appear ahead. But they couldn't be clouds, I thought, as they were much too small.

WHACK—WHACK!

Nearing the black puffs I encountered turbulence I couldn't believe. Only then did my slow brain record the fact that someone was shooting at me. Instinctively, I dove toward the ground and flew along at treetop height until I was away from the area. When I tried climbing again to cruising altitude, the firing began anew.

"Hey you turkeys, I'm a Yankee!" *Gad, what was I saying?* So, down on the deck again until I landed at Tallahassee.

When I entered flight operations, I was fuming. No one could understand why I had been shot at until an officer telephoned the chief of the coastal artillery forces. He stated that

The YP-61 was a night-fighter but one day she nearly whipped the author. Drawing courtesy of Bill Neale.

he "had not received any notice from anyone that a black, twin-boomed Focke-Wulf Fw-180 would be penetrating the United States coast." I started to wonder about us winning any war, but another officer appeared and showed me the current aircraft identification chart. There it was; in profile or from the ground, the YP-61 could easily be mistaken for the Focke-Wulf. It took another hour before I was assured there would be no further attacks on my body or airplane.

I taxied out for the final takeoff with a growing suspicion about my mission and a distinct revulsion to having heavy lead trying to find me. I wondered if anything else would go wrong.

I shouldn't have wondered.

As the takeoff roll accelerated and the airplane become airborne, the pilot's seat came loose. In the YP-61, as in no other flying machine, the seat track slides the pilot about six feet rearward for exit up the radio operator's position. As the seat slid, my left hand automatically pulled the throttles back to about half-power. Now, I had a 40,000 pound piece of metal barely hanging in the air and a row of high trees coming up fast. Somehow, I managed to kick the throttle levers to full power and scramble back to the controls. The seat was still in the back, so I squatted foolishly on the cockpit floor and used those wonderful spoilers to climb and turn until a safe altitude was reached. Then expecting anything to happen, I trimmed the airplane, raced back and frantically retrieved the seat.

Recently, I told this story to a Quiet Birdman fellow-member, Max Stanley, Northrup Aircraft's famous Flying-Wing test pilot. Max was very sympathetic, even admitted the same thing had happened to him.

"But it sure had a great roll-rate, didn't it?" He added that during WW II in the Pacific Theater, no pilot had been lost in a P-61 due to enemy action.

What could I say? But I imagined a score or so of pilots receiving Purple Hearts because of lacerated scalps.

I said, "You are right, Max. It sure did have a great roll-rate."

(Ugh)

32 FLYING THE P-38

It was the fall of 1941 and I was watching one of the last air meets of Southern California being held at the Santa Anita horseracing track in Arcadia, California.

The YP-38 came across the infield, low and with a peculiar windsound that exceeded the thrumming of its powerful Allison engines. Test pilot Milo Burcham executed several lazy, vertical-climbing slow-rolls. I had no idea then that in less than six months, I would be flying the same type of airplane.

My logbook shows that on March 8, 1942, I flew P38E, Air Force serial number 41-12071, as pilot in command for a total of one hour and 45 minutes. As I'd imagined when watching the airplane fly a few months earlier, piloting it was a near-sensual pleasure. I can assure you that anyone with a few hours PIC in a light twin-engined plane of today could easily check out in a P-38.

To one who'd been flying mostly lightplanes, the P-38's specifications were impressive. Its wing spanned 52 feet and it was about 37-feet long. It would gross out at 14,000 to 18,000 pounds, depending upon the armament or bomb load it carried. It could fly more than 1,500 miles at altitudes of 35,000 feet and climb like a rocket. At first it had 1,220-hp engines; later the P-38L would have engines of 1600 hp each.

For nearly a year I would alternate in delivering either Douglas A-20s or P-38s from our Long Beach, California, airbase to the Newark Airport in New Jersey. Each plane would average about 10.5 to 11.5 hours per trip. The 22-hour DC-3 airline ride back to our base was boring. Then I never wondered if there was a war going on, for how could I tell? It didn't seem legal that a young pilot should have so much fun.

After ferrying a few of the P-38s, I managed to ask Lockheed's chief test pilot Milo Burcham a few questions about the plane. I wanted particularly to know if he approved of the Air Force's request that we take off with only 40 inches of manifold pressure, what setting he used, and what were his personal techniques for single-engine procedures? Also, I was quite curious as to how one would bail out of the fork-tailed machine in an emergency.

Milo was helpful and candid, but surprised that the military wanted such low power settings for takeoffs. "I use 60 inches of boost on takeoff," he said. "Then, if an engine quits, you do a grand chandelle up and around and back to the runway with safety. I also urge pilots to lift a dead engine to maintain heading rather than to use rudder. With an engine out, you have only half the airplane's normal rudder control. Push too hard or too quickly and it will snap."

He further advised that if a bailout were required, the pilot should try to exit over the leading edge after jettisoning the drop tank and feathering the engine. I listened carefully to this man who was so wise and skilled, as a later experience would prove.

Our only radios for delivery flights were simple, Mickey-Mouse affairs that were located exactly where the rain poured in during flight. Of course, as soon as they became wet, they failed. Consequently, most of our P-38 deliveries were either VFR or climbs to on-top conditions.

As we flew this great airplane, some of us made astonishing discoveries. I learned that between Long Beach and Winslow, Arizona, I could slow it to about 120 knots with half flaps and ease over the rim of the Grand Canyon. Then after clearing the rim, I could dump it straight down the sheer wall, finally adding power with a vertical climb back out. And to think I always have feared tall buildings!

One day while I was landing at Winslow ahead of four other P-38s, my attention during the approach was concerned with smashing a horsefly that was buzzing around the cockpit. When I landed and looked ahead I learned too late I was running out of runway. (Dumb, I know!) Nearing the end, I used full right rudder and full left engine power. The airplane made a mightly broadsliding turn exactly like a midget race car might do. The other idiots behind me saw the fun I was having, so they landed and imitated my racing turns. All of us caught the same thought at the same instant, for we then proceeded to have a dirt-track race around Winslow's airfield. We stopped only because TWA's station agent flagged us down and complained that our dust had reduced the field to zero-zero visibility, and "how could his DC-3 land?"

Winslow became my favorite overnight stop and watering hole quite by chance.

On one trip, there were several of my P-38 pals along with me from Long Beach to Winslow and each of us would take turns trying to outdo the other in some aerobatic maneuver. Most such stunts were slow-rolls with multiple variations of

Author and P-38. (Note sensuous expression)

the theme. Few P-38 pilots ever held the airplane inverted for long as the oil pressure would drop and connecting rods would start flying through the crankcase. Sneaky me, I knew a trick they hadn't seen. Ahead of the pack, I dove for speed and when over the Winslow airfield, rolled inverted, cut the throttles to prevent rod failures and glided upside down around the pattern. Turning base leg, I then extended the landing gear "up" for its "down and locked position," and rolled back upright.

On the ground, was "Charlie," the owner of Winslow's most popular watering hole. He could hardly wait for my engines to stop before running to the airplane and shouting, "What a show! I know you come in here often so whenever you're in Winslow, the drinks are on me. And for as long as I have the bar!" He grinned his pleasure as I offered my gratitude. So, all during World War II, I was one of the few pilots who never went thirsty in Winslow, Arizona. Charlie—bless his rascally heart—went west a few years ago. Here's looking at you, Charlie! (hic)

In time, I became familiar enough with the airplane that I would put on a show at the barest hint of anyone who asked. No one ever called me down on my antics and I never thought much about the reason why I was never penalized for my actions until quite recently.

A Quiet Birdman friend in Dallas, Texas, recently told me the true reason I'd escaped justice. My C.O. at Long Beach for some time was Colonel Ralph Spake. He spent some time telling this QB friend how he would cover for me. "Whenever that red-headed devil would get in a scrape with his flying, I would take the call," Spake explained. "He was always doing inverted flying in the P-38. You know it won't do that! So, I'd tell the caller—sometimes a General of some base—that he was showing others what a fine airplane the P-38 was to fly. I never chewed Gerry out. What good would it have done? He'd simply do the same things somewhere out of sight." My friends said Col. Spake sighed. "That would be such a waste. You know he really did put on quite a show!"

Bless you, sir.

We discovered that by flying at altitudes over 25,000 feet, our groundspeed was phenomenal. Between Winslow and Amarillo, Texas, for example, we could shave a half hour off the time we normally used at lower altitudes. I made a few such flights but became bored with the lack of ground detail, so I continued my deliveries at lower altitudes.

Not all was gravy. As is inevitable with new airplanes, some things failed to work. My turn for an unwanted surprise came during several delivery flights.

On any icy morning in Columbus, Ohio, the wings of my

P-38 were heavily coated with frost; I assumed that with 8,000 feet of nice flat runway, the airplane would lift off without any problem. I was so wrong. With full power, I used all the runway and barely became airborne at the last moment. The madly shaking airplane taught me about frost the hard way.

Another bright day while cruising along at 10,000 feet between Amarillo, Texas, and Wichita, Kansas, the left engine on my P-38 caught fire. Heavy smoke came through the leading edge intercooler and into the poorly sealed cockpit. In seconds, I had followed Milo Burcham's advice and was squatting on the right leading edge contemplating my first emergency parachute jump. I had remembered to feather both engines and rid myself of the right drop tank. But what was I doing with my briefcase clutched in my right hand? Luckily the fire went out, but had I jumped, you know I'd have dropped the briefcase to pull the ripcord. What strange things we do in emergencies.

Taking off somewhat nervously from Bolling Field in Washington, D.C., on its very short east-west runway, an engine threw a connecting rod with a terrific bang and a great cloud of trailing smoke. But bless Milo Burcham, for I did my chandelle up and around and easily re-landed.

A week later as I sat waiting takeoff clearance at the old Pittsburgh's Allegheny County airport, I watched as a WASP (Women's Air Service Pilot) sped down the runway for her takeoff in a P-38. I saw the puff of smoke exit her cowling and saw her abrupt input of rudder as she became airborne. And I can still see her today as the airplane snapped onto its back and crashed in a huge pall of black smoke. If only Milo Burcham could have briefed her too.

In time, my number of hours at the controls of P-38s grew until my logbook showed over 300 hours' time. I remember and relive many of those joyous moments in the P-38, and I loved each one of them.

I wish you could have been with me—such fun!

33 DST, MOTHER OF THE TRANSPORTS

Whatever the venerable DC-3 was, or became in its illustrious climb through the halls of history, it owes its fame to the DST, the Douglas Sleeper Transport.

How little we know of our futures. Early in 1942, after delivering a Douglas A-20 to Newark, New Jersey, from our Ferrying Command base at Long Beach, California, I faced the unwelcome prospect of returning to base as an airline passenger. Though the DC-3 was the universally accepted airliner, it was terribly slow. Coast-to-coast flights averaged 22 hours—if the weather cooperated.

Enplaning at New York's La Guardia airport as dusk fell, I was pleasantly surprised to learn I'd been booked on one of American Airline's Douglas Sleeper Transports, the forerunner of the DC-3. Lucky me. If the weather cooperated, I would be able to sleep most of the way home.

Another pleasant surprise was meeting the flight's captain, George McCabe, senior pilot No. three with American Airlines. He advised me that the weather was fine and I should enjoy a good night's sleep.

After dinner was served and cleared, the stewardess made up the 14 berths. Mine was an upper, at about midship. Fortunately, all DST pilots were trained to fly the plane as smoothly as possible. As McCabe later would tell me, "The DCs are the world's easiest airplane to get up and down, but the toughest to fly skillfully." Except for the disconcerting safety-belt check by the flight attendant before each landing, the flight was pleasant.

Had anyone told me then that I would be flying this same airplane as pilot-in-command within the year, I would have questioned his veracity. But it did happen.

The genré of all Douglas transport airplanes began with the then-radical DC-1. With two engines instead of the usual three, like the corrugated Ford had, and sporting a low, cantilever wing complete with retractable landing gear and flaps, the DC-1 was a quantum leap forward in airliner design. It completely outclassed the newest Boeing 247D.

On the last day of the airmail contract flights before the Army Air Force would assume command, TWA president Jack Frye, and World War I ace Eddie Rickenbacker flew the original DC-1 from Glendale, California, Grand Central Air Terminal to Newark in the record time of 13 hours and four minutes. Alert airline executives immediately placed orders for the production version, the DC-2.

With six of the DC-2s on order, but seeing business escape to TWA's Curtiss Condor biplane nightsleepers, crusty American Airlines president C.R. Smith phoned Donald Douglas and said he wanted some of the planes he'd ordered converted into sleepers. Douglas rebutted that he already was behind on the DC-2 orders and turned Smith down. Considered one of the most persuasive airline executives, Smith argued persistently for Douglas to modify the DC-2 as he'd asked. Finally, he offered to order another 20 of the designs he wanted, sight unseen, in addition to the DC-2s to which he'd already committed. Douglas saw the light and agreed to proceed with a new design.

On December 13, 1935, tall, slim test pilot Carl Cover flew the first DST and declared it would surpass any airplane ever built. Actually, the DST was a completely different airplane than the DC-2. It was wider, heavier, faster and had a greater wing span. Passengers could walk erect in its cabin and those who flew it claimed it was a declawed pussycat.

On August 27, 1936, Douglas received its Approved Type Certificate, number 607.

American Airlines placed the DST into service in June of 1936. It was an immediate hit with the flying public. Smith was confounded to note that other airlines had placed large orders for a 21-passenger daylight version that Douglas would name the DC-3. Thus, the DST was the mother of all modern transports and gave birth to an airplane that would exceed 12,000 planes.

In time, I was transferred from routine delivery flights to the newly formed Army Airlines that all immediately renamed Snafu Airlines. My assigned route was from Long Beach, California, to Dallas, Texas, and all the stops in between. For my first flight, I was thrilled to learn I would command the former flagship Arizona. It still sported it bright aluminum exterior but was now owned by the U. S. Government. Somehow, the American Airlines logo, proclaiming "Flagship Arizona," was still on its nose.

I was fortunate on this flight to have Terry Beasley as my copilot; he'd been an American Airlines copilot before joining the Ferrying Command and was one of the very few on our base who knew how to operate the very weird DST steam-heater.

After having delivered brand new Douglas C-47s with their 1200-hp engines and all parts functioning perfectly, the old DST was a shock. My first light touch on the brakes while taxiing brought a bone-jarring brake lock. No matter how Terry or I touched the brakes, they would lock and jolt the tail off the ground.

Flying it, the first thing I noticed was that the controls jiggled rythmically with each bit of turbulence. On the control columns, deep grooves had been worn by thumbs and fingers over countless thousands of flight hours.

Arizona's propeller feathering system was unbelievable. I was familiar with the nice red buttons on modern airplanes which required simple finger pressure for automatically feathering the propeller; the DST had four large laundry-type valves above and to the rear of our heads. To feather an engine, one had to open one valve and then close it when the propeller was feathered. To unfeather, the procedure was reversed using the other valve. Imagine doing this under an emergency situation.

Landing the old airplane at airports on American Airline's routes, many of the senior pilots found their way to the airplane at ramps and offered remarks. George McCabe saw us at Tucson, Arizona, and asked, "Have you noticed its jiggle, lad?" I shook my head affirmatively and he added, "Poor old lady, she should have been put to sleep long ago!"

Senior captain "Pat" Patterson caught me at El Paso. "How are you getting along with the catchy brakes on that beast?" I gave a Bronx cheer and he added that he was glad he no longer had to fly it.

Though I soon moved to other duties, I never forgot the DST. As eccentric as the old plane may have been, there was a satisfying mystique about flying in the shadow of history's greatest line pilots. I told the other pilots I thought the airplane was haunted. I explained that whenever I made an instrument approach, it worked out perfectly and I knew I didn't fly that well. When the occasion demanded we penetrate a thunderstorm, it seemed the plane would select a passage that had the least turbulence. But I never forgave or forgot its impossible brakes.

Before the Flagship Arizona's retirement, it was estimated the airplane had worn out over 500 tires, 25,000 spark plugs, and 135 engines. To do so the airplane had to have spent more than 10 years aloft.

R.I.P., old girl.

Part 5

The Business About Learning

34 THE LATE NIGHT RUN

Certain years in everyone's life shine jewels in our memories. For me, 1933 had only one extraordinary factor, and that was my constant struggle to fly.

The real world outside my domain was concerned with other issues. In January of that year, Adolph Hitler became Chancellor of Germany. On March 3, Franklin D. Roosevelt was inaugurated as our new president. That same month saw Japan and Germany resign from the impotent League of Nations.

To me, March was eventful because Compton, California, where I lived, was shattered by a vicious earthquake. Many were killed, one of whom was my first serious girlfriend. I was unhurt though the Post Office I'd just exited fell down behind me. The quake hit as I swung my leg over the side of my Indian Scout motorcycle and kicked the starter. It first came as a roar, then as an explosion. It shook me so hard that my vision blurred and all turned a fuzzy yellow color. I felt the motorcycle being yanked from under me and heard it scrape the pavement as it slid about 20 feet into the curbing. The shaking seemed to go on forever. When it stopped, there was utter silence for about half a minute. The next sound was of dogs barking and then the sounds of people moaning, yelling, screaming.

I looked back at the rubble of the Post Office and saw a

man make his way through the debris to the curb near me and sit while holding his head and moaning softly. He was unaware that his right ear had been torn from his head. It was bleeding terribly.

However, even the earthquake soon had to take a back seat to my perennial thirst to fly. What was important to my aviation career that month of March was the repeal of the 18th Amendment to the U.S. Constitution. Though all could drink liquor, a few would sell it without Federal sanction. So bootlegging would continue. Big deal. Who cared? Not me, for I was concerned only with building up my flying time.

Renting airplanes then took money the same as it does today, and money was something I couldn't seem to get my hands on. Blame it on the Depression that was in full swing, but no one was hiring untrained teenagers. I had no idea that before April passed an unexpected event would take place that would dramatically change my life.

At our very tiny California airfield where I did everything and anything to fly, a particular Sunday had passed as many before it. During the day I had hustled fuel and radiator water for the passenger-carrying biplanes. The sun had set and I was alone.

My mind had been ruminating, grumbling that I'd not sold my motorcycle to anyone that day and I had to in order to keep my recently purchased Model-T. Busy, humming the tunes of the day as I scrubbed the bellies of the airports' two planes to a shine for the next Sunday, and rushing to finish before the gasoline burned my skin, I heard no sounds until the loud squeal of a brake startled me. When I looked for the source, I saw a Fairchild 71 monoplane sitting about 50 feet away. I recognized the design as that of the famous Alaska bushplane.

Where had it come from? How could it land without me hearing its engine? What was it doing at our cow-pasture airport?

Seeing me scramble out from under the belly of a biplane, the Fairchild pilot clambered out of the boxy cabin and waved a greeting. But when I moved to approach the plane, he motioned me away. "Son, would you mind waiting where you are until we unload?"

Unload? Unload what? What was he doing at our airport?

Smiling the ruddy-faced, stocky pilot in a gray flightsuit pointed to a large truck followed by a long limousine entering

The Fairchild 71 wasn't hauling pancake syrup. Drawing courtesy of Bill Neale.

the field's driveway.

As the truck drove to the plane's side, I watched as several men jumped out of it and began to unload cargo from the airplane. In moments they had emptied the plane of numerous, shiny, five-gallon cans. The pilot then quickly started the engine, took off and disappeared into the distance.

When I returned to my work, still awed by the unusual event, burning to ask questions but obeying their order not to butt in, one of the men in the limousine approached me. "Hi kid! You don't know what we unloaded from that plane, do you?"

"No sir." But I had a strong suspicion it wasn't pancake syrup.

The tall, well-dressed, muscular man studied me intently. "You fly?" He asked this in a friendly but authoritative manner.

"Yes sir, when I have any money. That isn't often."

"If someone asked you to help light the runway at night for a plane to land, would you do it?"

Uncertain, I stammered my answer. "I-I-guess so."

"Good!" He slapped me lightly on the shoulder. It seemed

he'd given me some kind of test and I had passed. Now, looking back, I wonder if he hadn't found me totally stupid.

He went on. "If I gave you $5 a week to shine your car lights on that fence bordering the field, would you do it?"

Five dollars! I gave him a brilliant answer. "Guess I would."

"And what would your parents think of you doing that at 10 o'clock every Wednesday night?"

"They wouldn't know, sir. I live in a room and board place nearby."

He seemed pleased with my answer, shook my hand vigorously and said, "It's a deal then. You start next Wednesday night. Make sure you are on time."

On the appointed evening at our field at 8 P.M., while herding cows into a small holding corral, I congratulated myself for being so early and faithful to my word. By 9 o'clock I had stationed myself and my Model-T Ford alongside the dirt runway where its headlights would face the fence.

Waiting, I wondered when the airplane would appear. What if the pilot couldn't find our cow pasture at night? What if he didn't show at all? What if I'd only dreamed all this?

Every few minutes I checked my pocket watch but except for the croaking frogs, mooing cows and barking dogs in the distance, it was quiet.

About five minutes before 10, I had the lights of my car turned on the barbed wire fence as requested. In the middle of a yawn, I heard a whistling sound that rapidly grew louder. Suddenly, with a whoosh, the Fairchild glided by me and expertly touched down a few hundred feet away.

Apparently, the pilot had overflown the area from several thousand feet high while slowly closing the throttle to simulate a night airmail plane passing through. But to glide down from a great height to a totally black airport except for an auto's weak headlights took a great amount of skill.

Of course, you know the rest.

Later on this hero of mine used that skill to become one of American Airline's finest captains. He flew to retirement and recently passed away. This man was one of the very few who ever knew how that wonderful year of 1933 allowed me to build up considerable flying time.

35 FOUR RHODE ISLAND HENS AND ME

In 1937, earning a license to fly was a drastically different experience than it is today.

To acquire a Private Pilot's Certificate now, one goes to a flying school and is taught by competent instructors who guide every move, through to the final flight test with an FAA examiner.

The current flight training process does not generate great emotional highs or lows. Progress is usually a steady, predictable climb to certification. We do not appear outwardly gleeful at carrying our first legal passenger, and obtaining the certificate often is considered a minor step along the road of achievement.

Let's travel back in time to pre-World War II days and see the difference.

My acquisition of a Private Pilot License was not considered unusual. In my first logbook several hundred hours were logged prior to the formation of the U.S. Department of Commerce and its original rules for civil flying. As most of my logged time was in unlicensed airplanes, carrying passengers or giving illicit flight instruction, it was not considered as meeting the new experience requirements. This was a hangover from the days when barnstorming died at the hands of government regulations. The new authority decided if you could only log time in licensed airplanes, then the unlicensed fleets would die out. They were right. Most of us in that category would have kept our illegal logs hidden—I did.

In May of 1936 I began to think seriously about getting a license to do some legal flying. The Hisso-powered, long-wing Eaglerock I flew filled nine hours of solo flying time that month.

When the older airplanes wore out and/or failed the new government inspections, they usually were scrapped. So went the airplane I flew, which presented me with a dilemma: How could I build up flying hours when my job barely paid for my room and board? But along with thousands of others, I freely offer my blessings to a gentleman named C. Gilbert Taylor. Still alive at this writing, he was the creator of the fabulous Cub trainers. (Later to become known as Piper Cubs).

At $4 an hour wet, it was the best flying bargain of its day. At the Long Beach, California, airport I discovered the fixed base operator would rent me his Cub at this price and throw in a lovely bound logbook filled with pages of data on the new Cub. A flight instructor named C. Hayes Marvin checked me out in one of their new E-2 Cubs. It was a squarish looking thing with a noisy rattling 37-hp Continental L-Head engine. It lacked side windows, tailwheel or brakes and it was without carburetor heat—but it flew!

To continue my flying, I had to overcome a great load of guilt about "liberating" a steady supply of my grandmother's Rhode Island Red hens to a nearby poultry market. Four hens ratioed out to an hours flying time in the Cub. As grandmother's hen population declined, my legally logged hours of flight increased. I can imagine what you are thinking, but can you imagine those times when learning to fly was such a passionate pursuit? Most of us simply had to fly—whatever and however. My plight was not unique.

July 19, 1937, arrived and Mr. J. D. McCutcheon, manager and flight instructor at the Compton, California, airport where I flew, thought I was ready for my Private Pilot flight test. By then, I had upgraded to a nice yellow J-2 Cub with the same engine but an enclosed cabin, brakes and a steerable tailwheel—pure luxury. I called it the Rolls Royce of the air.

No one knew what any flight test might include as each "inspector" asked for his own pet maneuvers. At best, it was a by-guess and by-gosh, hit-or-miss proposition. But Mac thought I was ready, as long as I didn't draw Mr. Hugh Brewster as the inspector.

So, I proceeded to Mines Field (now Los Angeles International Airport) and did my written test in longhand, taking nearly an entire notepad. To the question, "Explain Fog," I wrote over a dozen pages. Finished, an inspector scanned my pages briefly, nodded affirmatively and said to report the next day for the flight test. "Mr. Brewster will handle you," he said. My 24-hour fit of shaking began there. I did not get much sleep as the words "he will handle you," kept ringing through my head. Only when McCutcheon said, "You aren't going to die from this, you know" did I relax a little.

The next day, ready for the test and still shaking, I met Brewster. He was a huge bear of a man whose last assignment had been in Alaska where it was rumored he'd yelled so at a grizzly bear the thing had dropped dead of a heart attack. After hearing this and seeing the man in person, I hoped he would not yell at me. When he spoke, his great booming voice almost shook the ground. I felt his stare easily could cause body tremors.

After quickly checking my logbook for the required 50 hours of solo time, he roared, "Okay, take your airplane up over the west end of the field to 3,000 feet. Do a two-turn right and left precision spin and then a steep spiral to a spot landing. I'll be watching your every move from here!"

I may have saluted—I don't recall. But I do remember missing my recovery point on one of my spins and repeating it to the accompaniment of a hard lump in my stomach. Relaxed in thinking I had blown the test, I managed the spot landing.

Returning to the office, I walked with a head hung low and defeat showing.

"Hey, your spot was great!" said a nearby pilot.

"But I busted the test," I answered.

"Naw you didn't. How could you? The inspector was upstairs all the time you flew and arguing with someone. Hell, he didn't even see you!"

My turn for surprise. In moments I was standing before the big man. I listened as he made scathing remarks about my spin entries and my general flying ability. But as he did so, he was busy typing my brand new Private Pilot License, number 38481.

May the powers that be bless grandmother's chickens and forgive me.

36 CPTP, DAWN OF FLYING SKILL

In the course of any human endeavor, history has shown there rarely is a straight or even path. The art of flying as a developed skill came about through fits and starts, frustrating periods of no growth with a few explosive time frames of phenomenal progress.

Charles Lindbergh's flight across the Atlantic Ocean was one such thrust. The venerable DC-3 airplane was another. But the most astonishing leap forward in piloting skills, safety of flight and increase of certificated pilots came about in 1938.

President Franklin Delano Roosevelt saw clearly that a worldwide war was on the horizon. He was advised by civil and military authorities that the coming upheaval would cause a severe shortage of trained pilots. At that time, less than 4,000 new pilots were appearing each year. To offset this, Roosevelt created the Civil Pilot Training Program which was expected to produce at least 20,000 new pilots annually.

Perhaps one of my greatest good fortunes appeared through this effort. In March 1941, I was approved to take the CPTP Commercial Refresher course at Hank Coffin's flight school located at old Vail Field, the site of an original airmail field near Los Angeles, California.

My first shock came when toothpick-thin, salty and graying Joe Potter, my flight instructor, told me after our orientation flight that I was doing wrong everything he ever knew. And, he thought I possibly had invented a few more bad techniques new to him. Hearing that, I was about ready to return to my job as an aircraft welder at Douglas Aircraft Company, but he saved my day by affirming that, if I worked at it, the two of us might make me into a pilot.

I worked, sweated and agonized, but bit by bit, my flying improved under the constant instruction. With more than ten years of flying experience, I was just learning to fly. It was a common story. One month, two days and 23 hours of dual later, I passed my commercial test ride with CAA Inspector Jack Winder. This portion of my training alone lasted over an hour and a half. In May, six weeks later, I began the instructor refresher CPTP course under another stern taskmaster. After 12 hours of concentrated dual, I was pronounced ready for the flight test. I recall that the severity of the training had my feelings as wound up as if preparing for the battle of my life.

On June 4, 1941, I took the first half of my flight instructor's examination, again with Jack Winder. He demanded what I thought was a set of impossible tasks. Several days later, I finished the second half. I had flown a total of five hours for this single test. The maneuvers requested included such niceties as steep eight-turns on pylons, successive forced landings that had perspiration flowing off me, full power stalls of two oscillations, and spins out of turns, underneath and over the top. The spins had to be entered and stopped precisely on the point—no variation allowed. When I asked him to demonstrate a maneuver, he did so with accuracy even though he was un-

"Gentlemen, this is an engine!" CPTP instructor, Casey, advises students Joe Vaello (l) and Jim Harahan (r).

familiar with the Porterfield trainer I was using. At last it was over and I was a certificated flight instructor.

What a relief! And what a wonderful feeling to hang up my welding goggles and punch a time card for the final time at Douglas's Santa Monica, California, plant. Almost two years working on the swing shift had ground me down to a case of nerves.

Then, walking ten feet above the ground, I was hired by the Monrovia Airport, located east of Pasadena, California, as one of its CPTP flight instructors. My first class of 10 students would commence on July 1st. It had only been 90 days since I'd started my run of CPTP-sponsored refresher courses.

Waiting for my class to start, I learned the regimen of CPTP. There were manuals to study, student progress charts and logbooks with which to become familiar. Whoever were the nameless ones behind the planning should have been given medals. Time was certainly of the essence and it was pared to the bone. A CPTP student's every thought, move and upward step was analyzed, graded and expected to improve.

Students' personal logbooks were stored in open bins where all flight personnel had access. Any student could request a review of his or her logbook and read the remarks of the instructor. Each student was graded upon timing, planning, speed sense, coordination, judgement and progress. Attitudes were not omitted. There were spaces for comments upon how the student felt about the training.

Each lesson followed the regimen of well thought out planning. Instructors carried the current student's logbook on the flight and graded the indicated maneuvers on the spot. Lesson content always included a review, practice of the current maneuvers, and a demonstration of the coming lesson. The progress of young humans learning a complicated skill was phenomenal.

In less than 12 days of instructing, I had soloed all of my students. In another 90 days, and before that class would graduate, I would have entered more than 350 instructional hours to my logbook.

As with any human effort, there were unplanned events. One of my students with few solo hours was practicing figure eight turns around pylons in the practice area when the 65-hp engine of the Porterfield quit. The only level landing area within his gliding range was the narrow truck road running into a 200 foot deep gravel pit. Despite his few hours of experience, he managed a landing in the bottom of the pit without damage. The airplane had to be dismantled and trucked back to the airport. The student's primary concern was how he would be graded on the lesson.

Though time pressure was obvious to all who saw that war was on the world horizon, the CPTP safety record itself was an astonishing statistic. It proved to be 30 times safer to learn to fly within the Civil Pilot Training Program than by other means. Most students passed the initial private pilot phase in the allotted 35 hours of dual and solo. Non CPTP students trying for their private certificates would average 75 to 85 hours of flying before the testing.

A spin-off benefit of this program was that all who were in it became standardized in their training techniques.

After teaching the primary course, most of us went on to instruct the secondary, or aerobatic course with Waco UPF-7 biplanes. Without radio, all flight communication was accomplished via the gosport tube, a rubber hose-like affair that ran between the instructor and the student. At the instructor's end was a funnel, and the student had bulky earpads attached to his head like a headset.

Our teaching philosophy was that a student would learn all the technical aspects of flying on the ground and then prove his knowledge in the air. Queried before each flight, if any student did not have a clear concept of what he or she was aiming for, no flight took place.

The greatest bonus in the CPTP program was acknowledged by the instructors as the learning they got from teaching others.

Proof of concept was always at hand. With my first class of aerobatic students, I nursed them through the inverted flight acclimation stage and wasted precious hours. First, I would acquaint them with a snap-roll, then on to a half-roll with a few seconds inverted. It was evident that the students were fighting fear and it was impeding their progress.

Knowing I could not waste such time, I decided upon a more drastic approach, aware that some but not all students would take to aerobatics and nothing I could do would alter this fact.

The next student ready for his introduction flight proved that the blunt and brutal approach worked better. After a climb to 5,000 feet, I would take the controls and tell the student the mission of this lesson was to learn how to relax and trust the airplane. Then without further words, I would roll the Waco inverted and begin an extended glide earthward. In the mirror, I could see the student trying to clutch at anything available. Instantly, I would demand the student hang his arms out of the cockpit and into the slipstream. Ducking my head, I could look into his cockpit and see toes hooked under the rudder pedals. With my hand I would press his feet off the pedals and demand he allow his legs to float. In that way, the student would be totally suspended by the seat belt alone. The result became predictable with few variations.

Fear would possess the student at first. Then that would be followed by a fatalistic resignation. Later one explained his reactions. "When you made me hang by the belt alone, I figured I was going to die and there was nothing I could do about it. But then I realized you would die also, and it made me glad. And I forgot to be afraid anymore."

It worked like a charm. Somewhere on the inverted glide

downwards would come rage at the instructor but before rolling upright, a small smile would ensue. The remarkable realization swept the students into euphoria more than once. When they discovered that aerobatics were fun, the progress went on.

Our field was a mere 1,800 feet of gravel for a runway, located downhill with an elevated railroad track at the departure end. Our students became so adept that we would wager visiting instructors that our students could best them at spot landings. Our students always would win, because they knew nothing other than spot landings in that small airport. Monrovia to other pilots was known as "overshoots-ville."

In time, those of us who taught migrated to other fields of aviation. Johnny Holmes became a captain on Flying Tigers and a check-pilot. Our chief pilot, Bob Barlow, also went with the Flying Tigers, and I succeeded him as chief pilot at Monrovia. Barlow now lives happily on Santa Catalina Island. Bill Feast went with FAA.

Several of us went into the Ferrying Command at Long Beach, California, airbase. My worry-wart student "Smitty," who always thought he was verging upon being washed out, won medals during the war as a naval aviator and recently retired from flying Boeing 747's for an airline.

One of my female students became widely known in industry for her magnificent labels. All of you must have heard of Avery Labels. Phyllis Avery was an exceptionally fine student.

Those of us who participated in the era of the Civil Pilot Training Program wish aviation could return to such days when skill shone brightly.

37 ERNIE!

No, I haven't the slightest idea where you are now, Ernie (not a real name). I hope you are among the living but I seriously doubt it. Sure, I remember you . . . .

I recall when you told us about running out of fuel ferry-

Vultee "Vibrator" BT-13A used to train A.C.F.C. students in instrument flying. Drawing courtesy of Bill Neale.

ing a BT-13A trainer before you had completed your instrument rating. I can still see you laughing as you explained your plight to us at the Ferrying Command base in Long Beach, California. I can hear your boastful tone of voice as you told how it was to be flying on top of an overcast, lost, and hearing the old Wasp engine quit when your fuel ran out. I do remember shaking my head in wonder when you described how you looked down and saw that hole in the clouds—"Just one hole, mind you," then you laughed again as you told us of the runway intersection centered in the cloud-break. Indeed, Ernie, I'll wager the citizens of Prescott, Arizona, remember you too.

Quite a story.

What you do not know is that as I listened, I was not laughing with you. I knew still another story you were not telling.

When you were assigned to me for instrument training, I was a new and very green instructor. After previously having heard your tale of the Prescott incident, I was not expecting much from you. But I pushed that into the back of my mind, realizing every pilot can be expected to make one or two blunders in his flying career.

My best efforts with you fell far short. Time was running out for you to learn and I devoted more and more of it to ground instruction. Other waiting students resented you. I heard "dummy" said several times.

Funny, but you looked the epitome of a serious student. You were a bit older than the rest of us, perhaps almost 40. Your slight pudginess hinted that you did not move too fast. What black hair you had was a small semicircle around your pate. The rest of your head was a bald glare.

Then came the day when my boss, Captain Burt Bundy said, "Give me an evaluation ride on Ernie today. Either you tell me he'll finish in the allotted time or we'll return him to operations and try again in the future." That shook me up enough so on the next flight I tried even harder—too hard.

The day was typical of our Southern California coast in June. Strange, but I recall the date and even the number of the BT-13A. It was June 4, 1943, and the airplane we flew was number 42-22519. We had taken off at 9:00 a.m., and you wobbled up through the marine layer of clouds until we broke into the clear at 4,000 feet. You then went under the hood and I gave you my best instructional shot. I tried everything I could imagine to see if you would show any improvement.

Our lesson time ran out and I realized with some emotion that you would be my first instructional failure. Then at 5,000 feet I called for a letdown clearance and unexpectedly got one immediately. To save time in getting to the top of the undercast, I used the intercom and said to you, "Tighten your seat belt, Ernie, we're going down fast!" When needing a quick altitude loss, most instructors would execute a split-S. I rolled the Vultee Vibrator onto its back and started to ease the stick forward to slow the airplane.

But before I could do so, I felt the controls jolt severely. I looked into the rearview mirror, but you were not in sight. Immediately, I rolled the airplane back level and looked under the rear cowl to determine if you'd fallen onto the floor boards. There was no sign of you, Ernie, and my young heart nearly stopped.

What strange things we think of at these times. First, I repeated the date in my mind. Then it struck me that I'd lost a student. Actually, I then realized I'd probably caused a death. How had Ernie fallen out when I now saw the canopy was closed? Had it opened to let him fall, and then closed? How would I ever explain this to anyone else? Stupidly, I looked down at the undercast to determine if Ernie had left some sort of hole in the clouds. No hole. No Ernie.

I picked up the microphone to explain my emergency when my eyes caught a tiny movement in the rearview mirror.

I watched, petrified. Then I saw the tips of several pudgy fingers appear over the cockpit edge. Very slowly, a red, shiny bald head followed that was quite bruised. Attached was a very white, chastened face. I closed the throttle and he yelled, "I'll tell you back on the ground." We landed—a bad one in my emotional state—and taxied to the line. Then he told me the story.

"When you told me to tighten the belt, I reached down to fasten it. You see in these BT's, I've never had my seat belt fastened. I pulled it together as you rolled the airplane, but it lacked about four inches of meeting. I tried to hang onto the ends but that didn't work either. So, I fell into the canopy. When you rolled back level, I fell from the canopy into the bucket seat but upside-down and I got tangled in the chute straps."

"The chute straps?" (Oh, why did I ask?)

He grinned. "I didn't have the chute fastened either. So,

it took me quite awhile to get untangled and let you know I was still here."

To this day I cannot remember what I said and I would probably regret it if I could. But Ernie, if you are somewhere and happen to read this, I know you'll understand my meaning as I address this last sentence to you:

"Wherever you are, Ernie, please fasten your seat belt."

38 THE DOGFACES AND THE PBY

A young, brash military pilot easily could become smug about being listed as the "Commander" of a Catalina Flying Boat. Looking back I must admit the description fitted me, though even now I cringe at the tag. Young? Yes. Brash? I'm not sure. With people and until my later years, my behavior was mostly introverted. Only with the inanimate airplane was I overt in character.

Many deliveries of the flying boats to domestic and foreign points had been programmed by the chiefs of the Ferrying Command division of the U.S. Army Air Corps. Retitled the OA-10, the famous PBY was destined to inaugurate numerous air and sea rescue posts. Delivery trips were in the planning stage and pilots were going to be trained. But the usual bureaucratic lag fouled up the plans, and few of our pilots had been checked out to fly the big boats.

Navy brass at San Diego's North Island Naval Air Base had slowed the checkout process initially by demanding that our pilots take the Navy PBY training course. Ordinarily, this would consume 60 days. So, telephone calls and telegrams sizzled the wires between San Diego and Washington, D.C., until it was agreed by the generals and admirals that Ferrying Command personnel would check out their own pilots. And that was how I was assigned one of the first deliveries.

For once, it appeared as if the red tape had been sliced by the urgency of pilots going down at sea and needing to be rescued.

Casablanca, Morocco, had been selected as the staging

and training area for large numbers of Air-Sea Rescue Units. As this was under the aegis of the Army Air Corps, it became an army-oriented venture instead of a naval operation. This was the primary reason the airplane was redesignated as an OA-10, rather than the Navy's PBY Catalina.

As I'd been one of the first Air Corps Ferrying Command (ACFC) pilots qualified, and had successfully delivered one such plane to New York, I was then assigned a delivery to Casablanca.

A week was used to plot our routes, anticipate fuel needs, and receive secret briefings on how to avoid the Nazi's new submarine anti-aircraft traps.

The Germans had discovered that by duplicating a radio beam, our airplanes could be duped into using it for letdowns through an overcast and shot down by anti-aircraft aboard the submarine. With the P-Boat's greater range, it was assumed we could bypass the vicinity of Ascension Island where most of the attacks were taking place. That eased our fears for we'd learned that a few days after our orders had been cut, several ACFC pilots had been downed near Ascension Island by the German ploy.

Apparently, the United States and its Allies were unable to negate this method of attack on vitally needed airplanes being ferried from Natal, Brazil, to Dakar, Africa, via the overnight refueling stop at Ascension Island.

Consequently, the ACFC flying boat crews were ordered to stay well north of Ascension Island and make as few stops as possible. The Allied Forces were trying desparately to stop the juggernaut advance of Germany's persistent and brilliant leader, Field Marshall Erwin Rommel. The unbeatable weapon was airpower. Airplanes were the answer but they had to be flying in combat before military conclusions could be drawn. Our planners knew this and considered the ACFC deliveries to be as vital as combat. As a green crew never having faced bullets, we planned as carefully as we could.

But first, we had to pickup our OA-10 from the Navy at North Island.

A seaman picked us up from the American Airlines baggage section at the original airline terminal at Lindbergh Field's northeast side in a personnel carrier. We then were delivered straight to our airplane, parked on the crest of a seaplane ramp at the edge of Mission Bay. There, the Officer of the Day (O.D.), verified our orders and had us sign a receipt for the airplane.

As we clambered over and through the amphibian, inspecting all we could, I asked the O.D. why we could not takeoff from the air station's runway.

My question ruffled his feathers somewhat and he grimaced slightly as he said, "We've too much training traffic on the airfield. The Admiral doesn't want you army types getting confused with two-ball or three-ball runways———"

My copilot interrupted, "Just whatinhell is a, er, uh, three-ball runway?"

The O.D. studied his fingernails, turned his palms up and softly said, "See?" With a hunch of his shoulders to express his exasperation and a look that said we'd gotten the message, he left.

My crew and I stood there for a time feeling a loss of confidence in things nautical. When the copilot asked me what a three-ball runway was, I admitted total ignorance. In the background we heard a Chief Petty Officer (CPO), checking off the stores being placed aboard our airplane:

"Police whistle . . . typewriter with capital letters only . . . American flag . . . set of flex-seal pressure pots and pans . . . twenty-four hour clock . . . set of 3/8-inch drive universal socket wrenches . . . six canvas sea-anchors with ropes . . . Sign here, Lieutenant."

After the CPO left, the crew and I engaged in a spirited conversation regarding what we thought was a very strange list of items to be put aboard any airplane. My Sergeant flight engineer, asked one of the seamen standing nearby, "How come a typewriter with only capital letters?"

Smugly, the man answered, "so you dogfaces won't get your fingers stuck trying to type the word stupid!" So much for the remaining shred of dignity for the ACFC.

It was time for us to take off for our base at Long Beach. With the engines running and all my crew aboard and functioning, I shouted to the waiting launch crew standing at-ready, near the bow, "All set?"

The CPO opened his palms again as if to say, "How should we know?" Then as I moved to close the pilot's window, he yelled, "Don't forget to raise the landing gear, Lieutenant!"

"They can go to———" I said to the copilot as we were eased away and the mooring lines cast off.

Relieved to be free of our uncomplimentary and supercritical Navy helpers, we took a leisurely tack crosswind toward our mids-bay takeoff point.

My copilot radioed for clearance and I had scarcely brought the power to "takeoff," when our trainee flight engineer rushed forward. Whitefaced, he cried, "We're sinking. Look!"

As he pointed, I brought back the throttles and peered aft through the hull. "Gawd! There's a foot of water already." It was painfully obvious that the water flooding the hull was rapidly increasing.

I grabbed the microphone and radioed our predicament to the Bay Control tower. A different voice answered, cool, calm and deliberate: "I'm a Cat pilot, sir. Keep the yoke back and use full power. You might make it to the ramp." What he said was not reassuring but it was all we had.

As he'd suggested, I kept the yoke firmly against my chest and used full throttle. Our flight engineer couldn't leave his station in the wing-neck so the trainee had to race from stern to bow to report our latest sinking condition. "It's worse," he said with resignation and fear in his voice. "I don't think we're going to make it."

Gritting my teeth and wondering for a moment why we did not wear the life-preservers for our water takeoff, I also was confounded by the fact that with the nose high position, the plane seemed to be sinking all the more. As the copilot kept the tower informed of our turtle-like progress toward the nearing ramp, three proportional conditions were happening at once: as the bow raised higher, the hull sank lower and the speed decreased.

For awhile it seemed as if time was suspended as all of us stared fixedly at the upcoming ramp. Finally, I knew we'd make it, so lowered the landing gear and closed the throttles as I felt the clunk of the gear against the sloping ramp. In seconds, the ramp crew had fastened a line to he bow and was winching us further onto dry land.

All of us climbed out through the left blister ladder and gathered near the stern to investigate the cause of our dilemma. We watched as two very large streams of water poured out of the hull a few feet aft of the blisters. Where did it come from, I wondered as I heard a growing volume of snickering voices.

The somber looking CPO came to us, shaking his head in disbelief. "Well, you dogfaces really did it. Wouldn't you know you army types would try to take off with the flare-chute tubes open?"

Flare-chute tubes? How did we miss checking such an important item? And at once the answer came to us as to why the yoke-back, bow-high taxiing had only aggravated the problem. The more we'd lifted the nose, the more it pressed water into the fuselage.

Unable to think of anything intelligent to say to the copilot, I did manage to remark, "Hey, these navy people are wrong. 'Dogface' is a term for army enlisted men. We are officers."

He studied me for a moment then answered in a flat voice, "Sure, but we got their meaning pretty clear, didn't we?"

The next morning we accepted a different airplane as it was estimated to take a week to desalt the insides of the water-soaked PBY.

Have you ever seen at least 24 men—Army and Navy mixed—check two flare-chute tubes about 30 times?

39 ANOTHER CATERPILLAR CLUB ELITE

World War II was still a few years ahead, but the rumblings were being felt near and far. In the United States, there was an undercurrent of tension. Many secretly believed our nation would enter the conflict at some point. If that occurred, pilots—many, many pilots—would be needed.

The tempo of training increased. Soon there would be a Civil Pilot Training Program and the schools teaching military pilots would explode with growth.

Two of the fixed base operators at Long Beach Airport reaped a dramatic increase in activity. Aircraft Associates—where I flew—was one; Scott Flying Service was the other. Scott's chief pilot was 27 year-old Frank Averill. Randall Scott, head of the company, knew his employee to be a no-nonsense professional in his approach to flight instruction. Thoughtful and deliberate, a slender man with athletic build, Averill was intense about flying though he appeared easy-going to his associates. Always, his belief was that it was intelligent to profit from other's errors.

A few months earlier, a news clipping had caught his attention. It told of a San Diego, California, flight instructor who had fallen out of his airplane during an instruction flight. Louis Dale was teaching his student "barrel rolls" and had fallen out of the airplane. It said the instructor had hit his head on the high-wing and had barely recovered consciousness in time to open his parachute.

Frank Averill had found this account difficult to believe. How, he wondered, could a careful pilot permit such an event? Reading further, he learned the student, who'd acquired only 1.5 hours dual time, had managed to land the airplane. "Lucky," thought Averill and he dismissed the report from his mind.

I had not met Scott Flying Service's chief pilot, and that must be accounted as a small oddity since most of us who flew at Long Beach knew one another. My personal logbook of that period shows that on May 2, 1936, I had checked out for a solo flight in a Security-Kinner, side-by-side, low-wing monoplane. This was the same type favored by Scott Flying Service.

Sometime later, flying over Long Beach in the same type airplane, Averill was instructing student Don Farrell in the finer points of precision spins and loops. All was going well on the flight. Lovely weather. Smooth air. Routine. Ho hum.

Peering down to clear the area below, Frank noted they were at 3,500 feet high and above the open fields of the Bixby Ranch. Farrell was having a problem keeping the loop tight at its upper apex. Carefully, Frank had explained his errors. "Try it again," Averill ordered. "Tight, but not so you stall it on top. Okay, let's do it!"

Farrell concentrated upon the task and dove the plane for the loop. Averill noticed the entry was good. But as the airplane reached the inverted, he saw that his student had abruptly relaxed the back-pressure. Quickly, Averill reached for the stick to correct the error.

Too late.

Frank Averill felt a sickening sensation as he fell out of the inverted monoplane. What he had decided would never happen to him, in fact, had. His mind was still functioning well and he used it. Wisely, he delayed opening his parachute until well clear of the airplane's path recovering from the loop. Drifting down, he had time to speculate on why the seat belt had unlatched. As most belts were the old Army Air Corps types, anything could have caused the latch to unsnap: a brush of the hand, a sleeve caught, twisting in the seat.

Averill landed without injury on the Bixby Ranch where a motorist picked him up and drove him back to the airport.

Landing the plane safely, but with an extremely red face, Farrell emphasized he had not deliberately tossed his instructor out of the airplane. But the others already had received the news of Frank's successful leap so they ribbed the student unmercifully.

Again at the airport, Averill apologized to his student and everyone within earshot, though there was no data indicating he'd done anything wrong. Wrong or right, he had claimed some fame as another member of the famous "Caterpillar Club," albeit an accidental jump.

For the remainder of his aviation career, Averill was considered a bonafide expert on fastening seat belts.

Part 6

Sojourns Through the Land of Murphy's Laws

MURPHY'S LAWS

1. In any field of scientific endeavor, anything that can go wrong, will.

2. Left to themselves, things always go from bad to worse.

3. If there is a possibility of several things going wrong, the one that will go wrong is the one that will do the most damage.

4. Nature always sides with the hidden flaw.

5. Mother Nature is a bitch.

6. If everything seems to be going well, you have obviously overlooked something.

40 HOWARD HUGHES AND HELL'S ANGELS

One cannot mention the movie *Hell's Angels* without immediately associating the name of Howard Hughes. Though the actual filming began in October of 1927, the stimulus for this monumental creative effort was born much earlier.

When Hughes' father died in 1924, Howard claimed his share of the Hughes Tool Company that was producing an income of several million dollars annually. With his new bride, Ella, a member of the famed Rice family of Houston, Texas, Hughes headed for Hollywood, California, to investigate the movie business.

Freely spending money, it was easy for this newcomer to produce three motion pictures in a row. But success was not automatic. His first effort was so poorly done that the film was not released. The second attempt was classed as mediocre. A portent of things to come, Hughes' third try won an award for its excellence and earned its maker bundles of money as well. *Hell's Angels* would have lasting fame.

During this Hollywood adventure, Howard Hughes was spending his spare time at local airports. It wasn't long before another obsession engulfed him. He was determined to learn to fly. Apparently his future secretive ways were initiated during this phase of his life for he took flight instruction from several pilots at different airports without letting any of them know about the other. Later it was thought that he was less interested in merely soloing than he was quite concerned with learning all he could about flying. Again, another trait of his career was being expressed.

In 1927 Howard saw the film *Wings*. It intrigued him so much that he returned to see it several more times. He then told an associate, "I can certainly make a better flying picture than that."

Time proved that when Howard Hughes made a decision, the die was solidly cast. So began one of the most ambitious film making efforts Hollywood had known. Within the filming time of three years, Hughes would spend more than four million dollars, lease or purchase some 37 airplanes and have Otto Timm build several Avro trainer replicas from Curtiss Jenny parts.

In his film preparation, he tried to lease Roscoe Turner's Sikorsky S-29 to disguise and use it as a Gotha bomber. Roscoe, a wise promoter in his own right, refused to lease it but suggested that Hughes purchase it outright. This proved a wise decision of Turner's for the airplane crashed during filming. It was in a scene in which it was supposed to be shot down, spin behind a hill and then recover to land. Both Frank Clarke and Jimmie Angel refused to spin the plane and Al Wilson became the substitute pilot. When Wilson entered the spin, the wing spars promptly broke. Wilson tried warning the young mechanic in the rear of the fuselage to bail out. But Phil Jones was so intent upon making his smoke pots work that he was unaware of the emergency and fell to his death with the airplane.

Other unexplained events dogged the making of the picture. When an air service at Grand Central Air Terminal leased Howard Hughes their brand new Ryan M-1 mailplane, Hughes directed pilot Roscoe Turner and actor Ben Lyons to drop flowers over the site of the original Breakfast Club adjacent to the Los Angeles riverbed. Unfamiliar with the Ryan's fuel system, Turner set the fuel valve on a low tank before the flower drop.

After dropping the flowers, Turner zoomed skyward and the engine sputtered and quit. Too low to do anything but land, Roscoe Turner glided into the riverbed, dropped onto the soft sandy bottom and the airplane snapped inverted. With hundreds watching, both men unfastened their safety belts and tumbled unceremoniously into the shallow stream.

Other accidents followed. Dick Grace, known as the "crash king of Hollywood," suffered broken bones executing his contracted crashes for "Hell's Angels." Many of the airplanes were damaged in uncalled-for ground loops, taxi accidents and flip overs.

On one occasion the script called for a Tommy Morse scout to take off and then execute a sharp left turn around the camera's position. Chief Pilot Frank Clarke refused to fly the stunt and explained to Hughes that the rotary engine's torque at such slow speeds would flip the airplane into the ground. As no other pilots on Hughes payroll, would accept the mission, Hughes said he would do the job himself.

Clarke and the others warned Hughes that he was asking for trouble in that he had no experience with rotary-engined craft. Howard Hughes dismissed them and climbed into the Tommy and took off. And as predicted, the airplane dug its left wingtip into the ground and cartwheeled into total wreckage. Hughes' facial injury from the crash would bother him for the rest of his life.

Frank Clarke was heard to remark acidly, "Stunt pilots are born, not made. No one can make an eagle out of a duck!"

Coincident with his filming problems and the injuries from his crash, Hughes saw his wife Ella, bored with his preoccupations, depart for Texas. Almost relieved, Hughes settled a million and a quarter dollars on her for the coming divorce.

When the film was previewed as a silent movie, audiences were not impressed seeing violent dogfights in silence. Hughes faced the issue and reshot a major portion of the film, adding sound. For a greater impact, Hughes substituted his Swedish leading lady with an inexperienced but sultry-voiced blonde named Harlean Carpenter. As luck would have it, she later would gain renown as Jean Harlow and the film would turn into a blockbuster.

Thinking big, whoever was anybody in aviation, Hughes hired for Hell's Angels. Some who went on to even greater fame were: Jimmie Angel, Frank Clarke, Ray Crawford, Earl "Chub" Gordon, my cousin, Clinton Herberger, the famed crazy pilot Al Lary, and dour-faced Garland Lincoln. Frank Tomick and the unfortunate Al Wilson were also hired.

It is estimated that if *Hell's Angels* were to be filmed today the cost would run over a hundred million dollars. Even then it was a herculean effort that would earn Howard Hughes a healthy profit and a lasting success. It was a classic of such substance that a viewer today would be totally thrilled. And amazingly, this film was made over 50 years ago.

41 THE '30s GLIDER CRAZE

Some psychologists claim fads usually are started by emotions rather than conscious thoughts. If ever an American craze proved this, the glider-flying mania of the 1930s did.

It began shortly after the stock market crash of 1929. Though the crash was a monumental crisis for many Americans, there still were a lot of people who wanted to fly. But with the deepening Depression, a "chicken in the pot" became more vital than "an hour around the patch."

As people became more and more interested in flying, all it took to trigger the fad was for *Popular Mechanics* magazine to publish do-it-yourself plans for an American version of the German Zoegling primary glider. To avoid the foreign name, the author substituted "The Northrop Primary Glider." With a name sounding as if the great designer, Jack Northrop had a hand in the venture, the ploy worked.

In less time than you could say, "Snap me off the hill, Joe," primary gliders abounded in all shapes, sizes and configurations. As broad in spectrum was their quality of workmanship. Too many of the homebuilt contraptions could be classified as having dubious enough safety to being outright killers.

In my high school woodworking class, there were several under construction at once. We were fortunate that our teacher was also a pilot and knew the techniques of gluing and fitting together pieces of spruce. But the gliders in our class were exceptional, for I saw many species that gave one a feeling of horror simply to look at them.

On the Monterey Park hills near Los Angeles, California, I watched one built with an assortment of wood scraps and covered with varnished meat-wrapping paper make many flights. On closer observation, I saw that all the turnbuckles

Author ready to be launched off a California mountain in the Zoegling primary glider.

on the primary wire bracing came from a hardware store and ordinarily were used on screen doors. Made of soft iron, their strength was non-existent.

One foggy morning I witnessed the three owner/pilots experience a major problem. They had turned the glider over because the paper covering was wet and sagging heavily between the ribs. When the sun would dry one portion, they would turn the thing another direction to dry another part. When they were finished and had brought the glider back to its normal upright stance, there were many holes that had been punctured in the paper covering. Undismayed, the trio patched the holes with more paper and a generous helping of library paste.

It seemed everyone was flying gliders off hills. Some were auto-towed and many others were snapped skyward with long rubber shock-cords pulled by six to 10 people.

It appeared as if no one was exempt from the craze. It was common for politicians and entertainers to fly gliders for publicity photos. Many times these reaches for publicity backfired when the unskilled pilot broke a wrist or an ankle from an inevitable crash. I can recall watching a newsreel of a prominent state governor—who'd never before sat in a glider—attempt an auto-tow for publicity. The camera caught the glider climbing shakily to a few hundred feet high and then descending so fast than upon hitting the ground, his feet snapped off the rudder bar, breaking both of his legs.

Another newsreel gained nationwide notoriety as it showed a confident young pilot climbing aboard his frail, homebuilt glider for an airplane tow across San Francisco Bay. The idea may have sounded fine to everyone, but in moments after takeoff, the airplane's excessive speed caused the glider pilot-induced oscillations so severe the nose broke off behind the seat and he was thrown from the craft. Without a parachute, his thrashing and his terrified face were witnessed by a nation. But even events such as these failed to dampen the glider fad.

Many entrepreneurs tried to capitalize on the movement. The Ideal Airplane Company of New York City, a well-known model airplane kitmaker, realized that full-sized gliders could turn more profit than toys. They offered a complete set of drawings for a variation of the clumsy Zoegling for only $1.50. A flying buddy and I built one and discovered when launched from a 6000-foot-high mountain, it barely reached the foothills below. We were as dumb as the others.

Cessna Aircraft Company read the handwriting on the wall and advertised a complete primary glider for $398. Its ad headlined: "Glider pilots will be future transport pilots!"

The well-known Alexander Eaglerock Company of Colorado Springs, Colorado, sold a high-altitude primary glider for $375. It also tried to lure dealers for its product by promising a rebate of $225 for each three aircraft sold.

Bill Crawford of Seal Beach, California, watched the glider afficionados sweat and strain as they laboriously dragged their clumsy craft back to the takeoff point after each flight. He promptly came out with a primary glider powered by the dubious Szekely engine.It flew well so long as the engine ran—which wasn't very often! His design effort appeared in 1928 and though the glider did not find a ready market that early in the fad's history, he attracted enough financial support to enable him to design and promote a ghastly tri-engined, four-place airplane powered by three of the unreliable Szekelys. Publicity-wise, Crawford had thought to hire famed Jimmie Angel as his test pilot, but nevertheless, the venture failed.

The glider craze started in 1929 and rose to a crescendo in 1933. By 1935 it began to wane. After that, most gliders were being stored in barns and garages and offered for sale at ridiculously low prices before being consumed by errant rats. It was a great era for the very young or very poor aviation dreamers. Some of us would form a group of 10 or 20 interested friends, pool our resources and buy a glider. If we wrecked one—which frequently happened—we'd simply scrounge up the $10 or $20 to buy another.

Indeed, the glider craze was bizarre, although a few aviation types would use this as a springboard to greater things. From the thrill of the fad sprang many future pilots—Cessna was right!

Only the fad's excess was wrong.

42 WE-MITE, AN IDEA BEFORE ITS TIME

Brilliant idea! So proclaimed my enthusiastic flying buddies when I outlined my dream.

Though my concept of a super-light, powered glider had been tested in Europe, the United States would be some 40 years away from popularizing aircraft based upon this idea.

"Sound business thinking," said my two financial backers, who added, "Can't make money selling man-hours. You got it, sell machine hours only. The kit idea sounds great."

Our plan was to build a very light, powered glider and market it only in kit form. We intended to sell it in two stages: first, as a pure glider with a single-wheel landing gear. Presuming our customers would learn to fly the glider and then want the power package, we intended the final kit to comprise the 23-hp, two-cylinder-opposed, two-cycle engine; driveshaft; free-wheeling propeller; and, conventional two-wheel landing gear.

Without a large labor force and with mostly machined components, we expected a stable investment return and our customers would enjoy flying at a cost far less than that of the ubiquitous Cubs and Aeroncas proliferating the American scene.

So, we proceeded with the engineering and the structural work. An old flying friend, Fred Miller, assisted with the drawings and lofted the wing section for our rib jigs.

Our ideas had begun to solidify in 1936, but it was January, 1940, before we began actual construction of the We-Mite.

Though the We-Mite was my basic design, I was quick to admit I had borrowed many ideas from genius designer Hawley Bowlus and his Baby Albatross design. Our final craft didn't look much like Bowlus' glider. We stayed with the single aluminum-tube tailboom, but turned to a more conventional welded-steel tubing for the fuselage pod and the tail feathers. Using thin-walled tubing, we opted for brazing on most of the joints rather than welding and its chances of burning instead of fusing. That idea had been proven by the popular Franklyn secondary gliders.

Our wing was wood, two-spar with wooden ribs and a preformed D-section plywood leading edge. Easy maintenance dictated most of our design concepts.

Leonard Austin, one of our principals and the man for whom we named the small organization designed and built the power section from scratch because there was no such engine available. Aiming for greater stability than contemporary designs, Miller aided us by choosing an NACA 4412 airfoil which would blend into an NACA 4409 at the wingtips. With 1.5 degrees tip washout, it was expected to be very stable and forgiving in flight without a great loss of performance.

Gradually, the frustration of working long hours metamorphosed into an aircraft structure. Four of us did the actual work, while two others were our financial backers and one more handled the promotion.

As the basic glider neared completion, our backers made ugly sounds about pulling the purse strings tighter. Undaunted, we other four began working for Douglas Aircraft Company in Santa Monica, California, on their swing shift. Our excess wages were pooled and went into the project.

All who stopped by to check our progress were favorably impressed as the basic glider neared its completion. It looked like a good flying machine. The semi-tapered wings spanned 38 feet and offered a slight gull-winged effect. Empty weight, less the power package, was 250 pounds. Another 37 pounds made up the power package and landing gear conversion. Stall speed was computed at 25 mph.

We began an engine test program as the airplane's finish was drying and it became immediately apparent we faced a delay. The two-cycle valving was the culprit and a new rotary valve crankshaft had to be machined. So, we proceeded to finish the aircraft as a pure glider.

First assembly of We-Mite's components. Firm's publicist, Stu Potter in cabin.

At 2 A.M. on New Year's Day, 1941, my major partner, Glen Beets, and I stepped back and said, "She's ready to fly." At dawn we trailered the craft to a nearby field for flight testing. With the first few flights our elation soared. We-Mite had exceeded both our hopes and design expectations. It was the first glider I'd flown that could be "mushed" through an approach to a landing without stalling or falling off on a wing.

Yielding to the call of fun on the weekend, we proceeded to Lucerne Valley Dry Lake in the Mojave Desert and experienced some great soaring in light thermals. It seemed as if every flight we made proved the glider to be an exceptionally fine flying machine. Glen Beets learned to fly on these treks and the We-Mite put on many hours. Later, I soared above the Palos Verdes Hills near Los Angeles on slope winds and gained an altitude of 4,200 feet. Perfect.

And immediately, the bottom fell out of everything. Our great plans, our gut feelings of success, all flew out the window. It seems our backers had lost their investment money when Germany isolated itself from the Allied governments. Our budding ultralight stayed the glider it was. Glen Beets became an instructor at actor Harvey Stephen's military glider training school at Wickenburg, Arizona. Later, Fred Miller and I would join the Long Beach, California, Ferrying Command. Stewart Potter, our genius promoter, would become a process engineer of note. The We-Mite would end up with Glen Beets as partial compensation for his services.

Mark this the end of great dreams and use black to color the taste of bitterness in our defeat. But now, looking back from a perspective of over 40 years later, maybe we didn't fail at all. Perhaps we were right on target without knowing.

Though the war scuttled our efforts, it's possible that the success of today's ultralights and powered gliders may rest upon our pioneering shoulders.

Maybe we really did experience the impossible dream.

43 THE PHONY AIR RAID

The event at Pearl Harbor and our ignominious loss of most of the naval fleet was nearly three months behind us. Ten days after the start of World War II, I had been hired by the Air Corps Ferrying Command and was acting as the sole civilian-employment check pilot, flight-testing pilot applicants who wished to serve their country.

Many of us who were the early birds at the Long Beach, California, base lived in nearby motels. One in particular, the Circle Inn Motel, fronted a large, major traffic circle southeast of the airport.

Each night, many of us who lived there would gather in the motel's yard chatting and trying to speculate about our immediate futures. The tales were typical of young men unsure what the war meant to their futures—or, even if they had a future.

My ordinary day at the Long Beach base was filled with hours of flight-checks in the old Vultee basic trainer, the BT-13 "vibrator." Though one requirement for employment was 200-plus hours as pilot-in-command of airplanes over 200 hp, it was obvious that many who applied had padded their logbooks to meet the requirement. We termed this deception "Parker 51" time, after a popular fountain pen of the time.

One day when interviewing several applicants, I totaled their flying time for one particular Stinson SM8-A which was based at Blythe, California, and discovered it had flown 46 hours in a single 24-hour period. Caught with their collective hands in the cookie jar, their anguish was great. Stoics, all, none volunteered how such magic could happen. When I thought they'd been properly abashed, I said, "Well, men, what the hell? So there's a war on. Let's see if you can fly." My personal logs show that of over several hundred applicants flight-checked, a mere six had been failed.

That night in February of 1942, flying stories at the Circle Inn Motel abounded. It had been unusually warm for that time of year and many of us were reluctant to leave the cool outdoors and retire to hot, stuffy rooms. At about 10 p.m., a few mumbled about "hitting the sack," but as the camaraderie was satisfying, everyone lingered on.

Shortly after 10 P.M., we heard the first air raid sirens and watched as the entire area was quickly blacked out.

Was this the real thing? Were we about to be bombed by enemy planes?

Gossip had been rampant that the Japanese possibly would try to attack the West Coast. Phone calls came from the base alerting us that we were to stay put and await possible emergency orders.

Very soon all was in total blackness. For several minutes silence prevailed, then as if acting upon a signal, all hell broke loose. Searchlights penetrated the black sky. Minutes passed while the probing lights frantically swung to and fro as if trying to locate the enemy.

One of our group shouted, "Look! Airplanes!"

As he pointed, all of us watching saw the same sight: a flight of high-flying airplanes were crossing the area from west to east. At that moment, they were apparently over the Hawthorne-Compton area. The searchlights immediately found their targets; the airplanes were outlined in stark relief from the myriad shafts of brilliant lights. At what seemed the same instant, the still night was shattered by the pumping sounds of hundreds of anti-aircraft batteries.

For a while, we simply stood there too stunned to speak. Whistling pieces of shrapnel falling near us was unimpressive.

Then we agreed that the planes we were seeing was a flight of 13 airplanes composed of four flights of three vee formations—all centered upon a single, huge, four-engined bomber.

I remember shouting, "Those aren't enemy planes. Look, that bomber is the Douglas B-19!"

"Yeh! Crazy! Sure is!" the others chimed in. When one pilot demanded how I was so certain the big plane was the B-19, I admitted I had welded its landing gear and some of its engine mounts when I was employed at the Douglas Aircraft plant in Santa Monica.

Before long, we knew without question that the enemy flight we were witnessing was our own airplanes.

"Why are they trying to shoot down our own planes?" was the question asked repeatedly.

Then someone remarked, "Hell, look at the shells, they aren't exploding anywhere near the planes. They aren't trying to shoot 'em down!"

As ridiculous as the thought was, he was right. All the anti-aircraft shells were bursting some 2,000 to 3,000 feet below the formation. Obviously, the planes were in no danger, and also obvious was the conclusion that what we were viewing could only happen through some very careful and intelligent orchestration.

Easily, and without any change in their headings, the flight of planes droned away toward the east until they had outdistanced the lights and the anti-aircraft shells.

We learned there had been 1,433 rounds of anti-aircraft shells fired and that two Los Angeles citizens had been killed by the falling shrapnel.

The next day brought an even more ridiculous quality to the experience, which demoralized most of us who had witnessed the event. Secretary of War, Henry L. Stimson, was quoted as saying, "People in Los Angeles were seeing things. There was no raid, no airplanes—nothing! It must have been a case of mass hysteria."

But we witnesses agreed it was a shame we couldn't have flown one of the Ferrying Command planes to the March Field Airbase in Riverside, California. All of us would have given great odds that an interesting fleet of airplanes would have been found, plus a very large Douglas bomber.

To this writing, I cannot rid my mind of the sting that if we had been hired as rational, skilled pilots to aid our country, why was such an insult made?

Someone alive knows the story from the Washington, D.C. point of view. Anyone care to volunteer?

44 GLIDER CROSSES OCEAN

There are times in everyone's life, I suppose, when one is involved in doing his or her own thing and the world seems far removed. Such a time came upon me quite unexpectedly in June of 1947.

Then I'd have firmly rejected the idea that my image would be featured on the front page of the Los Angeles Times morning edition. That this event would springboard a feature story of my soaring pleasures in the distinguished *Look* magazine would have seemed equally ludicrous. But though I did not consciously cause any of these publicity highlights, they happened.

The cause of all this occured mundanely. At that time I was working with the Argentine government, assisting, their purchases of World War II airplanes and training their crews during the subsequent delivery flights.

Glider expert Henry Meyers heard I would be ferrying a surplus DC-4 from Augusta, Georgia, to Van Nuys, California. He told he'd become the successful bidder on two surplus Schweizer TG-3 sailplanes. He offered that if I would fly them to Van Nuys, I could take my pick, gratis, of either craft. How could I go wrong? In one easy step I could own a nice sailplane.

At Augusta, I readied the DC-4 for flight and stowed the two gliders aboard. At Van Nuys, I selected the original TG-3 Number One that had been the test vehicle for the later contract. Its nose was slightly shorter than the production prototype and the workmanship appeared superior.

So began a year of rebuilding and restoration.

The day for the test flight finally came, and with old buddy Fred Miller, I trailered to the El Mirage dry lake. The sailplane flew great and we enjoyed the first good thermal soaring we'd had in years. On one of my awkward landings Fred caught my ground-loop with his movie camera. He will still show it today to anyone who professes interest.

The first hint of coming publicity was when I was selected to fly the "Queen-for-a-Day" to the El Mirage glider contest in the TG-3. Perhaps wisely, the queen elected not to go so I urged a friend to substitute. I must say that the glider pilots of that time had no couth. Expecting a lovely queen to appear at their meet and instead having to take a fat and forty male substitute did not improve my image.

Later, while taking my friends for passenger rides at the Torrance, California, flight strip, Bob Stanley, a leading soaring promoter, asked if I intended to participate in the coming International Soaring meet to be held at Wichita Falls, Texas. "Sure," I said, "Sounds like a great chance to get my Silver 'C' soaring badge."

He grinned widely. "Great! Then you wouldn't mind helping with some pre-meet publicity?"

I should have known better but I agreed. Then he explained that his first publicity thrust would be to have me fly from Santa Catalina Island, 22 miles across the water to a landing at the Los Angeles Municipal Airport. Before I could say anything, he outlined how the event would be covered by the Los Angeles Times newspaper, an article would be written in *Aviation Week* by Alex McSurely; *Times* aviation editor Marvin Miles would

"Saludos Amigos"
prior to ocean flight.

be my passenger on the flight, and . . .

"Wow!" He made it all sound like Santa Claus was coming. Before I could catch my breath, Bob added that *Look* magazine would cover both the Catalina flight and my participation in the Texas meet. I was awed by such skillful promotion.

A few days later, on June 4, I was ready at the Torrance strip. My tow pilot was "Smitty," (not his real name) also arranged by Bob Stanley. The tug was Smitty's 450 Wasp-powered Stearman trainer. I told Smitty that I needed 14,000 feet over the Catalina Isthmus to make the flight. He admitted that he was suffering from a grand hangover but thought he could handle the mission. Bob smiled and told me that he'd also arranged for a Coast Guard PBY to monitor my flight in case I landed at sea.

Ready for takeoff, the first alteration of plans became known when a message from Marvin Miles arrived stating that he could not make the flight but would meet us at the point of landing.

My wife agreed to substitute for Miles but made loud noises about me risking her life in an unproven glider flight. When Smitty yanked us off the runway, it was immediately apparent that his hangover was a major malady. His flight path varied up and down alarmingly and his course was in the opposite direction. I gritted my teeth and used the sailplane to yank Smitty's tail in the directions I wanted to fly. He seemed to accept this glider-domination.

The climb to 14,000 feet was quite a chore with the sailplane and towplane yanking and pulling all over the sky. Way below we could hear the tired Coast Guard PBY struggling to climb to our altitude but seemingly stuck at 12,000 feet. When my wife asked where Smitty would go after we released, I said, "Don't know and don't care!"

We released and Smitty fell off in a steep curving dive. His heading appeared as if he might make Japan but certainly not the mainland.

Gliding toward the mainland and our proposed landfall at Palos Verdes hills, we cruised at our minimum sink rate and reached Palos Verdes with 7,500 feet of altitude remaining. Then we made a shallow dive to Los Angeles Airport. Alerted beforehand, the tower sent us a steady green light and I landed upon a parallel taxiway and coasted to a stop in front of the waiting cameras.

"Where's Smitty?" were my first words.

Someone said, "He's okay; he managed to stumble into Long Beach airport. He phoned and said as soon as he has some more coffee, he'll fly here."

Marvin Miles was waiting as was Alex McSurely, and two gorgeous Hollywood starlets. Instant or not, the fame was looking and feeling good.

All of it came true. We did enter the contest and placed a low number 40 due the demands of *Look* Magazine's photographers. But that is another story and if you read on, I'll share it with you . . . .

45 HOW TO EARN A SILVER C

The story of how any individual earns the coveted FAI (Federation Aeronautique Internationale) Silver C Soaring Award must include those who contributed to the effort.

When I brought the Schweitzer TG-3 sailplane, their first experimental model, back to Los Angeles, California, the next step was to restore it to flyable condition.

In June of 1946, new automobiles were not available to the buying public so dealerships were doing whatever they could to stay afloat in business. A truck sales agency was happy to rent me their unused showroom as a bright, warm and airy sailplane-restoring-workshop.

In my spare time away from a flying job, I began the task of restoring the TG-3 which I named "Saludos Amigos." First, it had to be stripped to its bare bones, and then patiently brought back to mint condition. Much of the menial labor was in removing old finishes and preparing surfaces for the new coatings.

Each day as I worked there would be spectators young and old, the same as if a new building were being excavated for a foundation. Most wanted to talk flying, few offered to help. One morning a young man about 14 years of age on a bicycle appeared and sat watching me work for the balance of the day. He studied my every move with an intensity that finally caught my attention. I winked at him, said "hello" and returned my attention to the task at hand. At my greeting, he'd nodded his head.

The next day he was there again, sitting in the same spot but had brought with him a brown-bag lunch. My attention turned to curiosity. After watching me for several hours, he introduced himself.

"I'm Lorry Wilkinson," he said with solemnity. "I want to learn how to fly. If I helped, would you teach me?"

Though grave, his tone of voice was respectful. But as I'd heard such offers many times before, I gave him the standard answer I'd given others.

"Sure, if you really help me and work hard, I'll teach you what I can."

This time was different. I was fooled. Not only did Lorry help me but he was skilled and used tools capably. I worked him as hard as if I'd been paying him top wages and he produced. With his help, I could see the glider would be ready to fly ahead of schedule. In the past, such well-meaning helpers would work one or two days then disappear forever.

Young Lorry, black-haired, lean and intensely serious about his dreams, was going after his goal as though he would kill to insure its realization. I thought him mature for his age and easy to be with. Despite his seriousness about things aviation, he would laugh long and loud if my joke was worthy. He admired the young ladies who walked by the showroom. I considered him good pilot material. When I talked to him of basic aerodynamics, flight techniques and piloting skills, he'd listen but continue working. To myself, I made a promise to help him all I could.

On October 16, 1946, Lorry graduated from a plain bicycle to one with a rickety engine powering its rear wheel. As he rode up and parked, he told me he had some money he'd saved and asked if I would give him his first flying lesson.

With my auto in the shop for the day, both of us rode the powered bike to nearby Western Airport. I was glad I sat behind him on the fearful ride so he could not see my totally chicken expression. The contraption we rode appeared to me as if it had been glued together with gobs of Jello. Watching him dart through the traffic, I thought he might become the world's best fighter-pilot.

At the airport, I rented an Aeronca Tandem trainer and

gave Lorry his first flying lesson the same as I'd done hundreds of times in the past. He was a joy to teach and his delight at being able to handle the controls and make the airplane go where he wished was obvious. Back at the shop, he dropped his usual stoic pose and babbled away for the remainder of the day.

I gave Saludos Amigos its test flight at El Mirage Dry Lake in the Mojave Desert. Except for needing some lead in the nose, all worked fine. Flying a real sailplane with its flat gliding angle and positive-control response was very satisfying when I thought back to the crude gliders of my past. And having a passenger to talk with was an added bonus.

When I had made the Catalina Island to Mines Field flight for Bob Stanley to publicize the coming International Contest at Wichita Falls, Texas, I had promised him (and myself) that I would participate in the contest. I thought the idea rational because earning a Silver C Soaring Award had been a frustrated dream of mine for as long as I'd been flying gliders and sailplanes. Official observers are at all sanctioned contests for FAI, plus experts to record barograph readings. All these services were gratis during a meet but costly to an individual working alone.

There were additional reasons for wanting to be in the contest. First, I had never been in one or competed with any other pilot in such affairs. Always eager to learn new things in aviation, I presumed the pressure of a contest would accelerate my flying skills and soaring know-how. And the story that Stanley had arranged with *Look* magazine about my participation sounded like fun too.

We arrived at Wichita Falls, Texas, on July 3, 1947. At the former Air Force Base, Sheppard Field, we signed in for the contest and were allocated our barracks assignments. With me was my wife, Lorry, and my old barnstorming father, Claude.

That first night when I was lying in bed and trying to picture what a contest would be like, I thought back a few weeks to the response I got when I announced to Pop and Lorry I might enter the soaring meet. To anyone listening, it would have sounded humorous as I tried cooling their overblown fervor about my competitive skills. Pop said, "You'll whip their butts." Lorry soberly nodded agreement.

Despite their fervor I felt compelled to bring their views in line with reality rather than hoping through a veil of fantasy. I explained the many reasons why I would probably wind up in the middle of the contest pack but not at either end. When I said that I was a novice compared to soaring greats such as Harland Ross, Gus Briegleb and such capable pilots, they frowned deeply. Even when I explained that the *Look* magazine's photographer would interfere with soaring tasks, they were unimpressed.

When I'd finished my sermon, Lorry and Pop waited a respectful few moments then burst forth with all their reasons why I was wrong. When they had exhausted their outburst, Pop ejected the gum he'd been chewing, scratched his nose as if adjusting the world's greatest smug expression then added, "You are my son. You'll whup their fannies. I know."

Waiting until Pop had finished, Lorry screwed his face into a parody of my father's and offered, "I've watched you fly. I can tell good eggs from bad ones. Besides, I'll betcha fifty cents you'll win second place at least!"

Drowsy, listening to the sound of the light, warm Texas breeze coming through the screened window, I thought back to the early days of gliding. I could almost feel the brisk Pacific Ocean wind flowing over the cliffs and hills of Palos Verdes. My first soaring experience had been in an open primary glider while dressed in light clothing. I was surprised during one flight to discover as I turned from releasing to glide over the Palos Verdes cliffs the hard thrust of lift under the plywood seat. It was staying up! And I did not come down until I discovered my body was so cold I had trouble moving the controls. An hour and a half of delicious soaring had been mine and I felt as if I had experienced the supreme delight any human could be accorded.

Then my thoughts drifted to the many trips into the California desert we had made in search of thermal currents. Most of us at that time had only read of such lifting cells over flat ground from the accounts of German pilots. How many times had I released from a wire-tow about 1,000 feet above a dry lake, felt the lift thrust the glider upwards only to lose it when I tried to circle in its perimeter? Our awkwardness and our slow reaction without adequate climb-indicators would cause us to rise on one side of the lifting core only to fall out of it on the other side. A 10-minute thermal soaring flight in those days was considered a true miracle.

In Europe, the FAI published the requirements for a new

soaring badge Silver C. For years we had been working to earn the A, B, or C badges that required simple flights about an airport area. Then the Silver C appeared with its requirement of a cross-country flight, an altitude gain of 3,000 feet plus and an impossible sounding endurance flight of five hours. At my first attempt to earn an official leg of the Silver Badge, there were only 15 such pilots in the entire world.

As sleep nudged, I wondered about many things. Was I good enough to even enter this event? Good or better than the average non-professional, I guessed. What, really, was I doing here in Wichita Falls, Texas? Simple: To capture that elusive Silver C. How many times had I tried? Five? Or, was it seven? Recalling the failed attempts brought a pang of sadness. First, I would save all the money I could. Then I would try to coordinate the proper weather, the official FAI observer and rent a sealed barograph for the flight in question. Then when all was set, more questions would follow. Would the wind blow hard enough to soar? Would it blow long enough for the endurance leg of five solid hours of soaring?

With all the planning, if the weather failed to cooperate, Murphy's Law won—you lost!

Two such failed attempts I tried to erase from my mind without success. The first, I'd been so excited at the great soaring lift, I'd forgotten to turn on the sealed barograph. On the second, I was careful to start it after takeoff but the thing failed during the flight.

Better forget the past, Gerry. you cannot let your fans down. Lorry and Pop are counting on you for some sign of success. How? What can you achieve? Who knows. That was all I recall thinking before I fell asleep.

For the first days of the contest, I watched the "pros" do their thing. Then in practice flights, I would try and emulate their actions. Each day I could see the improvement in my flying skill but it was far below that of the real competitors. As I'd suspected, the *Look* magazine photographer wanted such a variety of shots that my contest attempts became second priority.

On July 10, the clouds filled the sky with signs of good lift and their bases averaged 6,000 feet high.

Releasing from an airplane tow at 2,000 feet, I caught a thermal that pilots called a "boomer" and began to climb better than 600 feet per minute. By then I'd learned to center the sailplane in the thermal's core of lift, quickly and accurately, with Harland Ross' expert advice. He would watch and harangue me to tighten my turns. Finally, when I was doing thermal circles at a 60-degree bank, he was satisfied.

With the Sperry electric horizon I was able to stay in the lifting cell though flying blind in a cloud. That day I had reached 7,200 feet within a Cumulus cloud. I steered downwind when the lift eased and broke out into bright sunshine soon thereafter. It was now or never for a cross-country effort. I told my wife we were going for it. She nodded, saving words for another time.

Looking ahead over the country that was obviously lacking in nice flat airports, I pointed the nose toward the northeast. As we'd pre-planned, Lorry and my father had already started down the highways to intercept us at our eventual landing site. We used a plan in which at each town, the ground crew would stop at the local police and ask if "Casey, the glider pilot, had called in?" If I had not, they would continue to the next city. If I had landed, I would call the police and tell them our location. It worked to perfection. The police always helped and seemed to enjoy the different experience.

But now I was heading out into the unknown. How long could I keep this aircraft in the air? Where would I be when the lift failed—which it would as the sun set. Would there be a nice airport nearby at which to land? As no crystal ball had been invented by which to forecast these serious questions for soaring pilots, I would have to wait and see.

That the coming events were serious was without doubt. To glide far downwind trying for distance could leave a pilot facing a fast, downwind landing without first having the chance to survey his landing area. Many broken gliders proved this risk. To land at a choice spot when too high would lose distance points. It had to be an instant compromise when the situation presented itself.

Thinking about all this caused me to realize why the art of soaring was so fascinating. Compared to flying a powered plane, the difference was obvious: with an engine, you knew in advance most of your moves. With a sailplane, you never knew what the next second would bring to cause a change in your plans. The thrill was the constant quest of the unknown. Soaring then, was a perpetual mystery the enthusiasts worked at solving.

After two hours of soaring, using every thermal encountered to regain lost lift, we had covered no more than about 50 miles from the base as the crow flies. I tried to remember the miles required for the Silver C but the landing we must soon face forced the answer from my mind.

We were over Duncan Airport in Oklahoma, and the lift had failed completely. The air that had been full of chop and vertical currents was now flat. It was glassy smooth and a landing would have to be made soon.

Feeling we'd proven some kind of point and needed no further risks for that day, I elected to land at the nice, flat airport below our nose.

A final wingover to a landing and we were down. The airport manager treated me like a hero. "Wow! You flew a glider all the way here from Sheppard Field? I can't believe it!"

I asked him to sign my landing card and the mileage between here and Sheppard Field. Before he could answer, the elusive distance requirement for a Silver C came to me. I had been surmising it was 52 miles which would have made me one mile short, but it dawned upon my dulled sense that the requirement was for 31 miles. I felt good as I could now claim title to the distance leg of the Silver C.

Lorry and Pop soon arrived and we dismantled the glider and had it on its trailer in 15 minutes. Enroute back to Wichita Falls, I wanted the world to know of our good luck and my achievement. I babbled on and on like a boulder galloping downhill.

" . . . and then when we hit this fat Cu's bottom the climb indicator read— —"

"Hey!" Lorry cut in. "You didn't only make— —"

"As I was saying, this Cu then produced a climb— —"

"Gerry, you didn't only make your distance— —"

"What do you mean? . . . As I was trying to— —-"

"You didn't only make your distance, Gerry!"

This time I heard him for sure. "What do you mean. Are you trying to tell me I didn't get my Silver C distance leg, Lorry?"

He and Pop guffawed, then Lorry said, "Yeh, you did not make only your distance. You said you had reached 7,200 feet when you started toward Duncan, right?"

"Right, so—-"

"So that gave you an altitude above release of 5,200 feet.

What I'm trying to tell you is that today's flight got you *two* legs of your Silver C!"

I yelled at Pop who was driving. "Hey, Pop, slow down. Watch those bumps in the road. Be careful of the barograph!" This was one time I certainly didn't want Murphy's Law to spoil a great day.

That evening I turned the barograph in to Dr. Carl Lange who would record its markings and resmoke the foil cylinder for the next days flying.

The next morning he informed me that I had, indeed, been verified for two legs earned toward the Silver C. That evening, the three of us: Lorry, Pop and myself, managed to induce a fair quantity of cold beer through our bodies.

Ten more contest days would pass before I would get a chance for the final leg of the silver badge.

Each flight, each day, the cross-country flights grew longer, the altitude gained higher and the time aloft increased too. My points posted on the daily board showed that I would not end up the meet's dummy unless something terrible happened to thwart our plans.

Several days came when the weather was not soarable so contest events such as spot landings, aerobatics and the like were put on for the local spectators. On one such day, I had rigged up a blind flying hood for Saludos Amigos, and Bob Stanley had agreed to be my "precision-approach-controller" in an attempt to make the first blind landing ever in a sailplane. Stanley would ride in the glider's rear cockpit.

Releasing from our airplane tow at 2,000 feet over Sheppard Field, Stanley guided me verbally as to when to turn, fly right or left to align with the runway and where we were in relation to the base landing leg. To lose altitude to the approach position, I executed wingovers, full-oscillation stalls and steep spirals, all while flying blind with the Sperry horizon. Though it may sound and have looked impressive, actually it was very easy.

On the final approach, Stanley gave me headings right or left rapidly and precisely. I followed his instructions and soon he said, "You're three-feet high and centered on the runway." And a moment later, the glider touched the concrete and rolled out to a stop. As we had stopped within a fourth of an inch from the landing spot, we were awarded the prize for that too.

Bob and I congratulated each other for making the world's

first blind landing in a sailplane. No book has recorded the deed. We were famous only between ourselves and the few pilots who were flying in the contest. Even the *Look* photographer failed to capture the event. Ho Hum.

The next day was forecast to be a good soaring day for westbound distance flights. It was Lorry's time to fly as copilot and I told him I planned a goal flight to Vernon, Texas. He thought I could make a much longer flight but I showed him that with the point award setup they had, the 52-mile flight to Vernon as a goal would earn more points than a 100-mile flight straight out to an undetermined point of landing.

Next morning, we saw that Dr. Lange had nailed the weather on the nose. Before takeoff time, the Cumulus had dotted the Texas sky. The wind was picking up from the northeast and things looked rosy.

Behind us on the ramp was the sailplane I had helped Harland Ross build for actor Harvey Stephens, the "Zanonia," now owned and flown by a brilliant San Diego pilot, John Robinson.

We released before reaching the tow maximum of 2,000 feet in strong lift and circled toward the fat bottom of a bulging Cumulus cloud in company with five other sailplanes, one of which was the Zanonia. As we climbed, Lorry called my attention to the fact that we were being passed by Robinson. I marveled at the silky-smooth way the Zanonia sailed around us. Such elan!

"Tell me when we get close to the cloud bottom, Lorry."

"Okay."

I kept my attention on the climb indicator as the air was becoming quite choppy and it would be easy to lose the core of the small-diameter, but strong-lifting, columns of air.

"Robinson went into the cloud, Gerry, and there are still three sailplanes a little below us. You going to stay in the thermal?"

"Don't think so," I answered. "Too much chance of a midair in the cloud with all the sailplanes at once."

"Aw, come on. I have never seen anyone fly blind."

I crossed my fingers. "Okay, we'll give it a go." Seconds later we were in the cloud and the lift was increasing. I discovered that lift on the east edge of the turn was increasing with each circle, so widened the turn until the lift was again centered. Now we had double the lift as before. At 8,400 feet, the lift began to slow and I decided to leave the cloud. Soon we were in the blue sky again, heading west.

"Where is everyone" asked Lorry.

I made a forty-five-degree turn to the right so we could see to our rear. As we watched the flank of the cloud, we saw John Robinson spring out of its side about two-hundred feet below our altitude and in moments, the other three sailplanes appeared as if in formation at the same height we were flying. The moment the three pilots saw each other, they made wild turns to avoid colliding.

"Wow!" Lorry saw the picture at once.

My observation carried a warning. "Great fun but very dumb. Can you see the danger?"

His expression changed to concern. "Yes, we could have wrecked the glider and had to use these chutes we're sitting on. I'm sorry I asked."

I laughed. "Don't sweat it. It was the one who made the decision. I just learned something, too."

Three more thermals and we saw Vernon, Texas, appear over the nose. Lorry flew until we'd centered ourselves over the airport. It was a Sunday and we could see a large crowd of spectators all around the airport. I took the controls and began to do large wingovers to lose altitude for landing.

"Loop it, Gerry. Loop it!"

I made some remarks about the acid from the battery spilling and continued our approach to land. However, in my mind, I had devised a plan.

On the ground, we who had landed agreed to pay for an airplane tow back to Sheppard Field. Within the hour three 450-hp Steaman towplanes appeared to take us back to the contest base.

When the pilot of one ran out two tow ropes from the tail of his airplane, I realized he intended to tow two of us at once. Another first for me that had not been planned; how many had I faced so far in my flying career? So, big deal. I went through WW II flying about everything made for flying without any problem; okay, I would go along with this and wait to see what happened.

Watching the tow pilot, my qualms were calmed when I noticed that the two ropes were uneven in length. So, one sailplane would always be behind the other even if they could not keep their distance laterally from each other. There was still much to learn about this glider business.

On takeoff I was busy but not unduly so. As usual, Saludos Amigos handled well and responded to the control.

Flying at 70 mph, we were over our home base 45 minutes after departing Vernon. Enroute, our tow pilot had gradually eased up to an altitude of 5,000 feet which put us above most of the rough air. My plan made back in Vernon was solidifying.

We released and I began to execute some wingovers to lose altitude. Lorry shouted, "The air is smooth now. Why don't you do a loop?"

Hesitantly, I said, "well, because . . . "

"Come on, Gerry, give me a real answer."

"Well . . .," and as I hesitated, I increased our dive until the airpseed touched the red line, and then pulled back on the stick—hard.

At the top of the loop, Lorry realized what was happening and yelled like a homesick Indian. We did several more with his delight increasing each time.

At least one member of our crew now believed the contest was a fantastic adventure.

But, the last leg of the Silver C was still wanting, for I needed that last duration leg before I could enter that hallowed halls of the few elites.

On July 15, the day appeared favorable for our attempt. Cumulus began building early. First off on tow since I'd placed our ship on the line at six A.M., Pop and I were in the air at nine o'clock sharp. Using positive thinking, I had announced a goal flight to Paris, Texas, 150 miles east of Sheppard Field.

As we released, the lift was phenomenal. I asked Pop to check the barograph and be certain it was operating.

"It's running," he grunted. "You going into that cloud?"

"Okay with you?"

"Hell yes! Let's see what that fancy horizon thing you got will do. Besides, I've never flown on instruments."

We continued circling in the smooth, powerful lift and as we reached the cloud base, I lowered my head to fly by the instruments. As the air was still smooth, I reminded Pop how he once flew blind in the barnstorming days without any instruments to guide him. His laconic remark amused me.

"Sure, always trusted me. Don't know about these fancy gauges though."

We continued climbing at 800-foot per minute and I was

able to widen our turn considerably without losing the core. At 9,000 feet, the lift began to wane slightly. Another 700 feet and we departed the cloud heading east. Setting the glide for 46 mph, I allowed the ship to fly hands off and told Pop, "See? All play—no work."

"You or the gauges, Son?"

"My magic, of course. Your old times got to give way, Pop."

He grunted a non-intelligible answer as we left the cloud and broke into the bright sunshine. Above, the sky was a deep blue and below and around all sides of us were smaller clouds dotting every patch of sky.

"Damn!" Pop shouted. "Isn't that beautiful? You know, Son, if I had a cup of coffee and a piece of apple pie right now, I'd think this was pure heaven!"

"How about a restroom?"

"Naw, I'm doing okay. Got my bottle."

I added that when we landed I'd make sure he got some pie and coffee. But I said that in the meantime, he was my copilot and had to work for his ride, so to take the controls while I checked the charts.

It was amazing to watch the innate skill of my father appear when needed. His easy way of handling the glider's controls was better than the rough manner in which he flew powered planes. He seemed to know that sailplanes were feathery, birdlike creatures of flight and deserved his utmost skill.

Flying tailwind at 8,000 feet, we crossed the state highway and some major railroad tracks over the wee town of Belcherville, Texas. Both of us made a few caustic remarks about its name.

My charts showed we'd flown 45 miles with ease. Abeam the small town of St. Jo, with its newly painted gleaming white water tower, we reached the zenith of our flight by climbing in a muscular appearing cloud to 12,300-foot altitude. Soon we had crossed over the Gainesville Army Airfield where an AT-6 trainer buzzed us off our right wing. Leaving, the pilot wagged his wings in a tribute to motorless flight. The noise his engine made was thunderous—beautiful.

Over Sherman, Texas, we got very low. At 1,000 feet above ground I was considering landing in the city's polo field. Pop, peered around the sky and saw a buzzard circling lazily about 150 feet below us.

He pointed to the bird and asked, "You think that guy knows what he's doing?"

"We'll see—guess we don't." I eased the glider over to the buzzard, crossing through a downdraft in between that had me exactly at the bird's altitude when we arrived. Laying the right wingtip practically upon his feathered back, I used the bird as a pivot for our turn. At once we began a strong, smooth climb in the exact center of the thermal. The ugly bird moved his pink neck and his head to stare at us for a few moments then appeared satisfied we meant him no harm and continued turning while studying the ground below.

My father and I almost held our breath during this event. In some strange way, we felt a kindred sense with the buzzard but accorded him our greatest respect. Pop had another terse observation.

"He knows, alright. Might even teach us a thing or two. Hmmph."

I laughed. "To tell the truth, I think that guy could teach us things we haven't even dreamed of yet."

Topping that thermal at 5,800 feet, we realized the day was passing, the sun was lowering and the thermals were getting fewer and weaker. We caught two more thermals, and as we crossed over a small town named Bells, Pop looked at his watch, "Congratulations, Son. You are now a Silver C pilot."

I must have given a whoop or two but as the lift was now fast disappearing, my attention had to stay on the task at hand.

Between Savoy and Bonham, Texas, we flew over another circling glider and saw that it was my old friend Gus Briegleb in one of his own sailplanes. I circled over him but in less than ten turns the lift totally died. Both of us made a beeline for the airport at Bonham, Texas. Landing, we knew our flight had been 14-miles short of our intended goal of Paris, Texas.

On the ground, Pop lectured everyone in sight. "My kid made it, he did. Got him a Silver C. Chip off the old blockhead, I guess."

Time would ultimately prove that this trip to Texas would be the highlight of Pop's mature years. Though I'd placed 40 in the field of 100-plus contestants, neither Pop or Lorry said anything about it.

For young Lorry Wilkinson, the experience might have solidified a desire for aviation achievement and propelled him into a career. It is possible that any of you reading this could have been his passenger on one of Western Airline's DC-10's. After reaching seniority number 15 and flying as a scheduled airplane pilot for over 32 years, he is now retired in the state of Washington. Does he like to fuss around airplanes after all that experience? Maybe you can find him living on several acres of ground at a private airport with a few other flying types. His time is occupied building small airplanes—just for fun, mind you.

Look magazine got their story and I got my precious Silver C. I have number 83; it is classed as a pioneer award. Today there are Gold and Diamond C's but when I got mine, there was only one kind, brother.

If awards must be considered, I think back and realize the three of us should have received a feather or two from the buzzard who made our last Texas flight a success.

Wherever he is, I think Pop would agree.

46 ARGENTINE FERRY FLIGHT

The popularity of airplanes, as far as the public is concerned, is that they shorten distances by traveling faster. However, one flight I made, if compared to a walking mule, might have been slower.

By December 15, 1946, my crew and I were ready to deliver our first transport airplane for the Argentine Government to Buenos Aires, Argentina, from Southern California. The three of us: Teniente Benigno Andrada (Lieutenant Ben Andrada), copilot; Ken Steffe, the flight engineer/mechanic, and, myself went through the checklist and decided all necessities had been met. The Argentine Consulate in Los Angeles had assured me that diplomatic clearances for all probable landing points had been granted. When I asked them if I needed to carry a verifying paper, they smiled and said, "No."

Much of the preparation time had been spent tracking down the various visas with which to travel through countries enroute, and I thought all was in readiness except for the airplane.

Posing before departure. Second from left is Lt. Andrada. Next right: Author and Ken Steffe with members of the Argentine Purchasing Commission.

Our converted war surplus Army C-47 was now a sleek airline DC-3, Argentine identification LV-XFR. Military bucket seats had yielded to a sparkling airline interior. All components had been overhauled, radios equipped with international frequencies and dual direction-finders added. Only one item bothered me.

Before takeoff, I'd grumbled about the tires that though reported as new, were seriously weather-checked. When I asked the modification company's rep how long the tires had been in storage, he assured me they were new and serviceable. Walking away, he made a comment about pilots being "worry-warts."

After a picture had been taken of the crew standing in front of the airplane with members of the Argentine Purchasing Commission for my personal scrapbook, we loaded our bags and were off. It was January 30, 1947, 10 A.M., PST.

From the Van Nuys, California, airport we made our first night's layover at Mazatlan, Mexico. Officials at the Mexican Port of Entry had no prior notice of an Argentine airplane coming in. I gave the official in charge two aerosol cans of fly-killer and he granted our clearance. Well, I thought, I guess bureaucrats the worldwide are slow.

Next day we flew to Mexico City for our second overnight stay. Our handsome copilot, Andrada, had been away from Argentina for several months and told us he was in need of feminine company. Enroute from the airport to the hotel he eyed the young beautiful Mexican girls and announced he would stay in his own private room at the hotel and meet us for breakfast in the morning at the hotel coffee shop. We agreed he was a big boy and none of us his keeper, so, why not?

Next morning in the coffee shop our breakfast was on time; Andrada was not. After eating, we asked the hotel clerk for permission to examine Andrada's room. We thought it possible our copilot had overslept. But his bed had not been used and there was no sign of his personal luggage. Andrada was mysteriously missing.

I phoned the Argentine Consulate and explained our dilemma. They said not to worry, "Mexico City is such a friendly *simpatico* town. Go to the airplane and prepare for your flight. He will show up."

Ken and I arrived at the airport, checked everywhere we could but still no copilot. About 10, we'd checked enroute weather, filed our flight plan to Guatemala City and refueled the airplane. Andrada still absent, we decided we would leave without our missing companion.

As we were about to enter the plane, a taxi stormed up—tires squealing and followed by a cloud of dust. We saw Andrada climb out of the cab and start running toward the airplane. Ken had taken the right seat to fill in for the missing copilot. When Andrada approached through the companionway, the odor of stale alcohol almost made Ken and I drunk. His slurred speech, dragon-like breath and bloodshot eyes told us clearly where he'd been all night and what he had been doing.

I was angry. "Whereinhell you been? We were worried."

Andrada smiled inanely, rolled his eyes and blew a kiss at the sky. "Ah, that Martita! What a beautiful body! Ahhh!" I told him to get lost and he staggered into the passenger cabin, literally fell into one of the seats and was instantly asleep. Ken laughed and asked, "Don't you wish you were that young?"

"I am that young," I retorted. "My wrinkles came from flying too many tired airplanes, not from chasing girls."

"Tch-tch! Still want me to fill in for him?"

"Do you see anyone else around? Let's go."

Ten minutes later we took off for Guatemala. Volcano Popocatapetl drifted by our left wing. We studied the long streamer of snow flowing southeast off its peak. Still higher than our enroute altitude, it was impressive.

As we flew toward the Gulf of Tehuantepec, both of us would occasionally look back through the open cockpit door to check on Andrada. He was motionless, only his heaving chest proving he was alive. For some time Ken and I wondered about what Martita could look like, what type of equipment she carried to make her so volatile, and what her appearance could be after the obvious heavy night of jousting with *amore*. Our conclusion was that neither of us really wanted to know.

We flew through the Gulf of Tehuantepec with its perpetually rough air, across Tapachula Airport a mile inshore from the Pacific Ocean and then angled northeast toward our destination, Guatemala City.

Our copilot came to life and stood in the companionway between us watching the scenery. He still could not converse normally but would periodically utter, "Martita—Martita!" Ken and I agreed he made her name sound like a Gershwin rhapsody.

Guatemala Airport came into view and I tried calling the tower for landing clearance with my rusty Spanish. Though my language was faulty, when the tower answered their's was impossible to decipher. As I hung up the microphone, I said a very dirty word to express my frustration. Instantly, the cabin speaker boomed, "You guys Yankees? So are we. We have only a single runway, land to the north and cleared to land."

The three of us laughed as I reduced power for the landing. "Murphy won't get us today," I said.

I think the landing might have been one of the smoothest I've ever made in a DC-3. But as we slowed, a loud rumbling noise transmitted itself into the cockpit from the right wing area. Slowing more, the right wing began to sag toward the runway surface. Using a full rudder was still not enough control to prevent the airplane from easing off the edge of the concrete. I had negated the use of brakes for I had a good idea what was causing our problem and trying to brake would have been worse.

We were down. We were safe. And we certainly had a very flat tire on the right side. *Murphy, I hate you.*

So, we wanted to see Guatemala City? For twelve days we saw it. We visited nearby volcanoes. We went through the pink palace many times. We took in a movie until the bugs biting our legs drove us out. And when we'd seen all that tourists normally do, like all pilots we gravitated to the airport in search of familiar objects.

Ken examined the Guatemala Air Force's only pursuit plane, an ancient Boeing P-26, complete with wingtips nearly worn off due to the uncountable groundloops. As we examined the P-26, Andrada yelped and pointed toward the north end of the airport. There, struggling with the choppy air on its approach to a landing, was a Stearman duster biplane. Lower and lower, the pilot allowed the plane to get until finally the inevitable happened: he hit the top of a tall pine tree near the end of the runway. We made a move to run in that direction when we saw the airplane thump heavily to the ground, breaking its landing gear in the process. Several uniformed men ran out, warned us to return to the Airport Terminal area and proceeded toward the downed biplane.

A half hour later, as we waited for a taxi to return us to

the hotel, we saw the uniformed men—soldiers—bring the pilot out as they waited for an Army vehicle. The pilot recognized us as Yankees and told us his story. It seems when he clipped the tree, there was a Guatemala college student resting in its top branches studying for a coming exam. Of course, the student fell out of the tree when the Stearman hit it, and broke a leg. "Tex," the pilot, was immediately considered an "enemy of the people" and arrested. Seems he'd been hired to ferry the plane to the Canal Zone after its sale.

That night we visited the Argentine Consulate to learn if our new tire had arrived by air-freight. It had not but the Consul suggested we use his short-wave radio and send messages back to our home in Los Angeles. To be newsy, I said we were fine and told of witnessing Tex's weird event. Early the next morning I received an urgent telegram at the hotel. It stated:

> "GLAD YOU WERE NOT INJURED IN CRASH. CAN YOU GET OUT OF JAIL?"

To us, it was obvious old Murphy spoke Spanish.

By February 2, we had our tire installed and were enroute to the Panama Canal Zone. Deciding to land at David, Panama, for fuel, we ate sandwiches for lunch at the small coffee shop in the terminal building. The others had coffee; I had a bottle of Orange Crush. Studying our charts, we saw it was only about a five-hour flight to Guayaquil, Ecuador, from David if we flew direct and avoided landing in Panama. As we'd been warned by other pilots the paperwork involved for foreign airplanes was fearsome, we elected to make the ocean hop. Rational; it would avoid a paperwork delay and save us an entire day. The sole question would be how easy or tough the intertropical front would be.

As we taxied toward our takeoff point I saw that our Argentine copilot was looking more and more concerned. When I'd set the brakes, I asked, "So what is troubling you?"

He looked hurt. "I have never in my life taken an airplane over an ocean." His fear was obvious.

"Hey friend, we intend to go over the ocean, not in it. Its an easy flight. Relax." In the companionway, Ken Steffe added, "Sure, might even see some great naked mermaids out there!"

Andrada gave both of us a wounded-animal look, hunched

down in his seat and began to chew his fingernails. I felt sorry for him but thought we'd laugh about the hop later that day. We took off and climbed to our cruising altitude of 5,000 feet.

However, as Murhpy's law, "What can happen—will," was next up.

About an hour and a half into our flight, part of it on instruments, but apparently a stable day for the unpredictable front, I felt the pangs of intestinal distress. In full force, Montezuma's Revenge hit me. I gave the controls to Andrada and made a dash into the rear of the passenger compartment. With the door open, I could monitor the cockpit activity while trying to ease my own emergency.

Despite my concern over Montezuma's effects, I noticed whenever Andrada bent his head down and tried to fly by instruments the airplane began to go out of control. As I pondered this, Ken looked back at me and spread his hands in a "what now?" pose.

Having a few moments respite from my problem, I ran back to the cockpit and ordered Ken to sit in the left seat I had vacated. Understanding what I was about to do, Andrada was now clearly petrified.

Ken took the controls and looked at me for instructions. He was not a trained pilot but could fly passably in clear, smooth air. What we were rapidly heading into was choppy, blind-flying conditions with areas of very heavy rain.

"Keep your head down, Ken. Keep your eyes on the artificial horizon and nothing else. Make the little airplane on the dial stay level with its bar. Keep it level! Don't concern yourself about anything else. Do you understand?"

"Sure, I think I can do that."

He did as I'd requested and after a few minutes, I could see that he was capable of keeping the airplane level and in control despite the occasional chop. Then I ran back to my "duty-post" in the rear.

Between attacks, I would peer forward to assess the situation. Ken was busy flying, his eyes were riveted to the instrument panel. Andrada was gone. His body was slumped into the corner of the seat as far as he could get and I could see his shoulders shaking uncontrollably.

Fortunately, my problem ended after a half hour of our dilemma, and I returned to the cockpit to relieve Ken. Sneaking a glance at my copilot as often as I could between periods of smooth air, I felt total sympathy for him. A good pilot ordinarily, he knew better than Ken Steffe that if control of the airplane was lost due to unexpected turbulence, all of us could be killed. That fact plus his lack of experience flying transport airplanes and crossing strange oceans was too much for the way he was wired, so his circuits had blown. It has happened to others and will happen many more times in the flying business. I would not judge him.

Another 15 minutes and Andrada became aware the front had modified and the air was smoothing out though we still flew through cells of rain that smacked the windshield as if gravel had been shot at us from a gun. My pressured copilot looked at me. I winked and said, "What the hell you worried about? It ain't your airplane!"

That brought a laugh and a "thank you" from him. I then instructed him the same as I had Ken about the artificial horizon and added, "If you imagine its a hole in the airplane and you are looking through it, you'll think you're flying in nice clear air." And I turned the controls over to him then.

Andrada struggled for a few minutes as I urged him to relax. Shortly, he got the hang of what he was trying to do and a smile crossed his face. Once, he managed to take his eyes off the instruments to give me an appreciative smile. I had helped my Latin friend face the *toro of his fear*. And he had won.

At three hours and 30 minutes I turned one of the ADF's (Automatic Direction Finder) to Esmeraldas, Ecuador, and the needle promptly swung to "zero," denoting the landfall station was dead-ahead. Andrada shouted with joy. From the rear, Ken Steffe appeared and asked if we needed any expert help. Graciously, I thanked him.

When the hazy outlines of the coast at Esmeraldas came into view, I thought my copilot would weep again, but this time for joy. He asked, "Easy eh? Like a baby and a bottle?"

"Sure, any kid can do it—even you."

The crisis between friends had passed.

Dodging a few thunderstorms, we flew direct from Esmeraldas to Guayaquil, Ecuador. Landing, we made our downwind leg over the wide river adjacent to the airport and noticed a DC-3 sitting midstream. Apparently on some dark night with a very low ceiling, some poor pilot had missed his approach. The identification of the airline that was once painted on the plane's fuselage was repainted with the word "Ouch."

On the ground I ducked instinctively as we walked to the airport terminal from our plane. A noise like some giant electric razor had assaulted my ears. When we discovered its source, we were not relieved. We had met the equatorial version of the common June Bug. This version, however, was six inches long, about two inches across and an inch thick. At night it would slam into the sloping windows of the passenger terminal and fall dead in a growing heap on the ground. In the morning, farmers would come by with their carts, shovel up the remains and use them as fertilizer for their crops.

Later after a shower and some of the greatest-tasting beer any of us had ever drunk, we walked through the town. A street hawker approached me with a basket of shrunken heads for $25 each. I was horrified. Andrada engaged him in a spirited conversation in Spanish and ended with an amazed expression on his face.

"What gives?" I asked.

"I asked the man if he had any heads with *Rubio* colored hair like yours and Ken's. He said he didn't but if we returned in two weeks he could sell us a pair."

Our horror was complete. Was this a civilized world in which we lived? Was it actually possible that for $25, we could have two souls murdered to enable a street peddler to make a sale? I did not want to think so, but the experience has haunted me ever since.

The morning of February 14, Valentine's Day, we flew on in crisp, clear weather to Lima, Peru.

At Lima, we were faced with two additional problems: No diplomatic clearance was evident and Pan American Airways had no record of a letter of credit. Without the credit, we could not get fuel or use their "Aerophares" to navigate.

The diplomatic clearance situation was solved when I gave a pistol-grip spotlight for an auto to the highest official in evidence.In the morning, Pan American had gotten a telegram from their headquarters authorizing refueling but not their weather forecasting or homing-beacon service. Guess we couldn't have everything.

Next morning we departed for our fuel stop, a spit of land jutting from a miniscule town called Antofagasto. Wiser, I refrained from eating the great looking French-fried seafood served in the terminal building.

After a three-hour and 25-minute flight, we landed at Santiago, Chile. Adjacent to where we'd parked was a forlorn appearing Lancaster bomber that had been converted into an airliner. A Pan-Am pilot saw us inspecting it while we awaited ground transportation and told us its story.

It seems the British were inaugurating an airline flight direct between Buenos Aires, Argentina, and Santiago, Chile. On their flight, they had crossed the Andes Mountains at the airplane's ceiling, 35,000 feet.

"I think they fly their airplanes at whatever is their maximum ceiling," he said. "But when they made this first crossing of the Andes, they flew into a great big thunder-bumper storm that bent the airplane so badly its never flown again . . ." He paused, walked to a wingtip and added, "Look! And help me give it a push."

The four of us pressed the wingtip upward and to our combined astonishment, saw it flex as far as we could reach.

Ken Steffe was most appreciative of the apparent phenomena. He called our attention to a miracle. "If you look at the rivet holes anywhere on the wings, you'll see each one is stretched into an oblong. Nothing broke, but everything bent!"

(I wonder if the thing is still there.)

Next morning we were off early and climbing through the famous pass of the Andes. Cruising at 19,000 feet, without oxygen as our system had malfunctioned, we stayed on the right side of the pass. At its highest point, I took a snapshot of Mount Aconcagua—22,834 feet high—the highest peak in the Andean Mountain chain, studied the phenomenal "Christ of the Andes" statue marking the border between Chile and Argentina, and started the long descent over the approaching Argentine Pampas.

We landed at the Palomar Military Airfield among a gaggle of pre-WWII German Junkers, tri-engined trainers. Our DC-3 was the first modern airplane the Argentine Government owned.

We loved Buenos Aires. The expression "eat your heart out" was more than a cliche in a city where fine food is common. Dinner at the La Estancia steak house cost us a mere $2.15 each. We were served by two waiters, offered a cart with several kinds of soups, drank fine wine, sampled salads from another cart, ate until our eyes bulged from a Chateaubriand cut in thick slabs, nibbled at succulent vegetables, and stuffed our gullets in whatever space was left with pastries that were as light as feathers and obscenely tasteful.

Then we walked down Florida Street—blocked off for pedestrians only, bought fine Alligator purses and shoes at a pittance of their value and ended our evening sitting in a *Confiteria*, sipping liqueurs and listening to bandstands and orchestras that alternated classic and modern music. All this fantastic pleasure was contrasted by only one anomaly.

When the dictator in power at the time, Juan Peron was broadcasting to his people, loud speakers on street corners blared. and if anyone wasn't standing at attention and listening attentively, squads of police sought them out and clubbed them into unconsciousness.

But remember, this was back in the year 1947. At this writing, Argentina has one of the highest inflation rates of any country worldwide.

We left Andrada, happy as anything to be back in his beloved country. There were more airplanes to deliver and as that was my job at the time, I returned for the next mission.

For this first flight, however, it had taken us 19 days enroute and we'd logged 41 hours and 21 minutes flying time. Perhaps a lively mule could have beat us. But as pilots say, "If you have time to spare, go by air!"

Part 7

Potpourri

47 J-3 PILOT AND THE COLD FRONT

Most of us have heard the old cliche, "If it wasn't so tragic, it might be funny." Though the phrase has been around for a while, a personal experience emphasized its truth for me.

It was the summer of 1941 and the attack on Pearl Harbor by the Japanese nation was still ahead. I had recently acquired my commercial pilot certificate, my flight instructor's rating and had been approved to teach the primary Civil Pilot Training Program. To tie a ribbon on all this hard work, I'd even managed to obtain a job as an instructor with the Monrovia Airport Flight School, east of Pasadena, California. The sweat and tears and toil were behind me and I was tired. It was logical for me to reward myself with a short vacation.

My friend Del ran a small airport near Seattle, Washington, and suggested it would be a fine idea if I flew up there to see the great Northwest before nature dropped her winter curtain.

All went well with me and my rented Aeronca "Tandem" until I departed Portland, Oregon. A cold front was forecast to pass the Olympia area the same time I planned to be there. Local pilots thought I could make it CFR (Contract Flight Rules, now VRF), because the cloud spacing would be wide. It seemed safe enough to hear them talk although I had a gnawing feeling inside. New country and weather? I didn't know about that combination. But as this was an emotion rather than logical fact, I pushed aside the uneasy feelings and took off for the final leg of my flight.

When the Aeronca and I flew over the Toledo Emergency Airfield, I began to realize my scud-running experience was mighty poor. I zig-zagged between towering columns of cumulonimbus clouds and it wasn't long before I was hopelessly lost.

Slowly, I crept along at minimum flying speed through the dark rain curtains and the lowering clouds. Seconds seemed like hours until I saw a green field lying in a bowl of tree-covered hills. There I circled for 45 minutes until the storm had passed and I could see Olympia Airport in the distance.

After refueling the airplane and sitting until the total impact of the experience had filtered through my brain, I left Olympia and greeted my friend at his nearby airport. I related my experience and he admitted it was lucky I'd used my brains before it had been too late. I agreed.

My stay was as an ideal vacation should be—pure fun. I was introduced to "Gooey-Duck" digging on the low-tide sandbars of Cape Dungeness. I would not have believed a clam weighing several pounds was in our civilized world. The thing appeared as if it had grown an elephant's truck to its large shell. Del made a couple of gallons of savory clam stew from the one we dug out of its sand-locked home. Several airplanes had flown to the sandbar with us and I was concerned what the consequence would be if one of the planes refused to start. Del had me look inside the baggage compartment of his airplane and I saw that he had planned for such an emergency. Two coils of 200-foot long nylon tow rope were ready for one airplane to tow another home if needed.

The day before I planned to leave we heard an airplane had made a forced landing nearby. Several of us made our way into the soggy field where we saw a smiling, young blond pilot surveying his nosed-up J-3 Cub and its broken propeller. When Del asked what happened, the pilot said, "Nuthin' much. The engine quit so I glided around for a while until I saw the ground and landed."

My friend and I looked skyward. A very active cold front recently had passed through, leaving a ceiling of less than 800 feet.

"How high were you when the engine quit?" I had to know.

"Bout 4,000 feet."

Del and I couldn't believe what we were hearing.

"Were you in a hole up there?"

"Nope." He gave that insane smile again, "I was right in the middle of 'em."

I knew my mouth was hanging open. "For how long?"

"Until it ran outta gas. About two-and-a-half hours."

The others exchanged knowing glances. I was still determined to know more. "Whereinhell did you start from?"

"Yakima," he said, still smiling.

"And in the clouds?"

"Yep."

"Four-thousand feet, all the way?"

"Yep."

Trying to conceal a smile, Del tugged me aside and asked if I knew the elevation of Stampede Pass between Yakima, Washington, and Seattle. Indeed I did. I'd studied the Sectionals that showed the pass to be 3,800-feet high but surrounded by mountains more than 6,000-foot elevation. I walked back to the super-confident young man.

"You flew all the way, blind?" I had to hear it again.

"Yep!" His tone of voice was so proud.

All of us but the pilot stood silently for a few minutes knowing the CAA "Federales" would be there soon.

It wasn't a long wait before two Safety Agents showed up and questioned the brash fellow, who easily and proudly admitted the facts of his flight. Without being prompted, he told how, when the cabin windows had iced up, he had flown "hands-off" and steered a compass heading with his feet only.

One of the CAA men couldn't help asking, "And where in the world did you get that advice?"

The blond youngster laughed, "I thought you'd never ask. I read about it in a book about the old airmail pilots. It worked for them—it worked for me!"

Now all the mouths of those listening hung open. The CAA men started to ask more questions but thought the idea was useless so advised him of the many flight rules he'd broken. They claimed he was "a menace to himself, to society and to aviation," and suspended his student pilot license on the spot.

As far as I know, this man might still be alive. If he is, it only proves that miracles abound and old Murphy and his law must have been napping. Luckily, Del wrote to me later that the man had given up flying.

I thought of my own faux pas.

48 MISADVENTURES INTO CAA (FAA)

For a moment, let's consider one of the most blatant forms of advertising in our land: the military recruitment poster.

Personally, the sight of Uncle Sam pointing his finger at me as though I'd committed a crime has never caused me to consider joining our armed forces. I've seen children frightened by such visages.

It's doubtful most people make major life decisions through any form of advertising. In tracing causes in one's life there's always a chain of circumstances. As some accidents, we see a trigger-mechanism followed by a falling line of domino effects, each a significant segment of an overall cause.

At the end of 1947 there were subtle causes working within me to change my life's direction. With the Argentine adventure finished, I'd flown almost a year ferrying transport airplanes worldwide for airlines and governments. None of these planes were in safe condition, having sat in surplus storage areas over long periods.

However, the above fact was the cause of the ferrying business opportunities. For example: if an airline purchased a war surplus airplane cheaply and desired it to be at their home base or modification center, but assessed it as unsafe for their own pilots, guess who got the job of delivery?

This type of flying may have put food in baby's mouth, but only as long as papa-pilot stayed alive doing so. The probable end to such a gamble was not a happy conclusion. The least problem accompanying such flying was an ulcer. Constant stress was an ulcer's presumed cause and only a release from it invited a cure. I had one—a beaut.

Fed up, an unexpected telegram offered an answer to my problem.

I'd almost forgotten that I'd sent in an application to the Civil Aeronautics Administration (CAA) applying for a position

CAA Aero Center graduates. Author, 3rd., from left, kneeling.

as a Federal Aviation Safety Agent. When the telegram came offering me the job at a beginning salary of GS-10, I was eager to accept.

The CAA may not have been as gross as the military poster, but to many pilots who'd experienced similar types of flying jobs as I had endured, it was even more powerful. Civil Service offered a permanency, plus a promise of upward income. Coupled with these assets, there was flying action, safety, and an innate respect for the power and prestige inherent in the position.

January 26, 1948, I started my orientation class at the CAA headquarters adjacent to the Washington, D.C., mall. There in the shadow of the Washington Monument, for a full month, I and my fellow aspirants were fed an overblown diet of CAA history, methods of executing paperwork, policy, policy—and more policy. Having joined with a veteran's preference, there was a little chance I could fail the training. And if the flying phase at the Oklahoma Center found one flying passably, he could expect to be assigned a field post as an Aviation Safety Agent.

On February 28, my family and I arrived in Oklahoma City and rented a wee motel cottage 10 miles south of the city center.

As boring as the paperwork shuffling had been in the orientation phase, it was worth it to be back in the air. At the Center we would fly a wide variety of airplanes with numerous, capable instructors, bringing our skills up to razor sharpness and standardizing the maneuvers on flight tests.

An instructor who taught me the finer points of the Flight Instructor requirements was Ken Archer. Ken wasn't good—he was superb. After Ken's instructions, a student knew how to do a maneuver perfectly, could explain it in depth, and was able to spot weak or dangerous trends in the applicant he was testing.

That phase of the flying was almost as exciting as the two tornados that sped through a week apart.

The Oklahoma City experience was the good part of CAA—I regret to admit that all of it didn't evolve that way.

On March 3, we left Okalhoma City and headed for our first reporting section for further assignment to a district office. I was ordered to report to the 7th Region Headquarters in Seattle, Washington. We arrived there March 10.

Upon reporting to the R.O. (Regional Office), I was dismayed to find the building located in the skid row section of the city. The building was ancient and the offices were cold, drafty and perpetually musty.

I was introduced to my R.O. supervisors: Dave Nelson, Carl Rothenberger and Charlie Walker. Dave appeared the sober and quiet type. Rothenberger tended toward the acerbic. Charlie Walker had been with CAA almost since its inception and was acknowledged as "Peck's bad boy" of all the agents. Tolerating the R.O. and its paperwork, Charlie was happy only when he was in an airplane.

It appeared I was a problem. The R.O. had not been told by Washington that a new agent would be sent to them for field assignment so they faced a dilemma. Most of the field offices had a full staff equal to their workload. If the activity did not warrant an additional person, funds would not be allocated.

Near the end of April they thought I would be sent to the district office at Helena, Montana. When I learned this, I told Dave Nelson how I'd had a few confrontations with C.A. LeFever when I was teaching Civilian Pilot Training Program in Monrovia, California. Little did I know then he might be my boss at a future time. Dave, bless him, admitted that serving under LeFever would start me with two strikes. Hearing this, they shelved that plan.

Their final solution was to assume that if I was sent to the local General Aviation District Office (GADO), at Boeing Field, I would cause an increase in their paperwork, and thus would be justified in being added to the staff. No, I never did fully understand this type of government-ese thinking, either.

On the morning of May 1, 1948, I reported to my supervising agent at Boeing Field, Joe Princen. He introduced me to the other Airman Agents; Bob Jones, and ex-Navy pilot whose nose fit an eagle better than a human's, and Bob Phelps, who was tacitly considered the assistant to Princen.

As most of my life I had been self-employed, I was brash, and in looking back, realize my gung-ho attitude was grating to others. When I returned from coffee one morning, Jones and Phelps stopped their loud discussions as I entered the room. It was obvious they had been discussing me. All of us were momentarily embarrassed. For a few minutes we sat there silently.

Jones finally spoke to Phelps. "Shall we tell him?"

Phelps, a handsome man with wavy brown hair, full face and a beautific smile, laughed. "Hell yes! He's got to start somewhere."

"Wh—what's up, guys?" I asked.

Phelps tried to answer but both he and Jones went into a fit of laughter.

Jones stopped choking for a moment and said, "Lana Kurtzer needs his Flight Examiner rating renewed." And that inane statement triggered more loud laughter.

Dumb me: "Is he that bad?" I asked and knew that my expressions showed my doubt about their intentions.

My question increased the amount and volume of their guffaws, now almost hysterical. From the next office, Joe Princen heard the noise and came into our office. "What's with you guys?" he asked. "Nothing can be that funny."

A secretary passing the open door heard the commotion and peeked into the room. She waited, smiling. A few moments later, Spike Galvin, our crusty Aircraft Agent, heard the racket and came to the door to investigate. "What did these birds do, steal an old lady's cane?"

Phelps wiped his eyes and announced, "You'll never believe this. Ha-ha-hee-hee! Our brand new agent asked how *bad* Lana Kurtzer flies."

I couldn't believe it. Though I had no idea if they were discussing a man or a woman from the name, each time one spoke, it seemed to generate more laughter.

"Bad? Kurtzer?" Princen found the word to be incredulous.

Galvin snorted, "Send him—send him. Kurtzer will eat him alive!" And Spike returned to the other office chuckling happily. I felt they were discussing me as if I weren't there.

The secretary stifled her giggles and returned to the outer office. Joe could no longer talk as his laughter had almost doubled him. But he managed to say, "Sure, send Gerry. Great training!"

Obviously, I was not looking forward to the assignment, my very first with CAA.

Deeply concerned, inwardly upset and trying to hide it, I drove to the Kurtzer Flying Service, a seaplane operation at the south end of Lake Union. Tall, rigidly straight, a man with a regal bearing, Lana Kurtzer ushered me into his office and closed the door.

As Kurtzer sat in his chair I wondered who would be checking whom. To say his manner was imposing would be an understatement. Quietly serious, one who thought before speaking and then gave his message with carefully measured words, he smiled slightly and asked, "How much seaplane flying have you done, Mr. Casey?"

I hoped my reactive gulp was inaudible and thought about getting my original rating in a 40-hp Cub on floats and the PBY deliveries I'd made while serving in the Ferrying Command. A red flag in my mind cautioned this was not the time to talk about any of my flying exploits. Guardedly, almost a whisper, I answered, "Not very much, Mister Kurtzer."

"Hmmm."

As he studied me I looked at the photos of planes upon his wall. I heard the light tapping of his pencil stop and gave him my attention.

"So, you are here to check my flying?"

I sensed my answer could well be the pivot point of my entire CAA career. Before responding, I took several deep, slow breaths.

"Let's put it this way, sir," my voice was a bit shaky but cleared when I coughed. "If you show me some seaplane techniques that any pilot needs to know, we can consider your examiner rating renewed as of this moment."

Walking from his office, through the barn-like hangar and onto the float ramps, he may have given me an approving pat on the back—I do not recall. To this day though, I regard the ensuing flight as one of the highlights of my life.

Kurtzer took off toward nearby Lake Washington, a few miles east of his base. If I didn't goof up, I thought this man might award me a doctor-of-seaplane degree. Obviously, I was the student; he was the master.

As I observed his flying, I was amazed at the flawlessly smooth way he handled the under-powered and ungainly T-Craft floatplane. For one of the rare times in my aviation career, I observed a pilot who—in the truest sense of the word—*wore* the airplane. In the following hour I learned more about seaplane flying than I'd ever read in any book.

During my several years with CAA in Seattle, I was the agent usually chosen to renew Kurtzer's flight examiner rating. Unless Bob Jones and Bob Phelps happen to read this—which I hope they will—no one has known why the famous taskmaster of seaplanes didn't totally demoralize the brand new CAA agent.

* * * * * *

Investigating accidents was a grim, unpleasant part of the job. In the State of Washington, airplanes do not usually go down in nice flat areas where walking is easy. Many mishaps occurred when pilots flew beyond their capabilities in severe weather. And usually, the accident site was on some granite mountain top or in a thickly wooded forest, far from civilization.

The CAA often aided the Civil Aeronautics Board (CAB) which was charged with determining accident causes at that time (now NTSB). Heading the Seattle CAB office was Leon Cuddeback, former chief pilot of Walter Varney's pioneer airmail operation. I was fortunate that I had the pleasure of working with a man who had gotten his wisdom the hard way—by experience and much reasoning. His education to agents in CAA was a rare and treasured experience. His tales of the early airmail days were golden. But even this great man did not prepare me for the disillusionment I felt investigating some of the accidents.

Except for the local police or coroner, we were often the first at the accident scene. Many times it was a fatal accident and the victims were still at the scene. Too many times in our investigations, when we back-tracked the events leading to the time of the accident, we would learn the victims had large amounts of cash. Many flights had been people vacationing or making a long air journey. At the scene it was our responsibility to search for the pilot's flight certificates, airplane logs and other data. The shock to which none of us could ever reconcile was finding that the officials before us had "lifted" the money from the bodies.

No charges were ever made on these occasions and a further point of distress to me was finally accepting the fact that no bureaucracy ever admits to any culpability for its actions—no matter what. And I was a member of its best and its worst.

* * * * * *

Federal Aviation Regulations (FARs) were violated by pilots with regularity. All the FARs were promulgated to protect the public interest. Thus it was that the field agent sought to effect corrective action rather that purely punitive measures.

Sometimes a pilot would buzz a house and endanger the occupants and himself. There were flights when uncertificated student pilots would carry passengers illegally. On rare occasions, a mechanic or an approved air agency repair station would engage in an unsafe and illegal practice because of an economic crisis. In review, I can truthfully say that most violations filed by our office were warranted. A few were questionable. One or two, perhaps, were unwarranted.

Then there were the exceptions of some individual who flaunted the regulations, imperiled others' lives, but had enough political clout to escape the legal consequences. One in particular I remember.

We began to receive verbal complaints about a pilot who flew for a major lumber company located in our area. Other pilots and airport operators complained about his rude behavior when taxiing his twin-engine plane on small airports. Seems when he was ready to depart from his parking place, he would open his throttle wide and spin the airplane around brutally regardless of what was behind or near him. Bystanders suffered from eyes full of gravel and light fabric-covered training planes were often damaged.

When we tried to get written complaints, no one would comply with our requests. As a great number of those affected worked for, or indirectly made their living off the huge firm's business activities, they were afraid of retaliation. Without a written complaint, we were unable to process a violation. As in any deviation from a law, there had to be reasonable cause and actual proof before our office could act.

As time went on, we started hearing other types of complaints about this pilot. Pilots would see him climb into an overcast and make short flights without a legal instrument flight clearance from FAA Air Traffic Control. Now, his actions were extremely serious as he could easily cause a mid-air collision while flying in clouds. The other airplane could be an airliner or a military craft. Countless lives could be lost due to this man's contempt for others. Still without written complaints, we were stymied.

Then we got the lucky break for which we'd hoped.

An airline crew happened to see the man's airplane flying in and out of the clouds at their flight level, managed to read his identification number and alerted air traffic control. Immediately, the controller ordered all airplanes under his sector to take emergency headings away from the illegal airplane. A FAA employee of the Airports Branch then saw the lumber company airplane make a descent out of the clouds, circle and land at the airport. It was a remarkable coincidence that he had been at the right place at the right time.

Within the day we had six letters: one from the FAA employee at the airport, three from the airline crew and two from air traffic controllers who had a record of the emergency on recording tape. We went to work. I was chosen to accumulate the data and sign the violation form. Due to the seriousness of the matter, I urged the Regional Office to make an emergency suspension of the errant pilot's flight certificate. However, the political power of the lumber company was felt when the R.O. decided to let the normal course of events proceed. Meanwhile the man continued to fly and, we were told verbally, still flew on instruments without a clearance.

I received a few unidentified phone calls advising that I should cancel the violation or regret it. Then, the pilot stated before witnesses that his company was going to have me transferred to Alaska, or maybe Siberia. At times fate is amazing. For several years I had been operating a building contracting business and had been associating with the Special Agent in Charge of a Federal agency. When I informed him of the threats and admitted I was enraged, he advised me to cool it, that he would get it cleared up immediately.

Later, my friend and associate related how he had made one phone call to the lumber company's president and advised him of the penalties for threatening a federal officer. The entire affair suddenly cooled. The pilot was then given a one-day suspension during his CAB hearing, effective the day of the hearing. He continued to fly and I stayed in Seattle during the entire remainder of my CAA career.

The event changed my outlook for I could never afterwards regard my services as benefitting the public interest as it should have.

* * * * * *

There was one violation I filed that I regret to this day and has caused me anguish ever since.

While on a flight test, I witnessed an airplane in a practice area making simulated racing laps between two large trees in an open field. Curious, I took the controls from the applicant and glided down to identify the airplane and its occupants. When I was closer, I realized with a shock it was an airport operator I knew, respected and considered a friend. His school was an approved air agency and he was one of our Private Pilot Flight Examiners. His behavior was illegal and inappropriate according to the regulations.

In my office during the interview prior to filing a violation, he admitted he had pulled a dumb trick and said it would not happen again.

I worried for several days about the situation, but fresh from the fiasco of the errant lumber company pilot, I decided a violation should be filed with a recommendation for minimum penalty.

Others in the office said I was harsh and that corrective action had been achieved so why not cancel the violation.

I did not. My cohorts were right and I was wrong. The man in question was a bigger man than me for he bore me no ill-will afterwards. Maybe I should forgive myself for being a mistake-making organism they call a human being.

* * * * * *

Midway through my term with CAA, Lorry Wilkinson, one of my crew in the Silver C Odyssey, showed up in Seattle. He'd enlisted in the Navy and was stationed at nearby Whidbey Island Naval Air Station. By avoiding booze and girls he had managed to save $1,000 with which to buy an airplane. We found a good used Aeronca 7AC Champion from him and he bought it.

Each weekend he could get a pass, he would hitch-hike to Seattle where I would give him dual training. As I'd previously suspected, his aptitude was well above average. He soloed quickly and went all out to get the ratings that would eventually land him in the cockpit of an airliner.

When he was ready to take his Instrument Rating flight test, I elected to do the job. To avoid any rumors of favoritism, I gave him the severest test I'd ever handed to anyone.

In a Cessna 172 and under the hood, I had him do all the maneuvers required then ordered a special ending that would have demoralized most any applicant.

Pretending I was the controller, I issued him instructions

to make a ground controlled approach to an unused military flight strip. Only this one would be different. Instead of the usual breakoff from the approach a few hundred feet short of landing, I had Lorry fly right on down to the runway and make an actual landing totally by the primary blind flying instruments. Frankly, I wouldn't have believed it possible for any pilot to have landed the plane safely and then rolled to a stop while blind. But he did and he did it well.

Any of you might have recently ridden as passenger with him when Lorry was the Captain of a Western Airlines DC-10.

Occasionally we would be charged with giving a medical flight test. Here, the object was to fly with a person who had a physical handicap and determine if he or she could compensate for the deficiency.

Most of the medical flight tests were for people with diminished vision. We faithfully followed CAA's Manual of Procedure issued by the Washington brains that directed us to have another airplane, by pre-arrangement, fly a collision course on the side of the applicant's deficiency. If the applicant saw the airplane coming far enough away to take corrective action without surprise, the MOP stated he should be approved.

I'd given many of these tests and all the applicants had shown no problem. I gave one test to a one-eyed applicant who performed so well that I could not determine any difference between him and that of a person with normal vision. On the ground after the test I remarked on how well he had compensated for his problem. This delightful man then said, "I'll tell you a secret, buddy. We are always protecting our blind side. Had you checked me on my good side, we both might be dead from a mid-air!"

So much for the wisdom of the Washington types.

* * * *

My disenchantment with the CAA career came insidiously and irrevocably as far as I was concerned.

During my later days, we were furnished with a J-3 Piper Cub equipped with an angle-of-attack indicator on the wing. It was common for most light planes to have a stall-warning indicator that gave off a shrill sound starting about 10 percent above a stall then progressed louder as the stall deepened. In attempting to standardize all aviation maneuvers, CAA had granted an eastern college a study fund with which to investigate stalls and recommend a standard recovery method. When we in the field heard about this and began to demonstrate the relationship between angle-of-attack and stalls, we wondered why the experts at the Aeronautical Center in Oklahoma City hadn't been utilized.

But the good little boys that we were, we flew the Cub around our territory demonstrating what most pilots already knew.

When later, we agents received a bound volume describing the university's findings, we were all disenchanted. Reading in the section on "stalls during turns," we were aghast to discover the university had not investigated stalls in turns because, by their words, "they were too unpredictable."

Indeed, stalls inadvertently entered from steep turns are a significant cause of light plane fatalities at this writing. And they were so at the time of the university's study.

Worse, the non-professionals at the university urged CAA to advocate every pilot recover from stalls "with the nose on the horizon." This is still the procedure today but most pilots are aware an airplane "knows no horizon—only relative air."

Dead wrong. Dead pilots. Dead crazy.

When I wrote my opinions of the study as all the field agents were supposed to do, I challenged the study and angrily charged CAA with stupidity. I knew it was coming and it did—I was severely chastised.

Rebel that I was, on a few occasions I still was granted letters of commendation for my personnel file.

I was requested to formulate written tests for glider pilots—they had none at that time—and the meterology tests for the Commercial Pilot, Instrument Rating and Flight Dispatcher Certificates.

Even today, a few of my original test questions can be found on FAA written examinations.

In time, the irrational approach to serving the public by CAA became a heavy weight. As my contracting business was growing and being unable to get a CAA transfer to a warmer climate, I decided to return to the real world where a wise teacher would one day write on a blackboard before me:

"Institutions are born to serve an idea. As long as they do, they are viable. When they stop serving the idea and become self-serving, they are invalid."

This statement does not make for peace in our world today.

49 AN UNWANTED SOLO

It was still early in the morning and the Southern California fog lay as a cloying blanket over the small rectangular field they called the Compton Airport.

Even in those days the airport wasn't much to brag about. Flying from it were two Jennies, a Standard J-1 with an OXX-6 engine, and a Thomas Morse S-4 Scout once used by the airport's owner to give aerobatic performances. Somehow, an early model Vought biplane with a 300-hp Hisso engine had appeared on the field. No one seemed to know from where it came nor cared. Across the field where the airplanes would land and take off was a dairy, and the black and white Geurnsey cows were lowing softly, waiting to be fed. Their breathing left small blobs of fog above their heads.

It had been two years since the airport had started in 1925. At first the Compton, California, city fathers wanted to close it down. But after Jimmie Angel had given most of them a passenger ride in the airport owner's Jenny, they stopped their complaints. Two began to take flying lessons.

Offering the public a free show every weekend, the airport owner saw to it that Jimmie or Eddie Angel gave an airshow performance. If he was broke, Shorty Stark would make a parachute jump for $5. On one weekend, the airport owner paid him $20 and Shorty made four "breakaway" jumps with four 28-foot chutes. The crowd roared each time he cut a chute loose and dropped prior to opening the next one. All those watching said he was an idiot. But Shorty was no idiot. He packed his own chutes and stayed alive.

Ending their barnstorming as the "Angel Flying Circus," working the midwest, the entire family had migrated to the Compton area. Glenn, the father, had always managed to keep the family intact with his artisan skill as a carpenter. Parker had complete plans for a monoplane of his own design that would carry six people and be powered by a Wright J-5 engine. The family was convinced that if they could get a factory going to build and sell parker's design, they would all become rich.

Each member occupied a special niche for which he or she was best suited. Stable Eddie was generally in an airplane's cockpit instructing or giving aerobatic performances. Most of the family's's income came from Eddie Angel's flying. Jimmie Angel, the World War I flyer, explorer, test-pilot of note, entrepreneur, raconteur, and all-around promoter was the tribe's front man. His picture could always be found once weekly on the front page of some newspaper.

By then the Compton Airport had a wooden hangar with a packed gravel and sand floor. All the airplanes were tied outside as the hangar was used solely as a repair shop. In it, every day after school and usually on weekends, sat this kid—a child really—working diligently on an airplane engine. Though only a few months past his 12th birthday, he'd picked up an uncanny skill for scraping perfect fits on bearings for rods and crankshafts of the airplane engines. He could set the crankshaft on a Hisso or an OX-5 faster than any adult mechanic and his work was considered professional.

Often one of the adults would try to trap the boy by proclaiming that as he knew nothing about the technical aspects of gear depthing, he couldn't possibly do a satisfactory job of fitting bearings. But as the bumble bee technically cannot fly, the boy didn't even know what "depthing" meant. But he had this special feel for an engine, see? As this child could not explain his ability, neither could the adults around him explain the child's special talent. But he was good. His engine jobs lasted longer than most anyone's in the Southern California area.

His father, the airport's owner, knew a good thing when he saw it and always managed to keep an engine waiting in the hangar shop for the boy to work on. Each week, usually on Mondays, the boy would be paid for his mechanical services with a 15-minute airplane lesson. Lately, Jimmie Angel had volunteered to be the boy's flight instructor for as he told his brother Eddie, "It's an easy job flying with the kid. We figure he's got about 50 hours of time already. He flies the Standard around the field about as good as anybody. All I have to do with him is just sit."

Hearing this, the boy's father had warned the two brothers, "Well for gawd's sake, don't tell him that. He might quit scraping."

With the folding doors of the hangar open, the boy could watch all the airplanes take off and land. He knew the way each pilot flew and he could tell if a landing would be good or bad when the airplane was gliding over the wires.

One day, an extremely handsome pilot named Roscoe Turner came into the hangar and watched the boy at his work. After a few minutes, he asked, "Would you do an engine for me if I brought it in?"

"Sure," said the boy. What else was he doing anyway?

Turner had laughed and affectionately tousled the boy's bright red hair. "You sure got freckles!" he said. "Do they hurt?"

Both laughed. Turner then gave the boy a shiny quarter. The smiling boy held it in his hand, turned it several times, then asked, "Are you a famous flyer?"

Roscoe playfully cuffed the boy's chin. "No, not yet, but I'm sure working on it!"

So, here it was August 2, 1927. He was still scraping bearings—he didn't mind really—after all they let him fly every week. Once he'd said something about getting money and flying lessons and his father had told him, "You can quit anytime you want. There's a line of kids 20-feet long waiting to take your place if you do."

He never complained again.

Unknown to the boy in the shop, in downtown Compton at the local beanery, his father and three of the Angel family were having breakfast and discussing a long-held dream. Again the subject of promoting an airplane factory was probed.

"It takes money," said the boy's father.

"And that takes promotion," said Jimmie, who knew more about the subject than most people.

"We'd better get on with it then," said Parker.

"We're almost out of money—again," said Eddie sadly.

They bent their heads together and after 10 minutes of frantic discussion all had agreed on a plan. Jimmie left to phone the local newspaper and the others paid the bill and prepared to go to the airport.

In the wooden hangar at the field, the kid sat working at

the bearings. He uncapped the center one, turned it over and began to scrape where a thin smear of Prussian Blue appeared. In a few moments, he put the cap back on, tightened it, then looked at his face in the small inspection mirror. He wondered if he might ever look as fantastic as Roscoe Turner. But studying his front teeth, one slanted and both set with a slit between them, he decided he could forget that idea.

Hearing a car drive up, he bent again to the engine. Without entering the hangar, those from the auto busied themselves moving the nearby Standard biplane to the front of the hangar where they placed chocks under its wheels and checked its fuel and water. Jimmie Angel entered the hangar, nodded to the kid, picked up two short chunks of four-by-four redwood with metal straps dangling from a notched end and returned to the others. The kid, studying a rod bearing, had not noticed the chunks of wood were the same ones used to let very short people reach the rudder bar.

From the outside he heard his father's raised tone of voice. "Son, come out here!"

Wiping his hands, he tried to get most of the Prussian Blue off his skin. Then he tried to scrape that which had dried to a crust from his trousers. Frowning because he had not immediately responded to an adult's order, he ran to the assembled group.

Jimmie Angel had just left the Standard's rear cockpit where he'd installed the two pieces of redwood. When the kid neared, Jimmie said, "Get in the rear of the Standard."

"Yessir!" He was not surprised for often the pilots would use him to turn on a magneto switch when someone started an airplane engine.

Inside the cockpit and waiting, the kid watched his father approach, peer into the cockpit where he was sitting and order, "Fasten the belt, son."

"Yessir!" He ususally did as he was ordered although often he did not know why.

Eddie came up to him and asked, "You been getting this easy-flying airplane around the field?"

"Oh, yessir. Been doing it with you if you remember."

Eddie smiled that slow grin of his, shook his head with some secret amusement and muttered, "Yeh, for a kid you sure do all right. Guess you should with all the dual you've had and the brain-blatting you've had to listen to."

For a few minutes it was quiet so the kid sat quietly and imagined he was an airmail pilot. "Vruum! Vruum!" He made a noise meant to imitate a Liberty engine in a DH-4 mailplane and imagined the thunderstorm he had to penetrate to deliver the mail. Pausing in his meditation, he then looked to see if there was a thunderstorm at the field. No thunderstorm, just a few wisps of fog rapidly melting away from the strong sunlight.

Jimmie Angel returned to the boy and asked, "You got over 50 hours of dual, we think. Suppose you can take the Standard around the patch alone without getting into trouble?"

Dreaming was over. Reality was now evident to the boy. His eyes grew large and his mouth dropped open. He accepted the helmet and goggles Jimmie offered and put them on.

At last. At long, long, last he was going to solo.

For a few moments the kid wondered how the decision had been made. Screwing his face into a slight frown, he tried to recall if he'd asked anyone if he could solo an airplane. No matter, he decided. Right now it was apparent that questions were irrelevent. He was in an airplane and had been told to fly it by an adult who was his hero. A tiny smile raised the corners of his lips. How long had he been flying? He could not remember in his short lifetime when he had not been in or near airplanes. Airplanes and his breathing occupied the same space.

"Hey!" Jimmie ended the boy's reverie. "Get the switch ready." Then he nodded to Parker who had his hands on the propeller ready to swing it through for a start.

"Contact!" Parker yelled.

The kid turned the switch to "On," and leaned his head over the right side of the cockpit to face Parker. "Contact, sir!"

Parker gave the prop a mighty heave and it spun through two compression strokes, catching and firing on the second. The OXX-6 coughed a few times, belched clouds of blue smoke then began to settle into a smooth idle. The kid looked at Jimmie who was approaching the cockpit with further directions for the young pilot. His black hair waving from the wind of the idling engine, he clutched the boy's shirt collar, drew him closer to his face, and asked, "You know you can do this, don't you?"

The kid nodded affirmatively.

Raising his voice above the noise of the wind, Jimmie ordered, "Then you take this airplane around the field once, land it and taxi back to us. If you hurt this airplane one little bit,

"Pop" Casey is proud of the airport's new gasoline pump. Circa 1928.

I'm going to whip you real hard. You understand?"

"Yessir!"

"Then what are you waiting for—git!"

Parker and Eddie held the right wingtip by the struts as the boy added power. As the Standard swung the full turn toward the eastern end of the field, they let go and the boy added a quick burst of power and a punch of left rudder to point the nose downwind.

As most of the other airplanes of that day, there were no brakes on the plane or a tailwheel. Under the stabilizer at the end of the fuselage, was a stub of ash wrapped at its top with shock cord. Steering on the ground was effected by air passing over the rudder, either from forward motion or bursts of power from the engine. It was common knowledge that more airplanes of the era were wrecked in taxiing than ever fell from the sky.

As the end of the field neared, the kid gave the rudder bar redwood extension a hard push leftward and added more power. Turning into a light breeze, the plane wobbled over two bumps, then was aligned with the tire tracks laid by airplanes flying off the field.

There was no need to wait, so he added full throttle exactly as he had for what now had seemed an eternity. The object now was to gain enough speed for the Standard to fly. Keeping the ash control stick pressed forward against its stops, he waited for the tail to rise. It seemed to take forever but finally the fuselage was level with the runway and the airplane was accelerating nicely.

It wasn't long before the old biplane seemed to gather its skirts about herself and begin to hop from mound to mound. Feeling the lift build under the long swept-back wings, the kid allowed the stick to come toward him slightly. One last bump and the airplane was flying.

For a time he let the airplane gather some speed then raised the nose further when the sound of wires told him the proper climb speed had been reached. Quickly, he lowered his eyes to the instrument panel and saw that the tachometer was swinging between 1400 and 1500 revs. Exactly right.

Alert, hearing every sound, feeling the airplane's special throbbing transmit from the control stick into his hands and arms, and sensing the air around him, the kid thought it strange that no one was yelling at him from the front cockpit or giving wild hand signals for him to follow. He was alone, he knew that fact, yet it didn't seem he was alone for in his mind he could see all the faces of those who had taught him during the extended period of his training. All the faces were different and their voices that of individuals. But the differences produced a common, single theme: "Fly the airplane, kid. Don't ever let it fly you!"

"Betcher life," he said to himself as he lowered the nose over the black ribbon of asphalt road bordering the western edge of the field. His speed went to cruising and he pressed the controls to the left. Slowly, the biplane responded. When it was about a 30-degree bank and halfway through its turn, he reversed the controls and the airplane reluctantly eased out of the turn, now headed south.

Again he climbed and noted he was higher than usual. Of course, he decided, the friendly airplane in which he flew was enjoying the easy task of carrying a 12-year-old boy.

Turning left again for his downwind leg of the circuit, he looked down and saw that the faces near the hangar were all turned toward him. A few had their hands shading their eyes. With his left hand, he gave them a salute for he'd imagined their hands were saluting him.

Wouldn't it be fun, he thought, if I took this airplane to San Diego and delivered the mail instead of landing. Then he amended his thoughts as it struck him that the pokey old Standard only had a 100-hp engine, not a 400-hp Liberty. And he had no mail. It sobered him to realize that his moment of truth must include the fact that he was just a little boy trying to fly a big biplane around the field, alone. Then he gritted his teeth and ordered himself to stop thinking such dumb things. So, he was just a kid? But this kid was flying the airplane all by himself. He smiled, certain that none of his classmates could make that statement.

In a few moments it would be time to close the throttle for his approach to a landing. Lowering his head into the cockpit momentarily, he watched the familiar grains of sand skittering along the wooden floor. Lifting his eyes to each side of the cockpit, he saw the frantic rattling of the fabric against the routed ash longerons and the solid piano-wire bracing. All was well and he was ready to land.

Slowly, steadily, he eased off the power until he could almost count the turning blades of the scimitar-shaped propeller. Pressing the nose down to keep the wires humming at the same sound of his climb, he swung the nose over the wires bordering the field and aligned the plane with the landing area.

Alert, waiting, sensing the decaying airspeed, the boy felt the precise moment of stall approach and pulled the stick all the way back against its stop.

From no higher than two inches, the Standard dropped to its landing, rolled out straight then slowly taxied toward the single hangar.

What will they say? He wondered about this and then imagined he was as tall and as strikingly handsome as his friend Roscoe Turner.

At Jimmie's signal, he cut the switch and undid his seat belt. The others had gathered around the nose of the airplane and were discussing how the newspapers would respond to a repeat of the event the next day. Some were laughing. A few pounded his father on the back.

The kid climbed out of the airplane and handed the helmet and goggles to Jimmie. His mentor took them without a word and moved to the men talking around the nose of the plane. For some strange reason he felt like hugging his father but as he moved to do so, his father evaded his movement and said, "You'll get that Prussian Blue all over my pants."

"I soloed the Standard, Pop."

"Sure you did, and if you keep busy, tomorrow when the newspaper people are here, we'll let you take Grandpa up for a short hop."

"I flew it alone, Pop."

"Uh . . . yeh. You haven't finished the bearings on that Hisso, have you?"

"No but I— —"

"Well, you know what to do?"

Another pilot hearing this exchange, said, "You think you own the place just because you flew the Standard around the field? Kids are supposed to listen to the grownups, not talk about themselves. Right, Pop?"

The boy's father grinned slightly, "Right."

Inside the kid there was a bubbling fountain of things he wanted to say. But his instinct cautioned him to remain silent. Something about the experience seemed very bizarre to him but he couldn't seem to pin it down. He didn't really understand why the adults had made him solo and it never dawned on him to question their motives.

One thing though, he knew for certain: He was a real pilot and he would be for as long as he lived. No one, he silently vowed, would ever take that away from him.

And that was how the author of this book soloed.

INDEX